Annals of Information Systems

Volume 16

Series Editors
Ramesh Sharda
Oklahoma State University
Stillwater, OK, USA

Stefan Voß
University of Hamburg
Hamburg, Germany

For further volumes:
http://www.springer.com/series/7573

Annals of Information Systems comprises serialized volumes that address a specialized topic or a theme. AoIS publishes peer reviewed works in the analytical, technical as well as the organizational side of information systems. The numbered volumes are guest-edited by experts in a specific domain. Some volumes may be based upon refereed papers from selected conferences. AoIS volumes are available as individual books as well as a serialized collection. *Annals of Information Systems* is allied with the 'Integrated Series in Information Systems' (IS²).

Proposals are invited for contributions to be published in the *Annals of Information Systems*. The Annals focus on high quality scholarly publications, and the editors benefit from Springer's international network for promotion of your edited volume as a serialized publication and also a book. For more information, visit the Springer website at http://www.springer.com/series/7573

Or contact the series editors by email:
Ramesh Sharda: sharda@okstate.edu or Stefan Voß: Stefan.voss@hamburg.de

Dionysios-Dimitrios Koutsouris
Athina A. Lazakidou
Editors

Concepts and Trends in Healthcare Information Systems

 Springer

Editors
Dionysios-Dimitrios Koutsouris
School of Electrical & Comp. Engineering
National Technical University of Athens
Zografou, Athens, Greece

Athina A. Lazakidou
Department of Nursing
University of Peloponnese
Sparta, Greece

ISSN 1934-3221   ISSN 1934-3213 (electronic)
ISBN 978-3-319-06843-5   ISBN 978-3-319-06844-2 (eBook)
DOI 10.1007/978-3-319-06844-2
Springer Cham Heidelberg New York Dordrecht London

Library of Congress Control Number: 2014939517

Springer is part of Springer Science+Business Media (www.springer.com)

Preface

Information systems have great potential to reduce healthcare costs and improve outcomes. The purpose of this special issue is to offer a forum for theory-driven research that explores the role of Information Systems in the delivery of healthcare in its diverse organizational and regulatory settings. In addition to the embedded role of Information Technology (IT) in clinical and diagnostics equipment, Information Systems are uniquely positioned to capture, store, process, and communicate timely information to decision makers for better coordination of healthcare at both the individual and population levels. For example, data mining and decision support capabilities can identify potential adverse events for an individual patient while also contributing to the population's health by providing insights into the causes of disease complications. Despite its importance, the healthcare domain has been underrepresented in leading IS journals. However, interest is increasing, as demonstrated by the proliferation of healthcare tracks in IS conferences, special interest groups, and announcements of special issues among leading journals.

The healthcare delivery systems share similar characteristics with most service and productive organizations but also exhibit specific characteristics, which are related to the complexity and diversity of healthcare production, including the dissimilar ways healthcare professionals discharge their clinical tasks. New requirements and technological advances occurring in healthcare, information systems, and information technology have influenced the evolving role of healthcare information systems and related technology. Relevant aspects that took place in the evolution of systems and technology in order to appropriately support healthcare organizations are:

- The diverse organizational healthcare environment of information systems, which need to be adapted to multiple types of healthcare organizations.
- Dynamic changes in the required role of information systems, following changes in the role and dynamics of all levels of healthcare delivery and management.
- The need for integration of information systems within healthcare organizations, which are also organized as networks.
- Technological advances in systems structure and communications, facilitating the implementation of integrated healthcare networks.

This special issue covers cutting edge research topics of utmost real-world importance in the specific domain of healthcare information systems, and presents studies from leading researchers and practitioners in the field.

The covered topics include computer based simulation and modeling for healthcare treatment, training, and optimization, role of healthcare information systems in improving care in different national health systems, role of healthcare information systems in fostering improved health and healthier lifestyles, challenges and impact of data standards on healthcare delivery, role of information technology in evidence-based medicine, information systems in personalized medicine, e-health Policy, privacy, security and trust issues with e-health solutions, mobile healthcare initiatives and social media in healthcare.

This book is an excellent source of comprehensive knowledge and literature on the topic of distributed health and e-health applications.

All of us who worked on the book hope that readers will find it useful.

Dionysios-Dimitrios Koutsouris, Ph.D
Athina A. Lazakidou, Ph.D

Contents

Contributors

Vassiliki Andronikou   Institute of Communication and Computer Systems (ICCS), National Technical University of Athens, Athens, Greece

Sayan Chakraborty   JIS College of Engineering, Kalyani, West Bengal, India

Sheli Sinha Chaudhuri   Jadavpur University, Kolkata, West Bengal, India

Efthymios Chondrogiannis   Institute of Communication and Computer Systems (ICCS), National Technical University of Athens, Athens, Greece

Goutami Dey   JIS College of Engineering, Kalyani, West Bengal, India

Nilanjan Dey   JIS College of Engineering, Kalyani, West Bengal, India

Elazer R. Edelman   Institute for Medical Engineering and Science and Cardiovascular Division Brigham and Women's Hospital, Harvard Medical School, Boston, MA, USA

Dimitrios I. Fotiadis   Unit of Medical Technology and Intelligent Information Systems, Dept. of Materials Science and Engineering, University of Ioannina, Ioannina, Greece

Kostas Giokas   Biomedical Engineering Laboratory, School of Electrical and Computer Engineering, National Technical University of Athens, Zografou, Athens, Greece

Spyretta Golemati   Medical School, National and Kapodistrian University of Athens, Athens, Greece

Dimitra Iliopoulou   Biomedical Engineering Laboratory, School of Electrical and Computer Engineering, National Technical University of Athens, Zografou, Athens, Greece

George E Karagiannis   Royal Brompton & Harefield NHS Trust, Research & Development Office, London, UK

Georgia S. Karanasiou   Unit of Medical Technology and Intelligent Information Systems, Dept. of Materials Science and Engineering, University of Ioannina, Ioannina, GR, Greece

Nikos Katevas   Department of Automation Engineering, Technological Educational Institute of Sterea Ellada, Psahna, Evia, Greece

Vassileios D. Kolias   Biosim Laboratory, School of Electrical and Computer Engineering, National Technical University of Athens, Athens, Greece

Vassiliki Koufi   Department of Digital Systems, University of Piraeus, Piraeus, Greece

Dionysios-Dimitrios Koutsouris   Institute of Communication and Computer Systems (ICCS), National Technical University of Athens, Athens, Greece

Biomedical Engineering Laboratory, School of Electrical and Computer Engineering, National Technical University of Athens, Zografou, Athens, Greece

Fabrice Labeau   Department of Electrical and Computer Engineering, McGill University, Montréal, Canada

Athina A. Lazakidou   Department of Nursing Faculty of Human Movement and Quality of Life Sciences, University of Peloponnese, Sparta, Greece

Di Lin   Department of Electrical and Computer Engineering, McGill University, Montréal, Canada

School of Information and Software Engineering, University of Electronic Science and Technology of China, Chengdu, China

Flora Malamateniou   Department of Digital Systems, University of Piraeus, Piraeus, Greece

Bryan R. M . Manning   University of Westminster, London, UK

Lampros K. Michalis   Department of Cardiology, Medical School, University of Ioannina, Ioannina, Greece

Zina Nakhla   BESTMOD Laboratory, High Institute of Management, University of Tunis, Tunis, Tunisia

Konstantina S. Nikita   Biosim Laboratory, School of Electrical and Computer Engineering, National Technical University of Athens, Athens, Greece

Kaouther Nouira   BESTMOD Laboratory, High Institute of Management, University of Tunis, Tunis, Tunisia

Anna Paidi   1st Regional Health Authority of Attica, Athens, Greece

Georgios Papantonakis   Biomedical Engineering Laboratory, School of Electrical and Computer Engineering, National Technical University of Athens, Zografou, Athens, Greece

Alexandros Perrakis   Biomedical Engineering Laboratory, School of Electrical and Computer Engineering, National Technical University of Athens, Zografou, Athens, Greece

Maria Petridou   School of Computer Science & IT Jubilee Campus, The University of Nottingham, Nottingham, UK

Charalampos Platis   National Centre For Public Administration and Local Government, Institute of Training, Tavros, Greece

Mikaela Poulymenopoulou   Department of Digital Systems, University of Piraeus, Piraeus, Greece

Michael L Rigby   Royal Brompton & Harefield NHS Trust, Research & Development Office, London, UK

Michael Roughton   Royal Brompton & Harefield NHS Trust, Research & Development Office, London, UK

Michael Schroeder   Biotechnology Center (BIOTEC), Technical University of Dresden (TUD), Dresden, Germany

Vasileios G Stamatopoulos   Biomedical Research Foundation, Academy of Athens, Athens, Greece

John Stoitsis   Biosim Laboratory, School of Electrical and Computer Engineering, National Technical University of Athens, Athens, Greece

Anastasios Tagaris   Institute of Communication and Computer Systems (ICCS), National Technical University of Athens, Athens, Greece

Evanthia E. Tripoliti   Unit of Medical Technology and Intelligent Information Systems, Dept. of Materials Science and Engineering, University of Ioannina, Ioannina, GR, Greece

George Tsatsaronis   Biotechnology Center (BIOTEC), Technical University of Dresden (TUD), Dresden, Germany

Lida Tzachani   Royal Brompton & Harefield NHS Trust, Research & Development Office, London, UK

Theodora Varvarigou   Institute of Communication and Computer Systems (ICCS), National Technical University of Athens, Athens, Greece

George Vassilacopoulos   Department of Digital Systems, University of Piraeus, Piraeus, Greece

Stelios Zimeras   Department of Mathematics, Direction Statistics and Actuarial-Financial Mathematics, University of the Aegean, Karlovassi, Greece

Emmanuel Zoulias   National Centre For Public Administration and Local Government, Information Systems and Technical Support, Tavros, Greece

Chapter 1
Patient-Generated EHR Input System Trials: An Analysis of Perceived Benefits Across a Range of Disease Groups

George E. Karagiannis, Lida Tzachani, Bryan R. M. Manning, Vasileios G. Stamatopoulos, Michael Roughton, Athina A. Lazakidou, Maria Petridou, Dimitra Iliopoulou and Michael L Rigby

Abstract Information technology can play a decisive role in empowering patients. This paper presents the perceptions of three different patient groups from three different European countries over the use of pEHR, a web-based personal electronic health record service. The patients' perceived benefits were identified following the analysis of their responses to predefined questions related to different service aspects. Our results indicate that patients, irrespectively of their disease, expressed a rather positive attitude towards the use of the system. However, several issues should be addressed by decision makers prior to the large-scale implementation of web-based personal electronic health records. Further trials are needed to evaluate use of this technology for the benefit of patients and demonstrate that it can assist their clinical care.

Keywords Patient empowerment · Electronic health records · Web based pEHR

G. E. Karagiannis (✉) · L. Tzachani · M. Roughton · M. L. Rigby
Royal Brompton & Harefield NHS Trust, Research & Development Office,
Sydney Street, SW3 6NP, London, UK
e-mail: g.karagiannis@rbht.nhs.uk

B. R. M. Manning
University of Westminster, London, UK

V. G. Stamatopoulos
Biomedical Research Foundation, Academy of Athens, Athens, Greece

A. A. Lazakidou
Department of Nursing, University of Peloponnese, Sparta, Greece

M. Petridou
University of Nottingham, Nottingham, UK

D. Iliopoulou
Biomedical Engineering Laboratory, National Technical University of Athens, Athens, Greece

D.-D. Koutsouris, A. A. Lazakidou (eds.), *Concepts and Trends in Healthcare Information Systems,* Annals of Information Systems 16,
DOI 10.1007/978-3-319-06844-2_1, © Springer International Publishing Switzerland 2014

1.1 Background

An ageing population and very high costs are putting unprecedented financial and organization pressure to public and private healthcare providers, putting health-care systems nowadays into crisis (IBM 2006). Because of this crisis, health care systems need to make changes: "focusing more on the patient and what the patient can do to help to improve his own health care" (Falcão-Reis and Correia 2010). The shift from paper based to an electronic media-based society can open up new promising avenues that were not present a few years ago. Society and market forces also add more pressure in improving healthcare system and all stakehold-ers including governmental authorities conclude that the new system needs to be more patient-centric (Sarasohn-Kahn 2008). It can be said that these reforms are making patient empowerment processes more inevitable. Based on the literature "patient empowerment" notion implies the idea of patients being able to control their own treatment or care plans as well as their interactions with health care organizations professionals and institutions. The term healthcare "consumer" is widely used to refer to people who are both healthy and ill which also denotes a market-type relationship that extends beyond health settings (Harris and Veinot 2004). Information technology can play a decisive role in empowering patients since it can assist them in collecting and storing their own personal clinical in-formation (Munir and Boaden 2001). It can also support them in managing their personal clinical information according to their own preferences within specific - tailored to each case - parameters. Consequently, patients can access and distrib-ute their personal information promptly to the appropriate levels of care when this is necessary.

1.2 Objective

In this paper, we report on the perceived benefits over the use of the Personal Elec-tronic Health Record (pEHR), a web-based health records service, across three dif-ferent patient groups from three different European countries. Currently there are a number of different platforms specifically designed to enable patients to create their own Personal Health Record (PHR) like Google Health and Microsoft Health Vault. Furthermore, social networks can form a channel of discussion on matters related to patients' chronic diseases and other related issues. It is worth mention-ing that only on Facebook there are more than 500 groups where discussions on a number of different diseases and YouTube is part of this global trend with 36,000 videos on different aspects of surgery (Angelmar and Berman 2007). This new trend characterize the "popular phenomenon of Health 2.0 that is based on the use of social software and its ability to promote a partnership between patients, their caregivers and health professionals in health" (Sarasohn-Kahn 2008; Falcão-Reis and Correia 2010).

Table 1.1 Demographic characteristics of patients in the three countries

	All	UK	Spain	Italy
	N (%)	N (%)	N (%)	N (%)
	150 (100)	59 (40)	50 (33)	41 (27)
Age (years)				
<20	4 (3)	0 (0)	0 (0)	4/4 (100)
20–34	62 (41)	28/62 (45)	19/62 (31)	15/62 (24)
35–49	50 (33)	24/50 (48)	14/50 (28)	12/50 (24)
50–65	27 (18)	7/27 (26)	11/27 (41)	9/27 (23)
>65	7 (5)	0 (0)	6/7 (86)	1/7 (14)
Gender				
Male	92 (61)	43/61 (47)	30/61 (33)	19/61 (20)
Female	58 (39)	16/58 (28)	20/58 (34)	22/58 (38)

1.3   Methods

A web-based service that authenticates users, provides the personal electronic health record application and enables them to access and/or update their own medical information was evaluated during the five-month pEHR trial. A total of 150 inpatients from three different European hospitals in the UK, Spain and Italy, suffering from congenital heart disease, Parkinson's disease and type 2 diabetes respectively fulfilled our inclusion criteria. Literate patients who were physically capable of handling a personal computer and understand the logic of the software application were recruited for the purposes of our study. Each patient performed at least one full testing session before he/she was asked to evaluate the system. Individual training provided to each patient prior to the trial session of the system.

Our analysis is based on the collection of the patients' views using a structured questionnaire containing Likert type responses, ranging from 1 to 5, on different statements. To avoid question bias, both positive and negative statements were used.

In our statistical analysis, the characteristics and demographics of the study participants are summarized using n (%). Responses to each of the questions included in the evaluation questionnaire are summarized using n (%) and mean (SD). Each of the three hospitals that participated in the study received ethical approval by their local research ethics committee according to internal organizational procedures.

1.4   Results

In this study sample, the UK and Spanish subjects consisted of mostly male patients while female patients were more in the case of the Italian group. Most of the patient-users in all countries belong in the 20–34 and 35–49 age groups (See Table 1.1).

The majority of patients from all groups (63 %) stated little or no experience in using computers or the Internet. An approximately equal proportion of patients

Table 1.2 Patient characteristics towards the use of e-Health services in the three countries

	UK		Spain		Italy		All	
	N (%)		N (%)		N (%)		N (%)	
	59 (40)		50 (33)		41 (27)		150 (100)	
	Very familiar	Not very familiar/ Not at all	Very familiar	Not very familiar/ Not at all	Very familiar	Not very familiar/ Not at all	Very familiar	Not very familiar/ Not at all
Familiarity with using computers and Internet	26 (44)	33 (56)	27 (54)	23 (46)	2 (5)	39 (95)	55 (37)	95 (63)
	Yes	No	Yes	No	Yes	No	Yes	No
Previous experience in using e-Health services	22 (37)	37 (63)	19 (38)	31 (62)	6 (15)	35 (85)	47 (31)	103 (69)
Previous experience in using web-based services	20 (34)	39 (66)	30 (60)	20 (40)	1 (2)	40 (98)	51 (34)	99 (66)
Paying for web-based services	13 (22)	46 (78)	2 (4)	48 (96)	3 (7)	38 (93)	18 (12)	132 (88)

(69 %) stated they had no previous experience in using e-Health services. A similar trend appears in our three patient groups concerning the use of other web-based services (e.g. internet banking, emailing services, e-commerce applications etc). The majority of our patients (88 %) stated that they were using their other web-services for free (See Table 1.2).

The overall evaluation results of the pEHR service have been presented elsewhere (Karagiannis et al. 2007). It is important to clarify at this stage the underlying preliminary data of the particular analysis; the overall perception of pEHR has been infiltrated with the medical condition in each case. Thus the analyzed views below (See Table 1.3) are holding the influence of a major disease within.

Our data indicate the pEHR service to be an effective medium for the storage and management of data by different patient groups. In our questionnaire-based analysis, patient responses presented similar trends against the different evaluation aspects of the service, irrespectively of their type of disease. Overall, the three patient groups considered the service to have comprehensive and valuable content, remaining neutral regarding the long term potential of the service. Furthermore, with

Table 1.3 Service aspect evaluation with distinction by country and patient group

Service aspect	Strongly disagree [Score No: 1]		Disagree [Score no: 2]		Neither agree nor disagree [Score No: 3]		Agree [Score No: 4]		Strongly agree [Score: 5]		Mean	SD
	N	%	N	%	N	%	N	%	N	%		
Comprehensive content												
UK[a]	8	14%	9	15%	18	31%	21	36%	3	5%	3.03	1.13
Spain[b]	6	12%	17	34%	10	20%	14	28%	3	6%	2.82	1.16
Italy[c]	8	20%	10	24%	13	32%	7	17%	3	7%	2.68	1.19
Content value												
UK[a]	2	3%	13	22%	22	37%	18	31%	4	7%	3.15	0.96
Spain[b]	1	2%	9	18%	16	32%	20	40%	4	8%	3.34	0.94
Italy[c]	8	20%	12	29%	13	32%	6	15%	2	5%	2.56	1.12
Sufficient monitoring of medical condition												
UK[a]	7	12%	12	20%	20	34%	14	24%	6	10%	3.00	1.16
Spain[b]	2	4%	8	16%	19	38%	18	36%	3	6%	3.24	0.94
Italy[c]	2	5%	20	49%	12	29%	4	10%	3	7%	2.66	0.99
Potential to improve medical consultations												
UK[a]	1	2%	5	8%	16	27%	24	41%	13	22%	3.73	0.96
Spain[b]	1	2%	8	16%	7	14%	24	48%	10	20%	3.68	1.04
Italy[c]	6	15%	19	46%	13	32%	2	5%	1	2%	2.34	0.88
Future system use should be recommended by physicians												
UK[a]	4	7%	3	5%	16	27%	19	32%	17	29%	3.71	1.15
Spain[b]	4	8%	7	14%	18	36%	13	26%	8	16%	3.28	1.14
Italy[c]	19	46%	12	29%	3	7%	4	10%	3	7%	2.02	1.27
Long term interest/use in the system												
UK[a]	6	10%	4	7%	23	39%	19	32%	7	12%	3.29	1.10
Spain[b]	9	18%	10	20%	15	30%	13	26%	3	6%	2.82	1.19
Italy[c]	13	32%	10	24%	12	29%	4	10%	2	5%	2.32	1.17

[a]Congenital heart disease patients
[b]Parkinson's disease patients
[c]Type 2 diabetes patients

the exception of type 2 diabetes group (represented by Italy) that remained negative towards the potential to improve medical consultation, the sufficient monitoring of medical condition and the future use to be recommended by physicians, the other two groups seemed to be in favour of those three aspects.

1.5   Conclusion

The primary aim of our study was to identify the user requirements for the development of the pEHR service, which aimed to cover the clinical information needs of three different patients groups. Our secondary aim was to identify the patients' perception towards the future use of patient generated personal electronic health records. Personal electronic health records can gain the better off traditional consultations, and lead in establishing the necessary information arrays between patients, healthcare professionals and organizations. From the health services point of view, the implementation of web-based medical records that can be easily maintained by different patient groups can result in the delivery of a better-coordinated care and quicker access to patient generated data. From a patient point of view, the use of similar systems may improve the quality of care they receive as well as their self-confidence in dealing with their personal state of health. As expected, the wider implementation of Internet based health records in publicly funded healthcare systems is not an easy task for policy makers. Several issues should be therefore addressed, such as the reliability and the quality of data entered by patients, access rights and concerns about confidentiality, the fixed-value computerized options as well as the technical and network aspects.

Technology can play an important and decisive role in empowering patients by enabling them with the appropriate tools to secure and manage their data regarding their health, such as PHRs. Although there is a variety of options available for patients it is crucial to make extensive use of the OpenID protocol, together with smart carts and 'valet keys' or even biometrics constitutes a tentative approach that should be further explored and promoted (Ferreira et al. 2006). Moreover, it is very crucial for the doctors to be provided with an up-to-date health history of their patients in the right moment in order to provide more efficient health services.

The current research evidence concerning the measurement of the impact that electronic health records may have on the outcomes of clinical care is limited. This can be attributed mainly to the lack of a coherent framework for evaluating the impact of electronic health records on health care outcomes and costs (Neville et al. 2003). It should be also noted that the collaboration between the relevant stakeholders (e.g. healthcare providers, IT firms and patients) has been principally on identifying the appropriate user requirements and proceed accordingly with the systems development. These stakeholders must be involved from the beginning of the project in order to understand and define what combinations of technological and non-technological resources can provide sustainable benefit (Essen and Conrick 2008)

Future development of information technology means should take into account the complex/dimensional nature of diseases beard by its potential users so as to have a real impact in empowering them. As it has been stated, to generate information that is useful to decision makers, evaluations of hospital information systems need to be multidimensional, covering many aspects beyond technical functionality (Kaplan 1998).The provision of solutions that are responsive to individual needs will allow patients to equally participate in the clinical decision making process. Further trials are needed to evaluate use of this technology for the benefit of patients and demonstrate that it can assist their clinical care.

Acknowledgements We are grateful to the European Commission's eTen Programme, which co-founded the pEHR study as well as to all our pEHR project partners.

References

Angelmar R, Berman P (2007) Patient empowerment and efficient health outcomes. 2007 Jan: 139–162. http://www.sustainhealthcare.org/Report_3.pdf

Essen A, Conrick M (2008) New e-service development in the homecare sector: beyond implementing a radical technology. Int J Med Inf 77:679–688

Falcão-Reis F, Correia M (2010) Patient empowerment by the means of citizen-managed electronic health records: Web 2.0 Health Digital Identity scenarios. Stud Health Technol Inf 156:214–228

Ferreira A, Cruz-Correia R, Antunes L et al (2006) How to break access control in a controlled manner. In: Proceedings of the 19th IEEE International Symposium on Computer-Based Medical Systems (CBMS), pp 847–854

Harris R, Veinot T (2004) The empowerment model and using e-health to distribute information. Action for Health, Simon Fraser University and the Vancouver Coastal Health Research Institute, Vancouver

IBM (2006) Patient-centric: the 21st Century prescription for healthcare, Whitepaper, Healthcare and life sciences May 2006

Kaplan B (1998) Development and acceptance of medical information systems: a historical overview. J Health Hum Resour Adm 11:9–29

Karagiannis G, Stamatopoulos VG, Rigby M et al (2007) Web-based personal health records: the personal electronic health record (pEHR) multi centred trial. Telemed Telecare 13(Suppl 1):32–34

Munir S, Boaden R (2001) Patient empowerment and the electronic health record. Stud Health Technol Inf 84:663–665

Neville D, O'Reilly S, MacDonald D et al (2003) Measuring the impact of electronic health records projects on health outcomes and costs: an evaluation framework. Abstr Acad Health Meet. 2003, vol. 20, no. abstract no. 845

Sarasohn-Kahn J (2008) The wisdom of patients: health care meets online social media. California Healthcare Foundation, Oakland

Chapter 2
Utilizing Semantic Web Technologies in Healthcare

Vassileios D. Kolias, John Stoitsis, Spyretta Golemati and Konstantina S. Nikita

Abstract The technological breakthrough in biomedical engineering and health informatics has produced several Health Information Systems (HIS) and medical devices that are used on a daily basis in hospitals producing a vast amount of data. The data that are produced come from different sources and are not stored in a unified storage repository or database even in a single hospital. As a result of that the interoperability of HIS is limited, the retrieval of information is difficult and there is hidden knowledge that remains unexploited in vast and diverse pools of medical data. In order to overcome the above, scientific community suggests the use of the semantic web technologies. The semantic web technologies provide the tools that allow to process data in a more effective and accurate way, create the framework for interoperability between HIS and also integrate data from various sources with their semantic meaning

Keywords Semantic web · Ontologies · Biomedical ontologies · Healthcare services · Health information systems

2.1 Introduction

The technological breakthrough in biomedical engineering and health informatics has produced several Health Information Systems (HIS) and medical devices that are used on a daily basis in hospitals producing a vast amount of data. Although the systems and the devices have improved the healthcare services, the main issue that has emerged is the utilization of the produced data. The data that are produced come from different sources and are not stored in a unified storage repository or database

V. D. Kolias (✉) · J. Stoitsis · K. S. Nikita
Biosim Laboratory, School of Electrical and Computer Engineering,
National Technical University of Athens, Athens, Greece
e-mail: vaskolias@biosim.ntua.gr

S. Golemati
Medical School, National and Kapodistrian University of Athens,
Athens, Greece
e-mail: sgolemati@med.uoa.gr

D.-D. Koutsouris, A. A. Lazakidou (eds.), *Concepts and Trends in Healthcare Information Systems,* Annals of Information Systems 16,
DOI 10.1007/978-3-319-06844-2_2, © Springer International Publishing Switzerland 2014

even in a single hospital. In many cases one hospital has many Radiological Information System (RIS), Laboratory Information Management System (LIMS) and HISs which are not interconnected. In addition to this, the medical data have not a structured and unified form and, as a result, data are not utilized in an efficient and is very difficult to be retrieved. In order to overcome these issues several standards such as Electronic Health Records (EHR) and define abbreviation Health Level 7 (HL7) have been suggested and used by the HIS. However, their major limitation is that they do not contain the semantic information of the medical data in a form that can be easily processed by computers. Due to this, knowledge is hidden in vast and diverse medical data pools. The scientific community has suggested the use of the semantic web technologies to overcome the problems that are mentioned above. The semantic web technologies provide the tools that allow to process data in a more effective and accurate way, create the framework for interoperability between HIS and also integrate data from various sources with their semantic meaning. In the past years several ontologies and terminologies have been introduced, which are the core element of the semantic web, in healthcare for describing and integrating medical data such as Unified Medical Lexicon System (UMLS) (Bodenreider 2004), Foundational Model of Anatomy (FMA) (Rosse and Mejino Jr. 2003), Radiological Lexicon (Langlotz 2006) and International Classification of Diseases (ICD)-11 (Tudorache et al. 2013). Also new standards are evolving such as OpenE-HR (Kalra et al. 2005) which have integrated the main biomedical ontologies in order to provide to the HIS systems the capabilities of the semantic web that are mentioned above.

The mission of this chapter is to analyze how semantic web technologies can be integrated to the HIS systems in order to solve the integration of the medical data, to provide enhanced capabilities for retrieving medical data, to provide personalized healthcare services to patients and also how the research in medical and biomedical fields can be enhanced.

2.2   Semantic Web and Ontologies

According to Tim Bernee Lee the semantic web is a web of data that can be processed directly and indirectly from the machines (Berners-Lee et al. 2001). As a result of that many tasks will be automated, data processing will be more accurate, faster and can lead to greater exploitation of data by sharing and reusing. In health sciences and health informatics systems that leads to better information retrieval, discovery of new knowledge from unexploited data, enhanced interoperability between institutions and better health services for the patients. Core element of the semantic web is the ontology. Ontology has several definitions but in computer science ontology is a formal, explicit specification of a shared conceptualization (Gruber 1993). This definition implies that ontology provides a vocabulary which can be used to model a domain, that is, the types of concepts and objects that exist and their relationships between them. There are two types of ontologies: the reference or domain ontologies and the application ontologies. Reference ontologies represent knowledge about a particular part of the world in a way that is independent from specific objectives, through a theory of the domain (Burgun 2006). In the contrary application ontologies are designed to perform specific tasks and are narrower than the reference ontologies.

2.3   Main Biomedical Ontologies

In the past years several biomedical ontologies have been created. Most of them have been created to describe thoroughly a domain in medicine and biology such as FMA which describes the human anatomy terms and their relations. Other ontologies such as SNOMED-CT are used to model the clinical terms and processes in order to provide better communication and interoperability between HIS. The most significant biomedical ontologies will be described in terms of domain and use. Most of the ontologies and terminologies are available through web services via the BioPortal.

2.3.1   Foundational Model of Anatomy (FMA)

FMA ontology describes the domain of human anatomy. FMA is a reference ontology which contains over 75,000 distinct anatomic types which cover the human anatomy from sub-cellular components to major body parts and the whole organism itself. The anatomic types are connected with more than 130,000 terms either as preferred names, synonyms or their non-English equivalents. FMA describes and defines the relationships of the types. There are over 2.1 million relationships which are grouped in more than 200 types of spatial structural and non-structural relationships. FMA is the basis of the human anatomy for many projects and also subparts of FMA are used for representing the anatomy for specific anatomy or application ontologies such as NeuroFMA, MEDICO (Möller et al. 2009), SEMIA (Kyriazos et al. 2011) and others.

FMA was developed and maintained by the Structural Informatics Group from the University of Washington and is currently at version 3.1 and its format is OWL. FMA is available either with the use of the web services and widgets from BioPortal or it can been downloaded as a file from the Structural Informatics Group[1] site.

2.3.2   International Classification of Diseases (ICD-10)

ICD-10 was endorsed by the Forty-third World Health Assembly in May 1990 and came into use in World Health Organization (WHO) Member States as from 1994.

---

[1] http://sig.biostr.washington.edu/projects/fm/AboutFM.html.

The classification is the latest in a series, which has its origins in the 1850s. The first edition, which is known as the International List of Causes of Death, was adopted by the International Statistical Institute in 1893. WHO took over the responsibility for the ICD at its creation in 1948 when the Sixth Revision, which included causes of morbidity for the first time, was published. The World Health Assembly adopted in 1967 the WHO Nomenclature Regulations that stipulate use of ICD in its most current revision for mortality and morbidity statistics by all Member States.

The ICD is the international standard diagnostic classification for all general epidemiological, many health management purposes and clinical use. These include the analysis of the general health situation of population groups and monitoring of the incidence and prevalence of diseases and other health problems in relation to other variables such as the characteristics and circumstances of the individuals affected, reimbursement, resource allocation, quality and guidelines.

It is used to classify diseases and other health problems recorded on many types of health and vital records including death certificates and health records. In addition to enabling the storage and retrieval of diagnostic information for clinical, epidemiological and quality purposes, these records also provide the basis for the compilation of national mortality and morbidity statistics by WHO Member States.

ICD-10 is usually kept as a thesaurus but there is also an ontology of ICD-10 in OWL (Möller et al. 2010). The ICD-10 in OWL format can describe in a better and more formal way except from the terms and the relationships between the ontologies entities. As a result of that the query capabilities will be enhanced compared with a simple thesaurus. The latest version of ICD is ICD-11, which is under construction, and it is estimated to be available for use at 2015. The main difference from older versions of ICD is that there will be mappings and relationships to other ontologies, terminologies and classifications such as SNOMED-CT to provide semantic interoperability (Tudorache et al. 2013). Also the development will be based on an open collaborative tool (Tudorache et al. 2010) which will be used for authoring by medical experts from all over the world. ICD-10 is available through BioPortal at UMLS format via web services.

2.3.3   Radiological Lexicon (RadLex)

RadLex is created by the Radiological Society of North America (RSNA). The goal of RadLex development was to unify the variety of terminologies that radiologists use into one unified lexicon to serve all their needs. Additional to that is that the use of standardized terminologies is now vital in medical practice. The majority of the benefits that the HIS systems can provide in healthcare services cannot be exploited if the data are not stored using standardized terms in a structured format. Unfortunately, almost all radiology reports are stored in free text rather than in a structured format and due to this radiologists struggle to follow the changes in health care systems which are based on informatics innovations. RadLex provides a uniform standard for all radiology related information.

RadLex development started in 2005 and today the 3rd version of Radlex is available. RadLex includes many complex domains that are necessary for radiologists. These domains range from basic sciences to imaging technologies and acquisition.

The lexicon is organized into a subsumption hierarchy with RadLex term as the root. RADLEX contains over 7,400 terms which are organized in 9 main categories or types such as anatomic location, treatment, uncertainty and image quality.

Radlex provides a unified lexicon and it can evolve to an ontology but it is not an ontological framework. From an ontological prospective RADLEX has 3 limitations

- It is term-oriented and as a result of that it ignores the entities to which its terms project
- There is a lack of taxonomy grounded on biomedical reality
- The ambiguity and mixing of relations such as "is_a", "part_of", "contained_in"

For these reasons the application ontology FMA-RADLEX is proposed in (Mejino Jr et al. 2008).

2.3.4   Systemized Nomeclature of Medicine-Clinical Terms (SNOMED-CT)

SNOMED-CT (Stearns et al. 2001) is the most commonly used multilingual clinical healthcare terminology in the world and it provides the core terminology for the Electronic Health Records (EHR). The goal of SNOMED-CT is to encode the meanings that are used in health information in order to improve the healthcare services. SNOMED-CT covers most of the areas that are used in medical practice such as clinical findings, symptoms, diagnoses, procedures, body structures, organisms and other etiologies, substances, pharmaceuticals, devices and specimen.

The use of SNOMED-CT in Health Informatics Systems can lead to an interoperable EHR and due to that can enhance the interoperability between different HIS. Additional to that it provides a consistent way for indexing, storing, retrieving and aggregating clinical data across specialties and sites of care. SNOMED was created by the College of American Pathologists (CAP) and since April of 2007 is owned, maintained and distributed by the International Health Terminology Standards Development Organization (IHTSDO)[2].

2.3.5   Unified Medical Lexicon System (UMLS)

UMLS repository is consisted from biomedical vocabularies and ontologies that are developed by the US National Library of Medicine. UMLS covers most of the

_____
[2] http://www.ihtsdo.org/.

biomedical terminology and it consists of over 60 vocabularies with 900,000 concepts and over 12 million relationships among these concepts. The most notable vocabularies that are integrated in UMLS are SNOMED-CT, ICD-10, Medical Subject Headings (MeSH), Gene Ontology and others. UMLS covers from clinical terms to genetic information.

UMLS consists of 3 components. The first component is the Metathesaurus that is a repository of inter-related biomedical concepts. The relation of the concepts can be inherited from the structure or are manually created be the editors using the hierarchical or associative relationships. MeSH is used to derive the statistical relations between the concepts from the MeSH indexing terms in MEDLINE[3] citations. The knowledge of the repository is organized by concept. In order to achieve this the similar and synonymous terms are clustered together to a concept and then are linked to other concepts with relationships types that were described above in this section. Additional to that the concepts are categorized in terms of semantic types, which are assigned by the Metathesaurus editors. The structure of the Metathesaurus allows users to collect the various terms that name a concept, to extract the relationships of the concepts and to collect the concepts based on their semantic meaning.

The other two components of UMLS are the Semantic Network and lexical resources. Semantic Network provides the semantic types to semantically categorize the concepts of the Metathesaurus. Lexical resources such as the SPECIALIST lexicon[4] and programs are used to generate variants of the biomedical terms.

2.3.6   Open Biomedical Ontologies (OBO)

Unlike the ontologies and terminologies that are described previous in this section OBO is not an ontology itself but and ontology library and a framework for ontology developers. The purpose of OBO is to create an evolving set of shared principles for the ontology development at the biomedical field. Most of the ontologies that are created in the biomedical field do not follow the same principles in design and as a result of that the integration of them meets obstacles.

An ontology that is developed with the OBO principles must be open, orthogonal, syntactically well-specified and to share a common space of identifiers. Open ontology means that the use of the ontology and the data that are described by its terms must be free without the need of license. Additional to that is that the evolution of the ontology is open to community debate. Ontologies that are created must be orthogonal in order to add new annotations without the need of restructuring the ontology and also to exploit the benefits of the modular development. The well-specified syntax enhances the use of ontologies because it allows processing from algorithms. Crucial principle of OBO is the use of commonly shared identifiers. The goal of the commonly shared identifiers is to provide backward compatibility with legacy annotations as the ontology is evolving.

---

[3] http://www.nlm.nih.gov/bsd/pmresources.html.

[4] http://www.nlm.nih.gov/pubs/factsheets/umlslex.html.

OBO is comprised of over 60 ontologies and many are submitted as candidates. OBO is supported by the NIH Roadmap National Center for Biomedical Ontology (NCBO) through BioPortal[5](Rubin et al. 2006b). Except from the support by the NCBO the developers for a subset of OBO ontologies have created the OBO foundry[6] (Smith et al. 2007) which is a trial of the use of evolving principles in a voluntary basis by the participants. Significant biomedical ontologies such as FMA and Gene Ontology have been reformed with the use of OBO foundry basis.

2.4   Semantic Web Technologies and Ontologies in Healthcare

Ontologies in healthcare and semantic web technologies in general are used to share, integrate and reuse biomedical data to enhance diagnostic procedures, limit costs and to enhance research in biomedical field. In this section ontology based integration in the biomedical field will be discussed, how ontologies are integrated in HIS and how interoperability is promoted in healthcare with the use of ontologies.

2.4.1   Ontology Based Integration of Heterogeneous Biomedical Data

Data that are produced from healthcare providers are huge, unstructured and diversed. There are in many formats (images, free text, structured text) and stored in different systems that in many cases cannot communicate. Due to that the management and the retrieval of that data is very difficult and it is an extra burden for the quality of the healthcare service. A first to bring order to the chaos is to create distributed or centralized repositories of medical data. Although repositories are a first solution if the data are not integrated at a semantic level the access to that data remains difficult and also there is no capabilities for semantic search. Due to that the exploitation of the data remains low and hidden knowledge is at the exploited data.

The semantic web technologies can provide data integration in semantic level with the use of ontologies. This approach has been used in ONTOFUSION (Pérez-Rey et al. 2006) and Bio2RDF (Belleau et al. 2008). Core element of ontology-based integration is the domain ontologies. The domain ontologies are mapped with the data sources, which can be relational databases of RDF triplestores, or views that are derived from the data sources. The domain ontologies are used to provide a common vocabulary and also the relationships between the different concepts. Different elements from the data must be described only with concept names from the ontologies. As a result of that the semantically equivalent elements that are

---

[5] http://bioportal.bioontology.org/.

[6] http://www.obofoundry.org/.

stored in difference databases are now described by the same concept. The creation of such a semantic repository allows users to make semantic queries to a unified biomedical pool of data from one user interface and also allows the semantic integration of new databases.

2.4.2   Ontologies and HIS

HIS are informatics systems for managing the data that are produced in hospitals and healthcare providers in general. The core element of the HIS is the Electronic Health Record (EHR). EHR contains the personal info of a patient, patient history and also medical data that are derived from the subsystems of HIS. Additional to EHR there is DICOM[7] and HL7[8]. DICOM is used for the storing and transmitting of the medical images and HL7 is for exchanging, integrating, sharing and retrieving medical electronic information. The main issue of the HIS and standard that is used for storage, communication and information retrieval is that the data are not structured and unified. Even though the standards provide mechanisms for storing metadata these metadata are not based on standardized terminologies but they are in free text. As a result of that interoperability between institutions and even hospital departments is difficult, information retrieval is limited to text queries results and huge amounts of medical data remain unexploited.

Due to the above the integration of standardized terminologies and ontologies to standards is suggested as a solution. The main terminology which was selected was SNOMED-CT because it covers most of the areas that are used in medical practice such as clinical findings, symptoms, diagnoses, procedures, body structures, organisms and other etiologies, substances, pharmaceuticals, devices and specimen. Also SNOMED is used for structuring the reports at the EHR. The mapping of the current version of HL7 (HL7 RIM[9]) with SNOMED-CT is suggested (Ryan 2006; Ryan et al. 2007) for enhancing interoperability between HIS.

Additional to the above openEHR (Kalra et al. 2005) is created for enhancing interoperability between HIS and healthcare organizations. The community of openEHR focuses its work at interoperability between EHRs and HIS. OpenEHR inserts a reference model, which is called archetype, which models the clinical procedures (Chen et al. 2009) and the query language. That model in order to provide interoperability is designed to make use of external terminologies and ontologies such as SNOMED, ICDx, LOINC[10] and others. Also there are several works that are proposing the mapping of the archetypes with the Semantic Web Rule Language (SWRL[11]) (Lezcano et al. 2008; Viklund and Karlsson 2009) for better reasoning and information retrieval (Lezcano et al. 2011).

---

[7] http://medical.nema.org/.

[8] http://www.hl7.org/index.cfm.

[9] http://www.hl7.org/implement/standards/product_brief.cfm?product_id=77.

[10] http://loinc.org/.

[11] http://www.w3.org/Submission/SWRL/.

2.5   Use of Ontologies in Biomedical Research

Biomedical research has a broad spectrum of fields from Biology to Medicine, from Bioinformatics to Biomechanics. Due to the chaotic form of the data the exploitation of them and the production of information is very difficult. Many techniques are used from Artificial Intelligence such as neural networks, pattern recognition and data mining but the main drawback of them is that they cannot integrate the semantic meaning of the data they process. An example of that is the Semantic Gap (Hare et al. 2006) when low level features cannot be connected with high level features of the image. The semantic gap limits the power of the Content Based Image retrieval (CBIR) (Akgül et al. 2011) systems in retrieval and also hides important knowledge from the researchers. The major advantages that ontologies and semantic web technologies bring in biomedical research can be easily shown in the research field of epidemiology (Ferreira et al. 2013). The heterogeneous resources of epidemiology with the use of commonly shared concepts have a harmonized description. The terms of the resources are mapped to concepts that have defined vocabulary and relations among them. On the other hand the process of the data is done with the semantic relations of the concepts and the retrieval is more accurate and relevant. This is shown in several research works that use ontologies for annotating medical data (Kyriazos et al. 2011; Möller and Sintek 2007; Rubin et al. 2009; Möller et al. 2009).

A major field in biomedical research is the simulation models of Physiology. Simulation models of physiology and pathology as modeled and represented as a set of equations and graphical schematics. In current form of the models there is no link between the data, the equations and the graphic schema. Due to that the update of a equation or an alteration at the graphical scheme is a very time consuming task and also error prone. With the use of ontologies it is feasible to create a framework that in the same time can represent the graphical and the mathematical part of the model. Also changes that can occur in the mathematical model can be propagated to the graphical model and vice versa. As a result of that the maintenance and the extension is easier and is done in an explicit framework, which is given from the ontology. Several research works propose such frameworks in cardiovascular dynamics (Rubin et al. 2006a) and the VPH[12] European Commission projects create such frameworks for physiology and pathology.

2.6   Conclusions

Healthcare sector produces heterogeneous, diversed and huge data. Current information systems and health standards are not able to exploit the data in an efficient way. The main reason is that these systems cannot interpret the semantic content of the data and also the structure of the data and the metadata that describe them are not structured in a formal and unified way. As a result of that there is hidden

---

[12] http://www.vph-noe.eu/.

information that lies in the pools of data, retrieval of information is limited and also there is limited interoperability in between HIS and healthcare institutions. The drawbacks that are mentioned above can slow down diagnostic procedures, make integration of new data difficult and limit the research capabilities. The use of semantic web technologies and ontologies can create the infrastructure for homogeneous information access through the unification of data pools in a semantic basis, structure the data form and provide enhance systems interoperability. There are several ontology engineering tools such as Protégé[13] that allow the development of new ontologies and create ontology based mappings with data pools. Additional to that there are active communities such as OBO foundry and openEHR that through collaborative work set principles in creation of biomedical ontologies and clinical models respectively in order to promote semantic interoperability of data and systems. Moreover NIH has created NCBO BioPortal, which is a repository of ontologies, and are available through REST web services.

However there are some certain drawbacks in the use of semantic web technologies and ontologies in healthcare. One major drawback is that currently the mappings that are used in data integration with the use ontologies is made semi-automatically. Research community must focus in the creation of tools that can integrate with an automatically way the new data pools. Also the development of ontologies is not made with the same principles and due to this the alignment between them is a very difficult task. Finally the maintenance of the ontologies has to be made in a way so that every HIS has the most updated version. A solution of this is creation of web services that provide the ontologies and the terminologies as the BioPortal provides or the use of local sub-ontologies as it is suggested in (Sari et al. 2013)

References

Akgül CB, Rubin DL, Napel S, Beaulieu CF, Greenspan H, Acar B (2011) Content-based image retrieval in radiology: current status and future directions. J Digit Imaging 24:208–222

Belleau F, Nolin M-A, Tourigny N, Rigault P, Morissette J (2008) Bio2RDF: towards a mashup to build bioinformatics knowledge systems. J Biomed Inform 41:706–716

Berners-Lee T, Hendler J, Lassila O (2001) The semantic web. Sci Am 284:28–37

Bodenreider O (2004) The unified medical language system (UMLS): integrating biomedical terminology. Nucleic Acids Res 32:D267–D270

Burgun A (2006) Desiderata for domain reference ontologies in biomedicine. J Biomed Inf 39:307–313

Chen R, Georgii-Hemming P, Åhlfeldt H (2009) Representing a chemotherapy guideline using openEHR and rules. In: MIE. pp 653–657

Ferreira JD, Paolotti D, Couto FM, Silva MJ (2013) On the usefulness of ontologies in epidemiology research and practice. J Epidemiol Community Health 67:385–388

Gruber TR (1993) A translation approach to portable ontology specifications. Knowl Acquis 5:199–220

Hare JS, Lewis PH, Enser PGB, Sandom CJ (2006) Mind the gap: another look at the problem of the semantic gap in image retrieval. 607309-607309-12

---

[13] http://protege.stanford.edu/.

Kalra D, Beale T, Heard S (2005) The openEHR foundation. Studies Health Technol Inf 115:153–173

Kyriazos G, Gerostathopoulos I, Kolias V, STOITSIS J, Nikita KA (2011) semantically-aided approach for online annotation and retrieval of medical images. Engineering in Medicine and Biology Society, EMBC, 2011 Annual International Conference of the IEEE. IEEE 2372–2375

Langlotz CP (2006) RadLex: A new method for indexing online educational materials1. Radiographics 26:1595–1597

Lezcano L, Sicilia M-A, Serrano-Balazote P (2008) Combining OpenEHR archetype definitions with SWRL rules—a translation approach. Emerging technologies and information systems for the knowledge society. Springer, Berlin, pp 79–87

Lezcano L, Sicilia M-A, Rodríguez-Solano C (2011) Integrating reasoning and clinical archetypes using OWL ontologies and SWRL rules. J Biomed Inf 44:343–353

Mejino JL Jr, Rubin DL, Brinkley JF (2008) FMA-RadLex: An application ontology of radiological anatomy derived from the foundational model of anatomy reference ontology. AMIA Annual Symposium Proceedings, 2008. American Medical Informatics Association, p 465

Möller M, Sintek M (2007) A generic framework for semantic medical image retrieval. KAMC 253

Möller M, Regel S, Sintek M (2009) Radsem: Semantic annotation and retrieval for medical images. In: The semantic web: research and applications. Springer, Berlin, pp 21–35

Möller M, Sintek M, Biedert R, Ernst P, Dengel A, Sonntag D (2010) Representing the International Classification of Diseases Version 10 in OWL. KEOD. 50–59

Pérez-Rey D, Maojo V, García-Remesal M, Alonso-Calvo R, Billhardt H, Martín-Sánchez F, Sousa A (2006) ONTOFUSION: Ontology-based integration of genomic and clinical databases. Comput Biol Med 36:712–730

Rosse C, Mejino JL Jr (2003) A reference ontology for biomedical informatics: the foundational model of anatomy. J Biomed Inf 36:478–500

Rubin DL, Grossman D, Neal M, Cook DL, Bassingthwaighte JB, Musen MA (2006a) Ontology-based representation of simulation models of physiology. AMIA Annual Symposium Proceedings. American Medical Informatics Association, p 664

Rubin DL, Lewis SE, Mungall CJ, Misra S, Westerfield M, Ashburner M, Sim I, Chute CG, Storey M-A, Smith B (2006b) National center for biomedical ontology: advancing biomedicine through structured organization of scientific knowledge. Omics: J Integr Bio 10:185–198

Rubin DL, Mongkolwat P, Kleper V, Supekar K, Channin DS (2009) Annotation and image mark-up: accessing and interoperating with the semantic content in medical imaging. Intelligent systems. IEEE 24:57–65

Ryan A (2006) Towards semantic interoperability in healthcare: ontology mapping from SNOMED-CT to HL7 version 3. Proceedings of the second Australasian workshop on Advances in ontologies-Volume 72. Australian Computer Society, Inc., 69–74

Ryan A, Eklund P, Esler B (2007) Toward the interoperability of HL7 v3 and SNOMED CT: a case study modeling mobile clinical treatment

Sari AK, Rahayu W, Bhatt M (2013) An approach for sub-ontology evolution in a distributed health care enterprise. Info Syst 38:727–744

Smith B, Ashburner M, Rosse C, Bard J, Bug W, Ceusters W, Goldberg LJ, Eilbeck K, Ireland A, Mungall CJ, Leontis N, Rocca-Serra P, Ruttenberg A, Sansone S-A, Scheuermann RH, Shah N, Whetzel PL, Lewis S (2007) The OBO foundry: coordinated evolution of ontologies to support biomedical data integration. Nat Biotech 25:1251–1255

Stearns MQ, Price C, Spackman KA, Wang AY, SNOMED clinical terms (2001) Overview of the development process and project status. Proceedings of the AMIA Symposium. American Medical Informatics Association, p 662

Tudorache T, Falconer S, Noy NF, Nyulas C, Üstün TB, Storey M-A, Musen MA (2010) Ontology development for the masses: creating ICD-11 in WebProtégé. In: Ciniano P, Pinto HS (ed) Knowledge engineering and management by the masses. Springer, Berlin, pp 74–89

Tudorache T, Nyulas CI, Noy NF, Musen MA (2013) Using Semantic Web in ICD-11: three years down the road. In: The semantic web -ISWC 2013. Springer, Berlin, pp 195–211

Viklund H, Karlsson H (2009) Clinical decision support rules in an archetype-based health record system: combining Archetype Query Language (AQL) and Semantic Web Rule Language (SWRL). Linköping

Chapter 3
Exploiting Ontology Based Search and EHR Interoperability to Facilitate Clinical Trial Design

Anastasios Tagaris, Vassiliki Andronikou, Efthymios Chondrogiannis,
George Tsatsaronis, Michael Schroeder, Theodora Varvarigou and
Dionysios-Dimitrios Koutsouris

Abstract Clinical trials often fail to demonstrate beneficial effects and might overestimate the unwanted effects, with their results having low external validity. They focus on single interventions, whereas the clinical practice environment comprises various features that affect the efficacy, feasibility, duration and costs of a clinical trial. In this chapter we discuss PONTE, a platform which effectively guides medical researchers through clinical trial protocol design and offers intelligent services that address clinical needs, such as effective inclusion/exclusion criteria specification, intelligent search through a wide range of databases, clinical findings and background knowledge, and automated estimation of eligible patient population at cooperating healthcare entities. To the best of our knowledge, and to date, the PONTE platform is the first paradigm of an automated system that can effectively guide clinical trials protocol design, by linking data with drug, target and disease knowledge databases, clinical care and clinical research information systems, and guiding the users automatically though the whole pipeline of the clinical trial protocol design.

Keywords Clinical trial protocol design · Semantic-enabled technologies in life sciences · Electronic health records · Patient selection · Eligibility criteria · Semantic interoperability · Ontology alignment

3.1 Introduction

3.1.1 Clinical Research and Clinical Trials

All novel chemical and biological entities planned for human, use as therapeutic, diagnostic or preventive agents undergo rigorous in vitro and in vivo animal

A. Tagaris (✉) · V. Andronikou · E. Chondrogiannis · T. Varvarigou · D.-D. Koutsouris
Institute of Communication and Computer Systems (ICCS), National Technical University
of Athens, Athens, Greece
e-mail: tastagar@biomed.ntua.gr

G. Tsatsaronis · M. Schroeder
Biotechnology Center (BIOTEC), Technical University of Dresden (TUD), Dresden, Germany

D.-D. Koutsouris, A. A. Lazakidou (eds.), *Concepts and Trends in Healthcare*   21
Information Systems, Annals of Information Systems 16,
DOI 10.1007/978-3-319-06844-2_3, © Springer International Publishing Switzerland 2014

experimentation, before entering the phase of clinical development. Of 5,000 compounds that enter pre-clinical testing, only five, on average, are tested in human trials, and only one of these five receives approval for therapeutic use (Kraljevic et al. 2004). The clinical experimentation stage on human subjects is the last one in the chain of drug research and development, prior to approval by the regulatory authorities and marketing authorization granting. Because they involve humans, clinical trials pose scientific as well as legal and ethical challenges.

Today, the clinical development stage is comprised of *3 phases*. **Phase I**, in which a relatively small number of healthy volunteers or patients are enrolled (usually 30–70). The aim is to examine the pharmacokinetics, the bio-distribution and the clearance of the drug under investigation, and to *determine the safe dosing scheme*. Such studies last between 1 and 2 years. More than 1/3 of novel entities are eliminated during this phase. **Phase II**, in which a larger number of patients is enrolled (usually 100–200 per study). The aim is to *confirm the safe dosing scheme* derived from the Phase I and to *detect evidence of efficacy*. Phase II studies go for 2–3 years. Approximately half of the novel entities will be eliminated during this phase. Finally, the aim of a **Phase III** study is to *provide conclusive results* about the *new treatment compared to standard care*. This is done through (multinational, multicenter) randomized controlled clinical trials. Randomized controlled clinical trials have become the "golden" standard to assess clinical efficacy and/or safety, especially when the benefits are modest but worthwhile. Hence, they have formed the basis of regulatory guidelines and audit standards. Randomized controlled trials are based on power analysis which determines the chance of detecting a true-positive result. Today, a study is considered as adequately powered if it has at least 80 % chances of detecting a clinically significant effect when one exists. To calculate a study's power to detect a given effect, variables are being used, including the number of participants, the expected variability of their outcomes and the chosen probability of making a false positive conclusion (type I error). Reformulating these variables allows one to calculate the number of study patients needed to detect a clinically important effect size with acceptable power. Usually 500 up to low thousands of patients are being enrolled per study. Phase III studies last 3–5 years each. Up to 2/3 of the drugs tested will not successfully finish Phase III studies. Overall, of the thousands of molecules entering pre-clinical testing, less than 9 % will ultimately reach the market (Kraljevic et al. 2004).

3.1.2   Pharmaceutical Clinical Development Alone is a Lengthy and Costly Process

Over the years great debate has been taking place concerning the therapy development timeline, the invested resources as well as the reduced R&D productivity; i.e. the number of therapies which reach patients vs the number of investigational therapies for which research is held. In the past decades, the annually increasing financial and temporal resources spent on research did not reflect an increase in the success

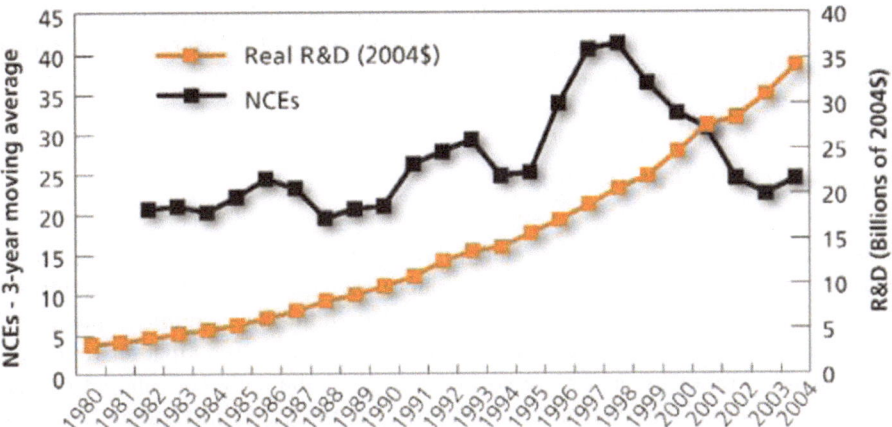

Fig. 3.1 Comparison of R&D costs versus launch of new chemical entities (NCEs). (Source: Tufts CSDD Approved NCE Database; PhRMA)

rate of therapy (clinical) development. Various factors have attributed to the drug R&D "inefficiency", including tighter regulations and adhesion to traditional, quite often obsolete, clinical trial design methodologies, in which studies that cannot reliably detect effect sizes may be defined as underpowered. Such studies are regarded as unethical and are not accepted neither by regulatory authorities and often nor by publishers. Despite their promise, newer adaptive design methodologies in clinical trials have not proved—at least yet—to be adequate to deliver new drugs sooner (and cheaper) to patients.

This delay that patients face in accessing new treatments comprises a major R&D cost in the drug industry. More specifically, the average cost for treatment development is *more than € 1 billion*—with recently reported figures indicating the overall required investment reaching even € 8 billion (Herper 2012)—with almost *one third* being accounted for clinical testing. Moreover, the development timeline of a new drug is on average 11.3 years (about 4.3 years for its discovery as well as pre-clinical research and development and about 7 years for clinical trials and final approval). In the meantime, a reduction of the number of new drugs entering the market has been observed with the R&D costs continuously increasing over the past years. According to CBO (2006) the main reasons for this reduction in productivity include: (i) the general trend towards larger and lengthier clinical trials, (ii) increased project failure rates in clinical trials, (iii) more time-consuming pre-clinical research processes, (iv) costs related to advances in research technology and (v) scientific opportunity (Fig. 3.1).

Moreover, even when the drug is marketed, despite the prior multidisciplinary excessive effort, time and money spent, the *drug's safety and efficacy profile* is continuously monitored through risk management plans, pharmacovigilance schemes, post-authorization safety and efficacy studies and meta-analyses. It is not unusual that warning letters are being issued to health professionals, that the summary of product characteristics is being altered or that the drug is being removed from circulation, based on data accumulated during the marketing of the drug and not during the clinical development phases.

3.1.3   Drug Repositioning

Within this context and with the reduction of drug approvals, the intensified competitive environment that blockbuster products are requested to survive within and the gradually reducing funding for new research within the field due to the global financial shrinkage, *drug repositioning* comprises a current trend that pharma companies tend to follow to gain more profits from drugs that either are about to go off patent or are already off-patent. Gathering data on potential application of drugs to new diseases and disorders is nowadays not only a means for evaluating the effectiveness of new medicine and pharmaceutical formulas but also for *experimenting on existing drugs and their appliance to new diseases and disorders.*

According to empirical studies, the number of medicines introduced worldwide containing new active ingredients dropped from an average of over 60 a year in the late 1980s to 52 in 1991, only 31 in 2001 (Van den Haak et al. 2002) and around 20–25 new licensed drugs per year over the past years (Fisk and Atun 2008). Aspirin and beta blockers comprise two most well-known examples; initially, aspirin was known for its analgesic, anti-inflammatory and antipyretic properties. However, aspirin's effects on blood clotting (as an antiplatelet agent) were first noticed in 1950 and since the end of the 1980s, low-dose aspirin has been widely used as a preventive drug for heart attacks. Interestingly, beta blockers, which were considered to be detrimental for heart failure, appeared to be beneficial and have changed the adverse course of heart failure. At the same time, the overall number of new active substances undergoing regulatory review is gradually falling, whereas pharmaceutical companies tend to *prefer launching modified versions of existing drugs*, which *present reduced risk of failure and can generate generous profits*. This approach extends to the ongoing attempts by pharmaceutical companies to extend the period of time under patent protection for a given drug and its associated family of products. This phenomenon has been even more intensified by the world economy shrinking which *causes reduction in the allocation of funds for new research vs repositioning of existing medications for new uses.*

3.2   Needs and Challenges in the field of Clinical Research

The overall clinical research landscape presented in the previous section encapsulates a series of *unmet needs* which in turn *pose important challenges* that the ICT world could at least partially address. Given the complexity and length of the processes included in clinical research, the analysis of these needs comprises a heavy task. However, there are 3 (three) major aspects in clinical research which significantly affect the research outcome; (i) the scientific question itself that the research efforts aim at answering, (ii) the considerations taken and design decisions made for mitigating patient risks and (iii) the intelligent patient selection.

3.2.1 Formulating the Research question

The difficult aspects of clinical trial design are concerned with the typical clinical investigator who would benefit greatly from having access to a comprehensive, interactive clinical trial design system. Current practice, both commercial and open source, tends to focus on providing access to discrete elements of the design process, e.g. patient registry, power calculation for number of subjects required, trial element checklists, and trial form templates. Most investigators are confronted with a complex path from trial concept to trial design and approval, particularly those dealing with the potential for international trial coordination, differences in administration by ethics committees, privacy concerns, confidentiality, informed consent and regulatory bodies, e.g. EMEA (European Medicines Agency) and FDA (Food and Drug Administration), along with the actual design of the trial structure, establishment of trial arms, primary and secondary endpoints and adverse event identification and reporting, Drug Safety Monitoring Boards and review, and most recently, the potential for implementation of adaptive trial design with interim data analysis and modification to inclusion/exclusion criteria, etc. It is, hence, crucial (for a system developed to support clinical trial design) to integrate all of these elements within its scope as well as, to provide access to just-in-time knowledge bases that include disease, drug and target information, ongoing clinical trials and potential issues around intellectual property concerns.

Such an approach, would primarily serve the purpose of aiding the Principal Investigator (PI) to formulate precisely and unambiguously the main research hypothesis based on which, the clinical trial will be designed, as well as to provide automated support towards addressing all of the aforementioned issues and viewing the hypothesis from all the necessary scientific angles. A typical flow within such a system, that would be able to support the formulation of a crucial research hypothesis, would examine the original hypothesis in question from three main perspectives, prior to the actual research question formulation, and would be able to provide in an automated manner scientific findings and support for documenting them:

Disease Focus
a. Determination of the *mechanisms of action of the associated disease*, towards investigating the potentiality of examining existing drugs in its therapy (drug repositioning),
b. Identification of all patients' *co-morbid conditions*, in order to consider drugs that may handle this complexity,
c. Examination of the *side effects of the drugs* that are under consideration, towards identifying potential therapy combinations,

Drug Focus

a. Understanding of the*metabolism of the drugs* that are considered,
b. Observation of responses in*past clinical trials* of single drugs or combination therapies for the disease under examination,
c. Consideration of*analogues of the examined drugs*, in order to minimize the side effects.

Target Focus

a. Analysis of the*critical biochemical pathways and processes* of the candidate targets, that may reveal additional opportunities for drug application into non-targeted diseases, but also blocking of pockets that are needed for the considered drug-target bindings,
b. Observation of*specificity differences* and/or opportunities to select alternative targets in a pathway in order to *maximize efficacy and specificity*.

The aforementioned angles may be considered as crucial towards formulating the research question that will constitute the basis of the clinical trial design. The main challenge in this regard is that a system that may encompass automated mechanisms to aid the Principal Investigator in formulating and revising research questions, with the aim to maximize the probabilities for a successful clinical trial by considering these three aspects in tandem, *should be able to harness the plethora of the publicly available document and knowledge sources*. It is precisely at this crucial design and architectural switch that technologies such as data and text mining, natural language processing, and semantic-enabled (e.g., ontology-based) computational approaches should be considered, which promise to extract and associate knowledge from heterogeneous data, both in nature (e.g., structured vs. unstructured), but also in content (e.g., protein, drug and disease databases).

3.3   Patient Safety

Clinical research findings quite often substantially *deviate* from the outcome of the treatments' application to clinical care (Taylor et al. 2007), limiting this way the validity of the trials' results and the medical community's understanding of how widely these results can, in fact, be applied while ensuring **patients' safety.** In particular, treatments with high efficacy may be limited by severe side effects, efficacy may be "lost in translation", side effects of treatments may be underestimated or treatment benefits may be overestimated. As an example, (Evans and Kalra 2001) indicate in their research that trials aiming to prevent stroke using antithrombotic therapies among patients with atrial fibrillation have recruited as few as 20% of eligible patients, often excluding older patients, women and people with previous cerebrovascular disease, which in turn leads to uncertainty about the actual benefit of such treatment in these groups. In fact, results of drug trials may show that mortality rates are lower than 3 %, whereas in real life this rate may prove to be greater than 25 %, placing the patients' safety in great danger!

Poor trial design, lack of proper funding, lack of access to and linking with important and complete data, such as real-world patient data over years, a non-representative patient sample recruited for the clinical trial and the inability to predict off-target effects and potential at-risk populations comprise main factors driving to these major problems seriously affecting *patients' safety*. Clinical trials usually focus on single interventions, whereas the clinical practice environment includes various features such as intercurrent illnesses, psychological status, compliance and concomitant therapies that need to be taken into account (Wilcken et al. 2007)—a fact that is driven mainly by the *non-representative sample of patients* recruited for participation in clinical trials. The latter has two major aspects and is strongly affected in two steps during the clinical research lifecycle; *specification of eligibility criteria* in study design and *patient recruitment*, with the latter being presented in the next section.

The eligibility criteria (aka *inclusion* and *exclusion criteria*) describe the characteristics that the potential study participants should have as well as the population to which the study results are applicable. They ensure that novel therapeutic approaches are investigated, in terms of safety and efficacy, on similar groups of people and they determine the extent to which the study results are generalizable. They also comprise a safety measure, by ensuring exclusion of any person for whom the study will have "known" or expected risks which outweigh any possible benefits.

Lack of models and standards, which could guide the expression and specification of eligibility criteria, leads to a series of problems which affect study outcomes, costs and research potential. Hence, great variability in the criteria across trials is met, whereas researchers often face difficulty in evaluating, comparing or replicating studies. Moreover, important aspects are ignored or underestimated, such as lifestyle, while there is a tendency towards strict criteria which restrict the study population and this way limit way the pool of available patients eligible to participate in the trial (and thus the recruitment potential) as well as the generalizability potential of the study results (affecting this way the market size to which the investigational treatment targets at).

3.3.1 Patient Selection

Selection and recruitment of a representative patient sample in clinical trials comprises an important step in the overall clinical research lifecycle, which significantly determines whether the trial will be successful. The traditional process followed by Principal Investigators (PIs) and researchers involves trial advertising, contacting hospitalized patients within their own clinic and/or hospital or search through the medical records of their own patients. Most of these processes are performed manually, are highly dependent on the PI's and researchers direct contact with patients, are time-consuming and quite often ineffective. The restrictions posed by the commonly applied processes lead to tremendous delays and/or failure to recruit the required sample size. In fact, only 15 % of clinical trials finish on schedule, while the rest face tremendous delays, preoccupation of the staff and disruption of the study timetable due to low participant accrual. Moreover, 60–80 % of trials do not meet their temporal endpoint due to problems in recruitment, whereas 30 % of trial sites fail to recruit even a single participant (Nitkin 2003). Recruitment of a patient sample less than the one required based on the study design, however, leads to not safely generalizable research results and quite often reduced ability of the study to detect efficacy. If the share of recruitment in the overall study costs—which goes between 30 and 40 % (McDonald et al. 2006)—is also taken into consideration, then overcoming the barriers for efficient, fast and effective recruitment seems to be an imperative need. This need is further intensified by pharmaceutical companies and clinical research organizations' needs.

Currently tremendous market opportunities for potential blockbusters may be delayed due to operational difficulties in clinical trial design and implementation. With limited patent lifetime protection and increased risk from generic competition, the onus on optimizing the most costly phase of drug development, clinical trials, looms as the key for enhanced return on investment in the industry and improving the long-term access to improved medicines for the patients and physicians. Many drugs designed for attacking very specific biological targets pose significant limitations in the medical profile of the patients eligible to participate in their clinical trials; lack of access to a large patient pool through proper linking of complex systems with disparate clinical care systems leads to operational delays and quite often to inadequate inclusion of critical study populations. This way patent exclusivity time is reduced and the most commercially productive phase of a drug's life cycle is significantly shortened with the pharmaceutical companies and the clinical research organizations facing many difficulties in gaining a competitive edge (Business Insights 2007).

Limited access to patient data comprises an important barrier towards this direction. In healthcare, *Electronic Health Records* (*EHRs*) and *Clinical Information Management Systems* (*CLIS*) are gradually being used for storing and managing patient health data, including demographics, therapies, disorders, genetics, and family history among others, with their main use focusing on treatment management. Nevertheless, their isolated development and poor linking, along with a series of privacy concerns, keep their secondary uses in other fields, such clinical research and epidemiology, rather limited. For clinical research, EHRs comprise a pool of patient data which could boost and automate the patient selection process as well as allow for enhanced post market research.

Regarding recruitment in particular, the innate characteristics of the EHRs in terms of semantics, structure and purpose pose a great challenge when aiming at their use for automated patient selection. More specifically, their different primary purpose of development and their isolated development of EHRs, at hospital and clinic department level, lead to EHRs of high heterogeneity at system, syntax, structure, semantics and interface/messaging level.

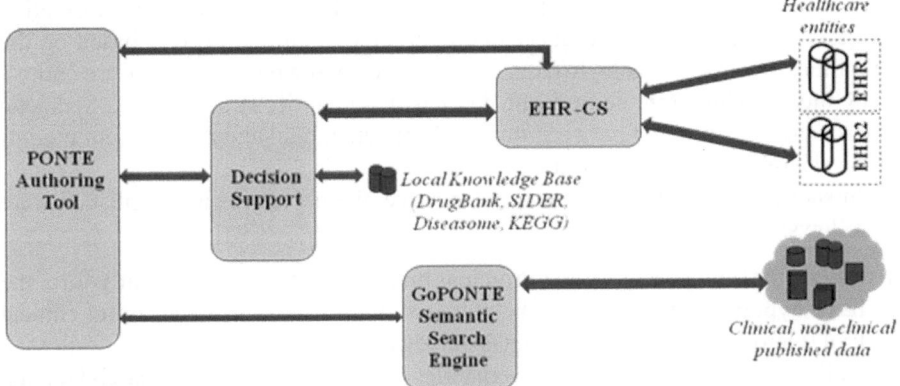

Fig. 3.2 Overview of the PONTE platform components

3.4   Combining Ontology-based Search and EHRs for Clinical Trial Designs

This section presents the methodology adopted by the PONTE platform[1] and the developed technologies in order to address the aforementioned needs and challenges.

In Fig. 3.2 we present the main PONTE components and their interactions. The PONTE Authoring Tool (PAT) constitutes the basic GUI and editor for the principal investigator (PI) and clinical researcher(s) in order to design a clinical trial protocol (CTP). The PI initiates the design of a new CTP, and the basic function is to set the parameters of the protocol, mainly a drug and a disease around which the clinical trial will be designed. The PAT is also the component allowing the research team to specify all of the CTP parameters, pertaining to the inclusion and the exclusion criteria (i.e., eligibility criteria). In order to present the user with automated suggestions during CTP design, PAT is aided by two components: the Decision Support System (DSS) (Tsatsaronis et al. 2012), and the GoPonte semantic search engine[2]. The GoPonte semantic search engine provides semantic annotation services, e.g., annotates with ontology concepts unstructured text, and also is able to *search and filter* all the MEDLINE indexed publications with the underlying ontology concepts. Finally, the EHR Communication System (EHR-CS) (Chondrogiannis et al. 2012) is responsible for (i) translating the *eligibility criteria set* within a clinical trial protocol into *EHR parameters* specific to the system of each healthcare entity having an established agreement with the clinical trial for acting as a recruitment site, and, (ii) providing the user with the estimation of the size of the patient population which satisfies the specified eligibility criteria at each such healthcare entity.

---

[1] The PONTE platform was developed as part of the PONTE EU project. More details about the project can be found at: http://www.ponte-project.eu/.

[2] Publicly available at: http://www.gopubmed.org/web/goponte/.

Hence, EHR-CS includes a set of mechanisms which perform query transformation (Tagaris et al. 2012); from a query expressing the eligibility criteria based on the Eligibility Criteria Ontology to a query formulated based on each healthcare entity's EHR model. Thus, this component deals with semantic, structural and syntactic heterogeneity issues met between the platform data model and the different models at the site of the healthcare entities.

In short, from the technological perspective, the objectives accomplished were as follows:

1. Offer a toolset in order for the Principal Investigator to more efficiently form the basic hypothesis and research the potential it has to lead to a successful clinical trial (Ontology Based Searching (Biomedical Domain))
2. Build models encapsulating the semantics of both the Clinical Research Domain and the Healthcare Domain using Ontologies, either by integrating existing ones or building new ones where needed. (ex. Global EHR Ontology based on HL7 RIM[3], OpenEHR[4] etc.)
3. Develop a language for expressing eligibility criteria
4. Convert eligibility criteria into EHR parameters enabling the search of potential study participants in healthcare records. (Ontology Alignment/Accessibility to EHRs and CLIS Data)

3.4.1 Semantic Searching in Literature

Clinical and non-clinical research findings are disseminated in the biomedical literature and in specialized databases. A possible architectural realization is based upon an existing semantic search approach (GoWeb)[5]. The GoWeb approach was extended and adapted to the two possible use cases within PONTE:

1. Having the search engine as an **internal Web Service** integrated with the Decision Support component
2. Use the semantic search engine as **Stand-alone application** and integrate the corresponding workflow in the overall solution.

In both scenarios, access to the various data sources using the Semantic Representation Layer and in particular the PONTE Ontology had to be in place (Roumier et al. 2012).

The workflow of the semantic search engine as an internal service integrated with the decision support component is described in Fig. 3.3 and starts with the user choosing one of the pre-defined questions suggested from the Decision sup-

---

[3] The Reference Information Model (RIM) is the cornerstone of the HL7 V3 development process, comprising a large pictorial representation of the clinical data (domains) and identifying the life cycle of events that a message or groups of related messages will carry.

[4] http://www.openehr.org/.

[5] http://gopubmed.org/web/goweb/3?WEB10O00h00100090000.

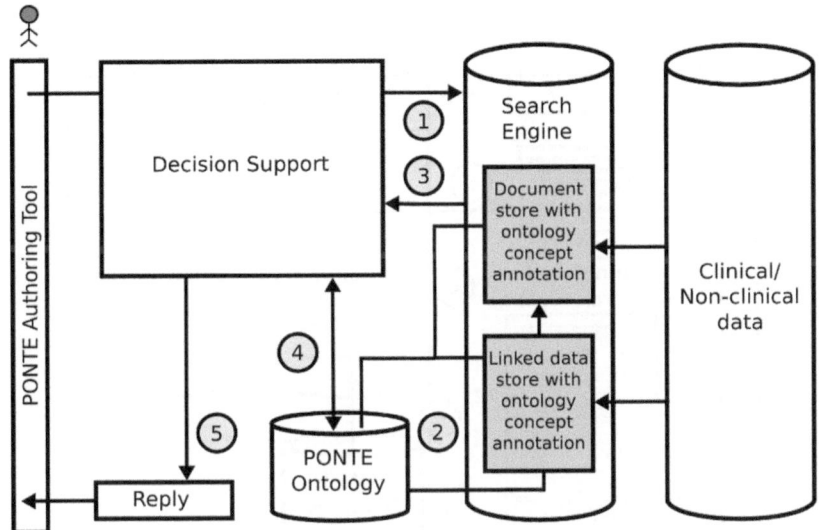

Fig. 3.3 Workflow of the semantic search engine approach as an internal service integrated with the decision support component

port component (1). The search engine component contains extracted research findings from textual sources and from relevant linked data sources that are linked to terms from the PONTE Ontology. The documents in the document store are indexed with the relevant ontology terms using text mining (2). The text indexes are created whenever new documents are added to the clinical and non-clinical data repository in order to speed up the literature retrieval task. On incoming queries, the search engine component selects from the indexed document store those documents that are annotated with the relevant terms from the PONTE ontology and with links to entities of external data sources from the Linked data store and returns a list of results (3). On the basis of the identified ontology entities and their annotations, the reasoning component provides decision support utilizing the semantics of the PONTE Ontology (4) and returns the results to the PONTE Authoring Tool (5). The annotated documents on which the decision support is grounded will be presented to the user to provide the highest possible transparency.

The second use case for the search engine as a **stand-alone** application used by the doctor for general research on the clinical trial topic is shown in Fig. 3.4. The figure displays the workflow of the semantic search engine approach as stand-alone application showing the main components and their interactions. The workflow starts with the user submitting a **query** via the search input field from the search engine started from the **PONTE Authoring Tool** (1). The search engine component selects from the **indexed document store** (2)—a subset of the **clinical and non-clinical data sources** (3)—those documents that are annotated with the relevant terms from the PONTE Ontology (4). Depending on the preferences the user may have selected via the PONTE Authoring Tool, the whole PONTE Ontology, only

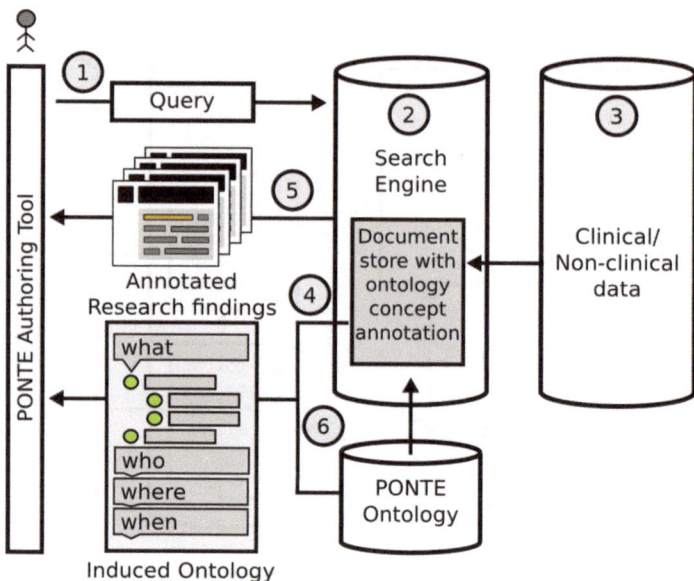

Fig. 3.4 Workflow of the semantic search engine approach as stand-alone application showing the main components and their interactions

certain parts, or only terms from specific underlying ontologies, such as GO and MeSH, are considered. The search keywords and the identified entities form the annotation are highlighted in the search results. Then the results are rendered and sent back to the search engine's front end started from the PONTE Authoring Tool (5). Based on the annotations and the ontology structure the tree representation is induced; top concepts are selected and sent to the front end (6).

Some of the information will come from Linked Data sources[6] which are semantic data sources accessible through Web Services using a semantic query language. The origin of that data will be displayed to the end user so that he/she can evaluate it according to the trust he/she has in its origin.

3.4.2 Eligibility Criteria and (Research focused) EHR Models

The **EHR model** (Chondrogiannis et al. 2012) has been developed as a semantic representation of the EHR parameters which comprise direct translations of, or are indirectly linked with, eligibility criteria. In other words, it *comprises the subset of the EHR which is of interest for the PONTE purposes*; i.e. applying eligibility criteria on EHRs for finding patients who could potentially participate in a study. This model acts as a *bridge between the eligibility criteria of the study and the*

---

[6] http://linkeddata.org/.

EHR data at the healthcare entity which could serve as a pool for study subjects. The reason behind the development of the EHR model is that the semantic distance between the eligibility criteria and the EHR parameters at each healthcare entity would require a heavy mapping process when (i) a new healthcare provider is linked with the platform, (ii) the EHR of the provider is updated (iii) the eligibility criteria supported are updated. Moreover, in many cases, it would result in great duplication of work. Hence, the EHR model introduces an intermediate step in the translation process which takes place only during system initialization and *requires updating only when supported eligibility criteria are updated.* By allowing the expression of the eligibility criteria in EHR-based terms, this model brings the criteria into a form which is of great semantic proximity to any healthcare entity and, thus, the linking of a new EHR to the system requires less mapping effort.

The **Eligibility Criteria model** (Chondrogiannis et al. 2012) comprises an ontological representation of the *inclusion and exclusion criteria* which may be specified for a study. Its development has been based on criteria extracted from clinical studies available at clinicaltrials.gov[7]. The need for developing these two models stems from the fact that the eligibility criteria describe the characteristics that the target population should have while the EHRs store information about the health status and progress of a patient. For example, a criterion for exclusion of a trial might be suffering from a cardiovascular disorder, whereas a patient might be suffering from acute myocardial infarction, a much more specific determination of a disorder. Both models have been developed as OWL ontologies.

It should be noted that for interoperability purposes, international standards and specifications have been taken into consideration and linked with the models, including HL7-RIM and OpenEHR, as well as international classifications and vocabularies (as Controlled Terminologies) for the various parameters, such as ICD-10-CM[8] and SNOMED-CT[9] for disorders, ATC[10], ChEBI[11] and PubChem[12] for active substances, HUGO[13] for genes, etc.

3.4.3 Eligibility Criteria Language

The eligibility criteria language allows the end user to formally describe an inclusion or an exclusion criterion using as a basis the Eligibility Criteria model. In fact, an eligibility criterion is defined based on the terms (mainly properties) of the Eligibility Criteria ontology by specifying one or more *restrictions over the range*

---

[7] http://www.clinicaltrials.gov.

[8] http://www.who.int/classifications/icd/en/ and http://www.cdc.gov/nchs/icd/icd10cm.htm.

[9] http://www.ihtsdo.org/snomed-ct/.

[10] http://www.whocc.no/atc_ddd_index/.

[11] http://www.ebi.ac.uk/chebi/.

[12] http://pubchem.ncbi.nlm.nih.gov/.

[13] https://wiki.nci.nih.gov/display/TCGA/HUGOgenesymbol.

```
<sdm:InclusionExclusionCriteria>
    <odm:Description>
        <odm:TranslatedText xml:lang="en-us">
            Eligibility Criteria of a Clinical Study
        </odm:TranslatedText>
    </odm:Description>
    <sdm:InclusionCriteria>
        <sdm:Criterion OID="001" Name="Males" ConditionOID="COND.MALE">
            <odm:Description>
                <odm:TranslatedText xml:lang="en-us">Male Subjects ...</odm:TranslatedText>
            </odm:Description>
        </sdm:Criterion>
    </sdm:InclusionCriteria>
    <sdm:ExclusionCriteria><!-- +++ --></sdm:ExclusionCriteria>
</sdm:InclusionExclusionCriteria>
```

Fig. 3.5 CDISC—inclusion-exclusion criteria

```
<FormalExpression Language="SPARQL" Content="EligibilityCriteriaOntology">
    <AskQuery>
        PREFIX rdf: <http://www.w3.org/1999/02/22-rdf-syntax-ns#>
        PREFIX ce: <http://www.semanticweb.org/ontologies/2012/10/CommonElements.owl#>>
        PREFIX eco: <http://www.semanticweb.org/ontologies/2012/10/EligibilityCriteriaOntology.owl#>
        ASK WHERE {
            ?person rdf:type ce:Person .
            ?person eco:sexAtScreeningCode ?sexCode .
            ?sexCode rdf:type ce:DICOMCode .
            ?sexCode ce:amountValue ?sexValue
                FILTER ( ?sexValue = "M" )
        }
    </AskQuery>
</FormalExpression>
```

Fig. 3.6 Formal expression of a criterion in SPARQL

of values in which they should belong to. Hence, for example, the Eligibility Criteria Ontology includes the property "Age at Screening" which is used for defining that *"the age of the persons eligible to participate in the clinical study should be between 18 and 60 years"*. For this purpose, a *syntax* is required for the representation of the above restriction. The representation of the eligibility criteria is based on the Design Model and Operation Data Model proposed by CDISC, which defines a wrapper for the criteria (Fig. 3.5).

The actual definition of the criterion is included in the element ConditionDef and the language used is SPARQL, given that the models are developed as OWL ontologies and is expressive enough for formulating the criteria. The following figure shows the expression of the criterion *"Include male patients"* (Fig. 3.6):

3.4.4 Translation of Eligibility Criteria into requests towards EHR

The PONTE approach for querying EHRs in order to find patients satisfying the eligibility criteria of a particular study includes a *two-level mapping* process (Fig. 3.7); from the eligibility criteria model to the Global EHR model (level 1) and from the latter to the healthcare entity EHR model (level 2). Alternatively, we name those two levels and the corresponding processes as *PONTE EHR Request Processor* and

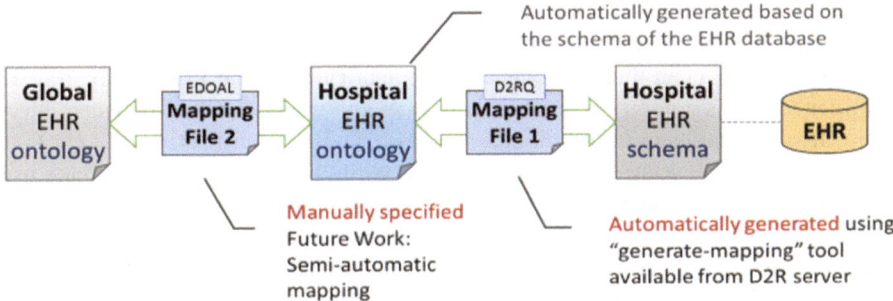

Fig. 3.7 Mapping between Global EHR ontology and the Schema of the EHR datasource

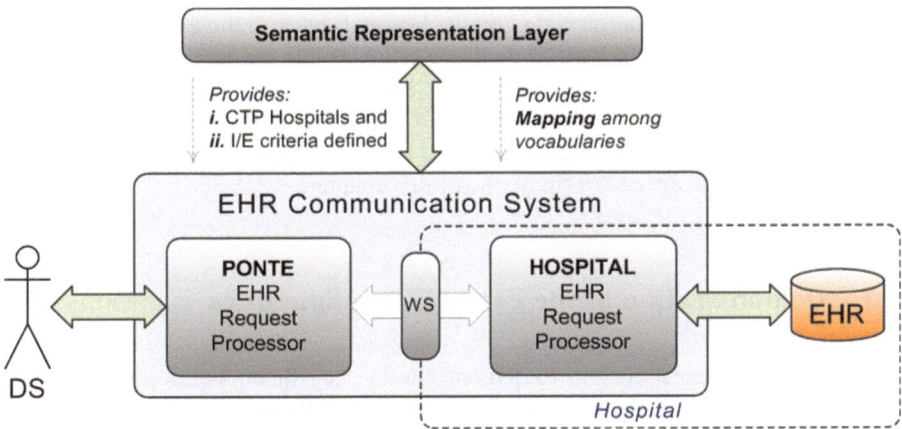

Fig. 3.8 Overall architecture of the EHR communication system

Hospital EHR Request Processor (see also Fig. 3.8). Given that the Global EHR model is aligned with other models such as OpenEHR and HL7 RIM, if a health-care entity complies with any of them then, automatic translation of the eligibility criteria is feasible and no further mapping is required. This scenario fits very well in cases where the hospital EHRs have adopted some kind of international classification systems (e.g., SNOMED CT, ICD10/9, ATC, LOINC) etc.

However, if the data in a hospital does not comply with a standard, there is the need for another level mapping with the use of a **custom dictionary** attached "at the side" of the hospital, which is responsible for translating the terms used within the specific EHR database, to one of the international standards adopted in PONTE. In fact, within PONTE, we have used international classification systems for gender (DICOM), disorders (ICD-10-CM), active substances (ChEBI), clinical & laboratory examinations (LOINC), etc. To cope with cases where EHR uses custom vocabularies (there have been many cases where the data is entered in the database by using words stemming from the native spoken language) a semi-automated procedure is needed to map and translate the local EHR terms used by hospital X to the corresponding terms of an international codification or classification schema. The resulting data can then be translated automatically by the **PONTE Semantic Mapper** which is a component capable to map and translate terms between international vocabularies or terminologies such as ICD-10, SNOMED, ICPC2 etc.).

This way, ambiguous mapping is avoided, while hospital EHRs that make use of standards can be connected easily to the PONTE platform. A **list of all hospitals** connected to the PONTE platform is attached to the *EHR Communication component*, which, amongst others, contains information about the type of connection with the specific hospital EHR and the *coding schema* used for the identification of concepts within each EHR (Fig. 3.8).

The **Web Services (WS)** at the end of each hospital are responsible for receiving a standard PONTE question and asking the EHR for the required data; then, sending the resulting data (provided by the hospital) back to the PONTE system in the PONTE predefined format. Thus these WSs are implementing the queries for that EHR database and are dealing with its specific structure, which the PONTE platform is not aware of. It should be noted that the communication between the PONTE platform and the healthcare entities' HER, encapsulates a series of security mechanisms, which are out of the scope of this chapter.

3.5 Demonstration of the PONTE functionalities

The following screenshots aim to demonstrate the key functionalities of the PONTE platform regarding the 3 aforementioned key challenges: (i) **Research Question**, which is addressed mainly by the *Semantic Searching and Filtering* (see Fig. 3.9 and 3.10), (ii) **Patient Selection**, mainly addressed with the *Eligibility Criteria and access/mapping to EHRs components* (Fig. 3.11) and finally (iii) **Patient Safety**, for which the PAT integrates all the platform's functionalities (Fig. 3.12) in a web tool offering a *Structured CTP Design methodology*.

3.6 Conclusions and Future Directions

Clinical research includes a great number of complicated processes which require the collection, filtering and intelligent processing of a wealth of distributed data. The continuously increasing costs combined with the rising societal need for fast access to effective therapies set the priority for the improvement of these processes higher than ever before. ICT comprises a promising vehicle towards the latter. Although the list of aspects in clinical research which can be significantly boosted by ICT is rather long, there are three major steps which significantly affect the research outcome and are of great ICT interest; (i) the specification of the scientific question to be answered through the clinical research, (ii) the study *design*

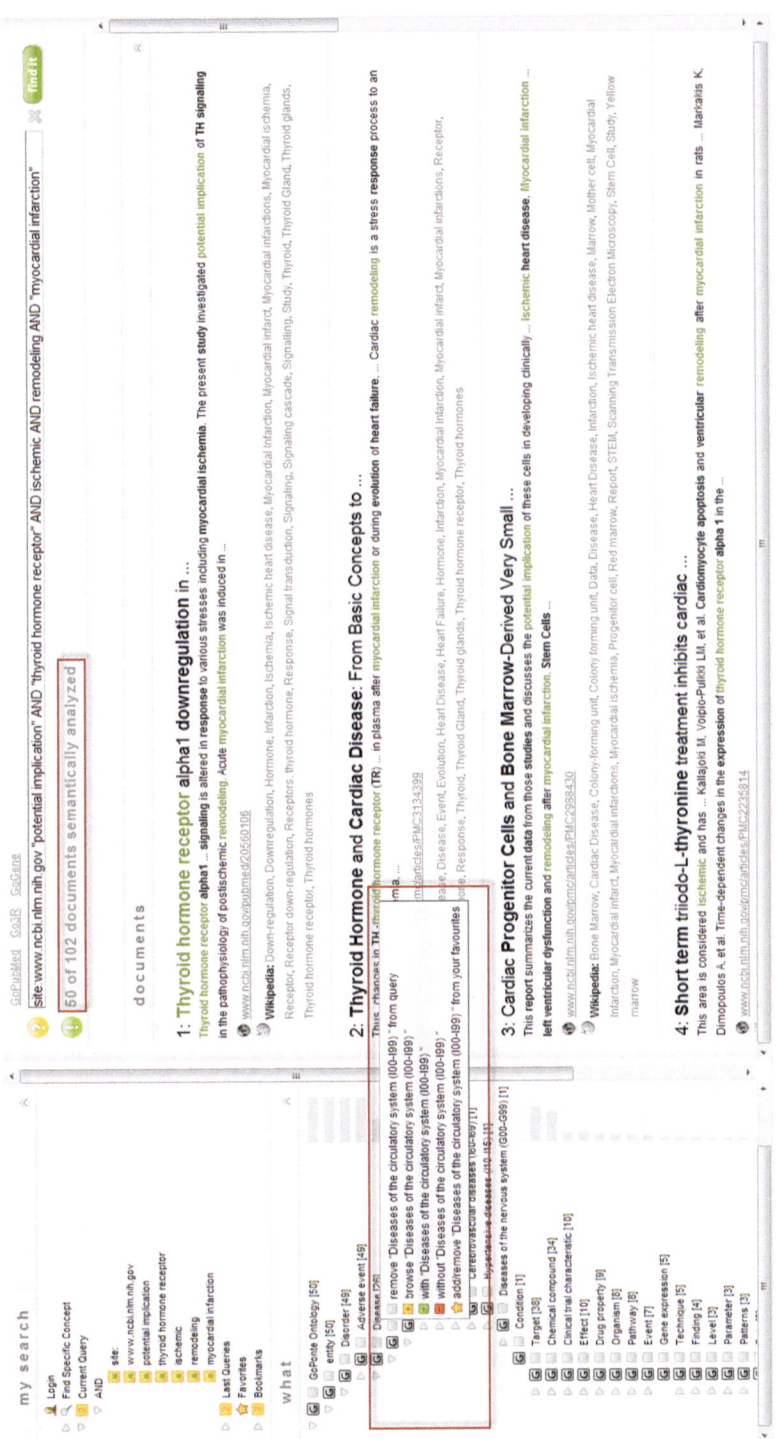

Fig. 3.9 Ontology assisted literature search through GoPONTE: "Potential implication of thyroid hormone receptors in the development of ischemic remodeling after myocardial infarction"

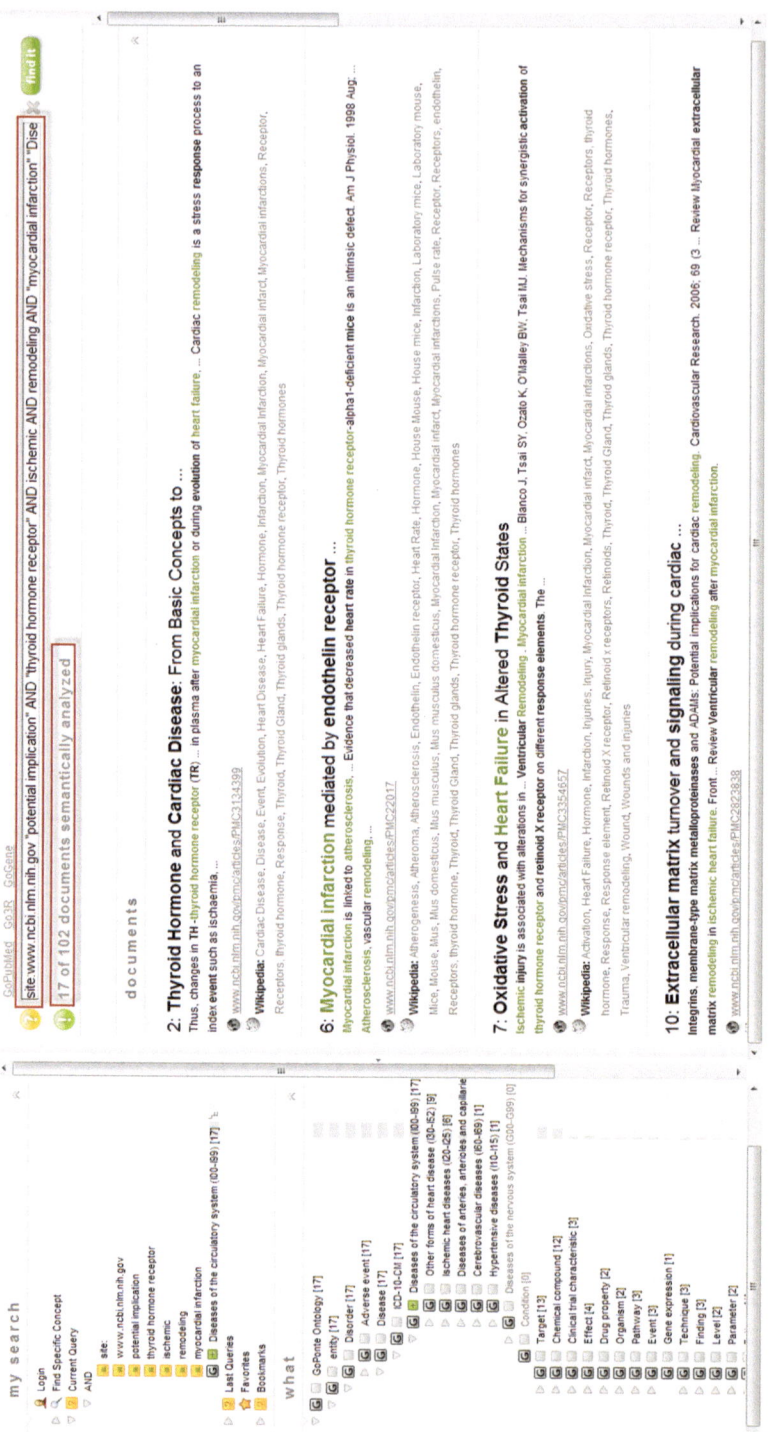

Fig. 3.10 Semantic filtering of results for diseases of the circulatory system

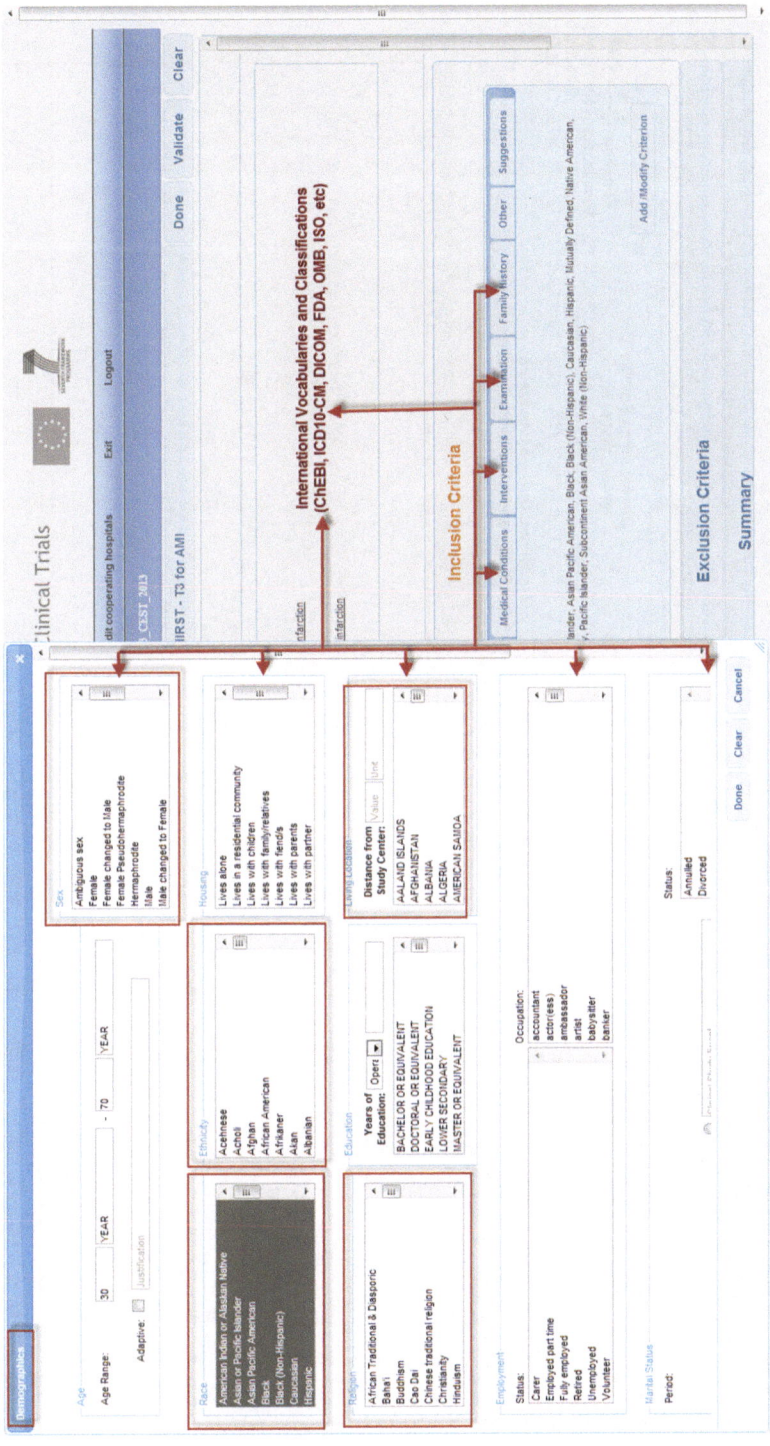

Fig. 3.11 Eligibility criteria specification: Demographics

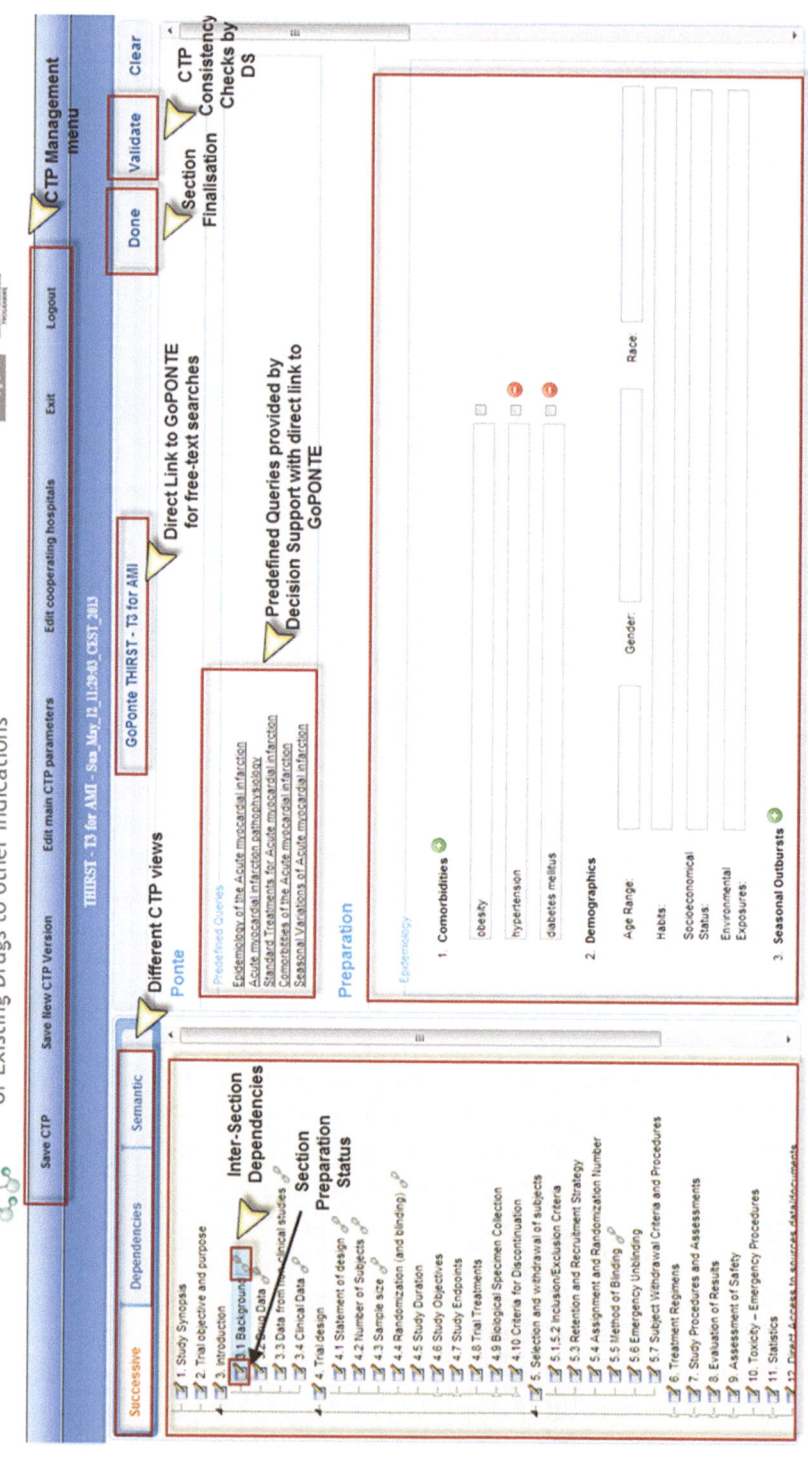

Fig. 3.12 PONTE Authoring Tool (PAT) integrating all platform's functionalities

decisions which ensure the safety of the patients both during the trial but also when the molecule reaches the market and (iii) the fast and intelligent patient selection. Within this context, PONTE is an example which has developed a series of novel mechanisms exploiting state of the art technologies, including Web2.0 and semantic web, which aim at facilitating clinical research with a particular focus on addressing these needs. Hence, GoPONTE offers semantically assisted access to literature for formulating a scientifically viable and novel research question. The two models developed, i.e., Eligibility Criteria Model and Global EHR Model, set the basis for the specification of unambiguous and complete eligibility criteria for a study, which take into consideration patient safety and targeted study efficacy and for the representation of these criteria into healthcare terms, respectively. Hence, along with a series of translation mechanisms, eligibility criteria are applied on EHRs (across various healthcare entities) allowing for the selection of patients who could potentially participate in the study.

Given the complexity and workload required for establishing the mapping between the aforementioned models but also the Global EHR model and the EHR of each healthcare entity linked with the platform, part of our future work will focus on developing a tool which will allow for the semi-automatic alignment of the Global EHR ontology and the produced EHR ontologies of healthcare entities wishing to connect to the platform. Moreover, the Eligibility Criteria model, and consequently the Global EHR model, will be continuously updated in order to be able to allow for the formulation of much more complicated eligibility criteria. Furthermore, effort will be made to further improve semantic search by enriching the ontologies it exploits with more terms and relationships as well as integrating improved data mining mechanisms.

References

Chondrogiannis E et al. (2012) A novel query rewriting mechanism for semantically interlinking clinical research with electronic health records. ACM, Craiova

Evans A, Kalra L (2001) Are the results of randomized controlled trials on anticoagulation in patients with atrial fibrillation generalizable to clinical practice? Arch Intern Med 161:1443–1447

Fisk NM, Atun R (2008) Market failure and the poverty of new drugs in maternal health. PLOS Med 5(1): 22–37

Herper M (2012) The truly staggering cost of inventing new drugs. Forbes, NY

Kraljevic S, Stambrook PJ, Pavelic K (2004) Accelerating drug discovery. Eur Mol Biol Org 5:837–842

McDonald AM et al. (2006) What influences recruitment to randomised controlled trials? A review of trials funded by two UK funding agencies. Trials 7(9):3–4

Nitkin R (2003) Patient recruitment strategies. Bethesda, Training workshop conducted by National Institutes of Health

Roumier J et al (2012) Semantically-assisted hypothesis validation in clinical research. eChallenges, Lisbon

Sahoo A. Patient Recruitment and Retention in Clinical Trials; Emerging strategies in Europe, the US and Asia. London: Business Insights Ltd; 2007 Jun p. 149. Report No.: RBI00152

Tagaris A, Chondrogiannis E, Andronikou V, Tsatsaronis G, Mourtzoukos K, Roumier J, Matskanis N, Schroeder M, Massonet P, Varvarigou T (2012) Semantic Interoperability between Clinical Research and Healthcare: the PONTE approach, Semantic Interoperability in Medical Informatics (SIMI2012) Workshop co-located with the ESWC2012, May 2012, Heraklion, Crete

Taylor RS, Bethell HJ, Brodie DA (2007) Clinical trials versus the real world: The example of cardiac rehabilitation. Br J Cardiol 14(3):175–178

Tsatsaronis G, Konstantinos M, Vassiliki A, Tassos T, Iraklis V, Michael S, Theodora V, Dimitris K, Nikolaos M (2012) "PONTE: a context-aware approach for automated clinical trial protocol design." In proceedings of the 6th International Workshop on Personalized Access, Profile Management, and Context Awareness in Databases in conjunction with VLDB, August 2012, Istanbul, Turkey

Van den Haak M, Sculthorpe P, McAuslane J. (2002) New active substance activities: submission, authorisation and marketing 2001. CMR International, Epsom

Wilcken NR, Gebski VJ, Pike R, Keech AC (2007) Putting results of a clinical trial into perspective. MJA 186(7):368–370

Chapter 4
Ontology-Driven Authorization Policies on Personal Health Records for Sustainable Citizen-Centered Healthcare

Mikaela Poulymenopoulou, Flora Malamateniou and George Vassilacopoulos

Abstract The citizen-centered paradigm requires that citizens are active participants in their healthcare processes. Personal health records (PHRs) empower citizens and allow them to manage their health and wellness by collecting life-long cross-institutional information from various sources. A virtual PHR is defined here as a collaborative platform, which is enhanced by cloud computing and Internet of Things (IOT) technologies, for sharing citizens' healthcare data typically stored in distributed, autonomous healthcare data sources as well as healthcare data stored by the citizen him/herself and assistive technology equipment; it can thus be considered as an entity on the network that, in addition to its own medical data, it can, be populated by relevant healthcare information on the fly at the moment of an attempted access. Although the requirement for integrating distributed, heterogeneous data sources for use by PHR services is challenging, pointing to the need for establishing a data sharing policy based on an interoperability platform, to resolve the heterogeneity among the data sources, new security challenges are induced due to the facts that citizens are the owners of their medical data and that various security policies are enforced on the various data sources. This chapter presents an authorization system for a virtual PHR, which is based on semantic technologies such as ontologies and is provided as a cloud service, to enable authorized access to integrated citizen information upon user requests. The system is based on the role and attribute based access control (RABAC) model and supports authorization policies of various granularity levels subject to area-wide constraints imposed by the health and social services involved.

Keywords PHR · Citizen-centered care · PHR authorization · RABAC

M. Poulymenopoulou (✉) · F. Malamateniou · G. Vassilacopoulos
Department of Digital Systems, University of Piraeus, Piraeus, Greece
e-mail: mpouly@unipi.gr

F. Malamateniou
e-mail: flora@unipi.gr

G. Vassilacopoulos
e-mail: gvass@unipi.gr

D.-D. Koutsouris, A. A. Lazakidou (eds.), *Concepts and Trends in Healthcare Information Systems,* Annals of Information Systems 16,
DOI 10.1007/978-3-319-06844-2_4, © Springer International Publishing Switzerland 2014

4.1   Introduction

Citizen-centeredness is about a higher level of citizen engagement to their health-care leading to better return of investment than the treatment of a disease after a diagnosis (Berwick 2009; Gajanayake et al. 2011; Wickramasinghe et al. 2012). In addition, citizen-centeredness empowers citizens with ownership of their health and social information, thus enabling them to grant authorization for access to appropriate third parties (Carrion et al. 2011; Cushman et al. 2010). Hence, one requirement for the realization of citizen-centered healthcare is the creation of appropriate services that integrate citizen health and social information from various, heterogeneous data sources so that it can be easily viewed and managed by interested, authorized parties (Kahn et al. 2009; Malamateniou et al. 1998; Poulymenopoulou et al. 2012). Virtual PHRs enable the creation of virtual healthcare workgroups organized around citizen-centered care as a collaborative network with the objective to improve citizens' quality of care (Bairs et al. 2011; Kahn et al. 2009; Kim et al. 2011; Malamateniou et al. 1998; Mori et al. 2012). Nowadays, virtual PHRs may be enhanced by the recent technological advancements of cloud computing and the Internet of Things (IOT) in an attempt to integrate citizen information from multiple health and social data sources, including data from medical devices or things of the citizen living space (Mahajan and Patel 2012; Said and Tolba 2012; Steele et al. 2012).

Although virtual PHRs can bring important benefits to citizens and support sustainable citizen-centered care, they pose additional challenges related to the protection of citizen information (Calvillo et al. 2013; Chen et al. 2012). The basic idea is to retain the citizen-centered concept of the PHR whereby the citizen is the exclusive security administrator for (owner of) his/her healthcare information, in a PHR and, hence, empowered to authorize other subjects to access it while not violating security policies of the diverse data sources (Li et al. 2010; Li et al. 2012; Pirtle and Chandra 2011). Hence, in a virtual PHR, an access request for citizen information needs to be evaluated by both the global (at PHR level) and the local (at the individual healthcare provider level) authorization systems (Blobel 2011) requiring a harmonization of the local authorization policies with the global (virtual PHR) authorization policy based on current legislation, ethical guidelines and personal preferences. This is mostly a semantic interoperability challenge that can be confronted by using ontologies for modeling security concepts which, in turn, should be mutually understood by all parties involved.

This chapter presents an authorization system for a virtual PHR cloud service that integrates health and social information over time from the citizen and sites of care in a structure (clinical documents) that is readily accessible. In particular, the virtual PHR cloud service is described as an entity on the network consisted of the following information categories: (a) the physically stored patient information contained in traditional PHRs, (b) the physically stored health information from medical devices connected to patient such as from assistive telecare systems, (c) the social care information retrieved on request from social care organizations; and (d) the health information extracted from various healthcare systems such as primary and hospital care electronic medical records - EMRs. Information of the latter two categories is extracted on the fly from relevant information repositories to populate the virtual PHR upon an attempted request for access The virtual PHR authorization system described here is based on the ownership paradigm and the role-based and attribute-based access control model (RABAC) enhanced by ontologies and ontology rules to create a semantic framework. Thus, it incorporates authorization administration and enforcement mechanisms for defining and enforcing citizen-centered authorization policies of various granularity levels subject to the constraints set by the various providers' authorization systems.

4.2   Related Work

Currently, there is a widespread international interest in modeling security and privacy services for healthcare, meanwhile extending the approach to health by including social care, prevention, fitness and public health in general (Blobel 2011; Calvillo et al. 2013; Trojer et al. 2012; Weitzman et al. 2011). Due to its particular relevance for this chapter, the focus is exclusively on authorization and access control services for protecting citizen dispersed personal health resources according to the citizen-centered concept. The citizen-centered paradigm encourages citizens to take an active role in the management and maintenance of their health. However, citizen-centered authorization policies have a potential to interfere with the tasks that a stakeholder has to execute, and therefore, conflicting with providers' goals. A successful citizen-centered authorization system should support individual data privacy according to citizen preferences and authorized citizen information flow during healthcare processes for better healthcare outcomes (Barua et al. 2011; Li et al. 2010; Martino and Ahuja 2010; Mohan et al. 2009; Ruotsalainen et al. 2012).

In healthcare security literature, a variety of citizen-centered security frameworks and access control systems have been proposed. For example, there has been reported an access control system of personal distributed health resources through the coexistence of access control policies defined by the citizen, providers and regional and international legislative organizations with a priority relation between those policies (Calvillo et al. 2013). According to this, provider policies apply only to resources and never to citizen information that is controlled by citizen-specified policies. In other studies, the use of electronic patient consents have been proposed, which are user-defined rules providing directives on how access to one data should be regulated, according to the features offered by the Integrating the Healthcare Enterprise (IHE) profile Basic Citizen Privacy Consent (BPPC) (Heinze et al. 2011; Zhang and Liu 2010). Other studies have suggested allowing authorized medical professionals to propose the disclosure of a health record in order to support the basic workflows of medical personnel or the stricter protection of citizen health records (Trojer et al. 2012).

In security literature different methods have been proposed for access control. The standard identity-based access control (IBAC) and role-based access control (RBAC) methods, are not sufficient for controlling access to large open systems like the virtual PHR service since potential subjects (e.g. doctors, nurses, pharmacists, family members, services, systems, devices) are many and unknown in advance, and hence there is no standard role definition (Calvillo et al. 2013; Ciuciu et al. 2011). On the contrary, the ABAC model gives greater flexibility in open systems but is more complex due to the large numbers of rules that needed to be checked for access decisions and the management of privileges, user permissions, and permission review for a specific user suffer from poor performance as large sets of rules must be executed (Mohan et al. 2009). Those limitations have led to a NIST call for the development of a policy-enhanced RBAC model, which incorporates attributes while maintaining RBAC's advantages called RABAC (Jin et al. 2012; Kuhn and Richard 2010). The RABAC model that combines the benefits of role-based (RBAC) and attribute-based (ABAC) access control models to synergize the advantages of each can better satisfy the security requirements for PHR authorization systems since it supports the specification of access control rules based on subject, object and environment attributes.

According to RABAC model roles are dynamically assigned to subjects in each session based on their attributes (context) and additionally, permission filtering policies are used to constrain the available set of permissions associated with the roles activated in a given session. This way the role explosion problem is avoided since it is not necessary to create multiple closely related roles to achieve fine-grained access control and policy administration is eased (Jin et al. 2012; Kuhn and Richard 2010).

Meanwhile, semantic technologies have been extensively used in the development of authorization and access control systems for modeling domain context information that has to be taking into account in authorization rules for allowing or denying a requested action on an object and for harmonizing diverse authorization policies that should communicate and exchange requests in the context of unified distributed security architectures (Blobel 2011; Calvillo et al. 2013; Ciuciu et al. 2011; Kayes et al. 2013; Shen and Cheng 2011). In particular, ontologies can serve to create common security vocabularies (attribute information) that can solve the semantic interoperability issues of diverse authorization policies. Semantic interoperability concerns mutual understanding of concepts by semantically matching the diverse local security concepts to those defined in the common ontology.

One of the most popular semantic tools is the Web Ontology Language (OWL) that allows the specification of domain knowledge by using classes in ontologies. Reasoners or inference engines work over instances of these classes, and this process allows inferring implicit information about the instances according to the domain ontology. Although simple inferences can be realized on OWL, a limitation in the reasoning process exists because OWL does not allow using more complex rules than the inheritance of classes. A special rule language such as the Semantic Web Rule Language (SWRL) allows modeling complex relations among classes and properties by extending the OWL expressivity (Blobel 2011; Ciuciu et al. 2011; Shen and Cheng 2011). Ontology rule languages take everything one step further in authorization systems. More than simple modeling attribute information, enable to model reasoning rules that are inferred to result new high-level attribute information based on basic attribute information and to model authorization rules that are inferred to result whether a requested access should be permitted or denied (Kayes et al. 2013).

Two of the most relevant initiatives for modeling policies and authorization rules and for supporting distributed and federated access control are the Extended Access Control Markup Language (XACML) and Security Assertion Markup Language (SAML) provided by OASIS. In particular, XACML is a general purpose, flexible, and powerful language for specifying and enforcing access control rules following the ABAC model. SAML is a language for interchanging information relative to security assertions, also defining a communication protocol (Calvillo et al. 2013; Sujansky et al. 2010). Moreover, there are other approaches for security in the healthcare domain like the technical specification ISO 22600, the HL7 RBAC approach, the Integrating the Healthcare Enterprise (IHE) and the Healthcare Information Technology Standards Panel (HITSP) (Kayes et al. 2013).

4.3   The Virtual PHR Concept

Current PHRs vary in scope and nature of functions, content and information sources and although those in general enable citizens to control their own health and social information, and some of them also integrate information from multiple resources, not all of them enable citizens to determine who else may access their information (Gearon 2007; Rostad and Nytro 2008; Sujansky et al. 2010). PHR services are basically divided into (a) standalone which enable citizens to collect and control their information into a (web-based, portable) PHR which is not connected to any other systems; (b) tethered which allow citizens to view their own information from the health care providers electronic health record (EHR) but citizens do not have control of their records; and (c) interconnected, which enable citizens to collect health information from multiple sources (hospitals, devices, services), enter their own entries and share information with different parties according to their sharing preferences (Kim et al. 2011; Zhang and Liu 2010).

The virtual PHR concept shares some features with the virtual organization (VO) concept originally developed within the business domain and later adopted by the distributed system architectures (Blobel 2011; Calvillo et al. 2013; Malamateniou et al. 1998). By definition, a VO is formed in order to accomplish an objective common to all the stakeholders. In the healthcare domain, this objective would be the health, well-being and social care of each citizen. The need for collaboration, coordination and integrated information sharing among multiple and dispersed providers and individuals in the health and social care environment has led to the introduction of virtual healthcare organization and virtual patient record concepts (Blobel 2011; Calvillo et al. 2013; Malamateniou et al. 1998; Mori et al. 2012). The virtual PHR concept as proposed in this chapter differs from the virtual patient record concept in that it integrates not only citizen health information from healthcare providers, but also social

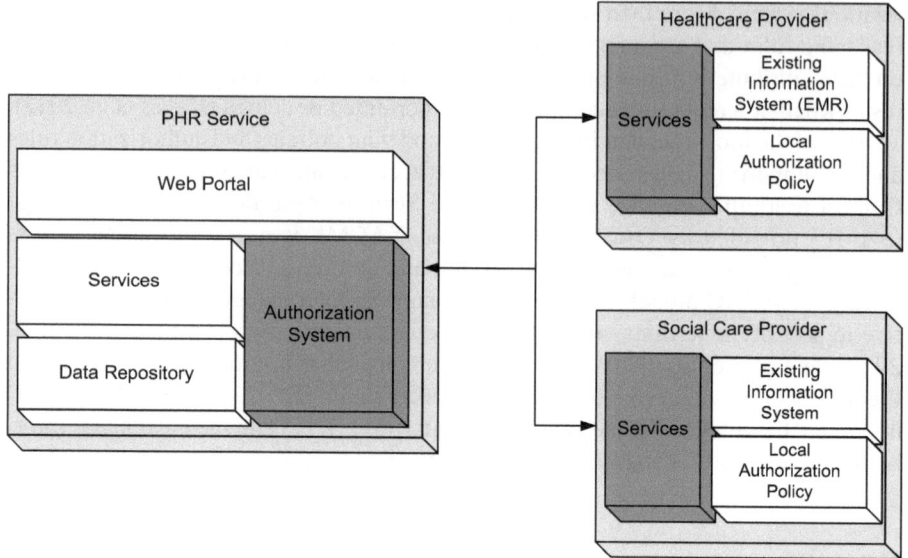

Fig. 4.1 The PHR service overall architecture

information as well as health information from a variety of other sources like the citizen, the non-professionals, the social care providers and the medical devices and enables information sharing according to citizen premises (King et al. 2012; Rigbya et al. 2011). This, in turn, enhances communication, collaboration and information sharing among citizens and providers and ultimately forms the basis for a citizen-centered collaborative healthcare environment (Calvillo et al. 2013; Malamateniou et al. 1998).

4.4   The Virtual PHR Service

Figure 4.1 shows the overall architecture of the document-based virtual PHR that is provided as a cloud service and incorporates the proposed authorization system. The service integrates citizen health and social information over time from citizens and sites of care in a standard structure such as the continuity-of-care (CCD) document schema (based on XML data structure) for structuring standard citizen XML documents (Gearon 2007; Steele et al. 2012). Due to the nature of XML, those documents are logically organized in a hierarchical way.

The virtual PHR service comprises the following:

1. A data repository that stores citizen information contained in traditional PHRs and health information transmitted by medical devices (information categories (a) and (b) of the proposed virtual PHR service) in the form of citizen XML documents,

2. A web portal, through which, citizens can access and manage their lifelong health and social information and set their sharing preferences,
3. A set of services that are called in order to store and retrieve citizen information to/from the data repository (information category (a) and (b)), and,
4. The proposed authorization system that enables modeling and enforcing citizen-centered authorization policies, that are consulted each time a subject requests an action on a resource (citizen information), through the web portal in order to decide if the requested action should be permitted or denied.

Additionally, in each social and health care provider connected to the virtual PHR there exist services that extract a pre-specified subset of citizen social and health information (e.g. an extended discharge summary including citizen critical factors like allergies extracted from EMRs) from social care providers and various health-care systems (information categories (c) and (d)), accordingly, upon subject request through the virtual PHR.

4.5   Virtual PHR Authorization Requirements

The proposed authorization system for virtual PHR services is based on the ownership paradigm and supports the creation of a global PHR authorization policy according to the policies determined by legislation and ethical guidelines, citizen-centered premises and local authorization systems policies. This system is build on top of the security features provided by the participating providers' authorization systems. Figure 4.2 shows the global PHR authorization policy.

More precisely, the proposed authorization system was based on authorization requirements of the virtual PHR service, such as:

1. Citizen information in the virtual PHR is structured in the form of XML documents and each document belongs to an information category of PHR. Each citizen document contains hierarchical XML data elements and each element falls under a category such as medications and lab results.
2. Citizen has read access to all his/her information existing in the virtual PHR.
3. The citizen authorizes subjects (e.g. healthcare providers) to add health and social information to his/her PHR.
4. The citizen can, at any time, revoke authorization he/she has given.
5. The citizen is the owner of all the information existing in the virtual PHR and controls access to this information according to his/her sharing preferences.
6. Access to the pre-specified subset of citizen information existing in social and health care providers systems (information categories (c) and (d)) is additionally controlled by providers' local authorization policies.
7. Authorization rules assign permissions to subjects at various granularity levels (e.g. for a citizen document or for specific XML data elements representing a category).
8. The citizen can delegate authorizations (e.g. in case of disabled people) and parents or legal guardians can take authorization to control information in case of infants/children.

Fig. 4.2 The PHR global
authorization policy

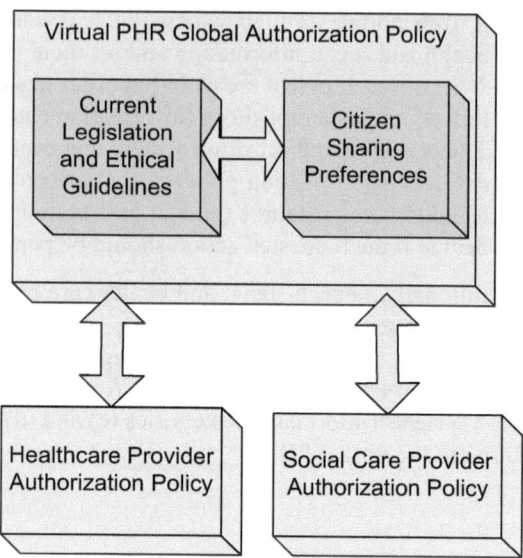

4.6   Authorization Policy Based on the RABAC Model

The proposed PHR authorization system is based on the RABAC model irrespective
of the diverse local authorization models of the participating health and social care
providers. Hence, the virtual PHR authorization policy contains both role-based
authorization rules and permission policy filtering functions (Kahn et al. 2010).
Role-based authorization rules indicate which subjects, in terms of role, are permitted to access which objects and under what conditions. The permission policy
filtering functions indicate which of the permitted objects, according to role-based
authorization rules, should be permitted to requesting subjects according to the current subject attribute information. In particular, the following attribute information
is considered in authorization rules (Shen and Cheng 2011):

- Subject attribute: A subject is considered an entity that requests access to an
  object and can be a person (e.g. citizen), a system or a device. Hence, subject
  attribute information include any subject-related information like the subject's
  specialty, role, provider, status, EMR system and medical devices IP, as well as
  subjects' social (e.g. friends, family) and proximity (e.g. therapist physician, attending physician) relationships.
- Object attribute: An object is an entity that is requested by a subject and can be
  an information category of PHR, a citizen document or an XML element of citizen documents. Hence, object attribute information include any object-related
  information like the object owner and time and location of creation, and
- Environment attribute: The environment attribute information describe the situational environmental at the time of transaction such as location and time of
  access request, as well as the transactional context (e.g. on duty physician).

In the proposed authorization system, authorization is performed according to the RABAC model, through the following process: In each session, subject-to-role assignments are dynamically performed according to subject current attribute information. Then, role-to-permission assignment is performed on objects according to role-based authorization rules. For each of the permitted objects, the corresponding permission policy filtering rules are executed in order to restrict access only to those objects for which the subject is permitted to gain access according to current subject, object and environment attribute information (Jin et al. 2012; Kuhn and Richard 2010). Those are performed with the following rules:

- subject-to-role assignment rules receive current subject and environment attribute information related to the subject and result in a general role that is meant to be assigned to the subject during a certain session. For example, a current subject attribute information consisting of "orthopedic physician" (medical specialty), "on duty" (time) and "at hospital orthopedic clinic" (location) will result in triggering a subject-to-role assignment rule that will assign to the user the role "hospital physician on duty",
- role-to-permission rules receive current roles of each subject and result in a list of permitted actions on objects. For example, a subject assignment of role "hospital physician on duty" will result in triggering a relevant role-to-permission rule that will assign (to this subject) permissions to read citizen information of information category (a) and,
- permission filtering rules receive the permitted actions on objects, objects attribute information and current subject and environment attribute information related to subject, and result in, an allow or deny decision for the requested objects. For example, the subject holding the role "hospital physician on duty" will be restricted by permission filtering rules to read only relevant health information to orthopedic health problem of information category (a).

With the use of RABAC only general roles (e.g. hospital physician on duty) are defined that are assigned permissions for information categories of virtual PHR and then filtering rules are used to constrain subject permissions to a set of citizen information existing in information categories according to object, subject and his/ her environment attribute information.

4.7   Authorization System Architecture

The proposed authorization system adopts the service-oriented architecture (SOA) design concepts and semantic technologies for interoperability purposes among diverse authorization systems (Calvillo et al. 2013; Kayes et al. 2013). In particular, as shown in Fig. 4.3, the authorization system consists of the following main components: the knowledge repository, the authorization policy administration and the enforcement mechanism.

Fig. 4.3 The authorization
system architecture

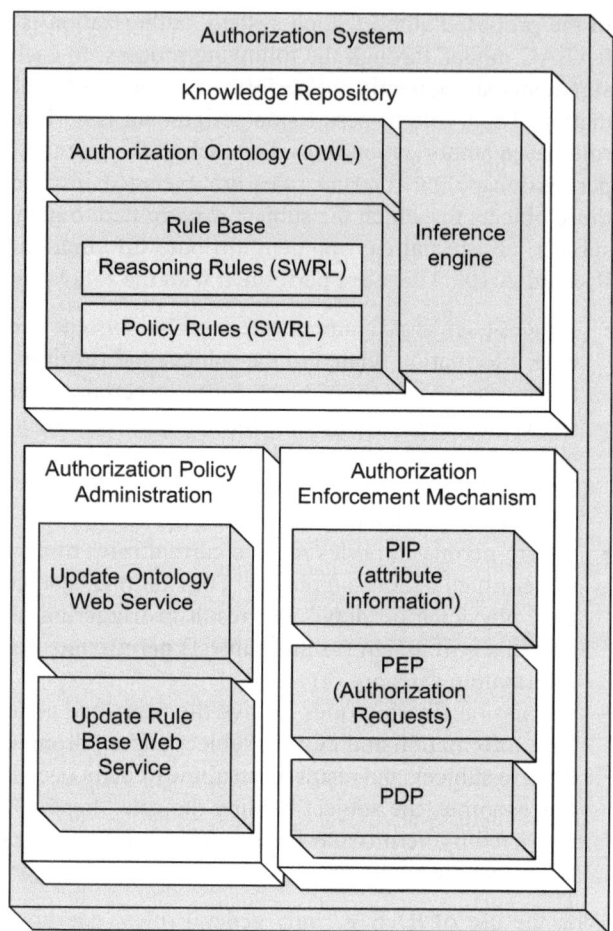

4.7.1   Knowledge Repository

The knowledge repository hosts the PHR authorization ontology, the rule base and
the rule engine. The authorization policy has been built in Ontology Web Language
(OWL) and contains the subject, object and environment attribute information, in
terms of ontology main classes that are further analyzed into a hierarchy of sub-
classes. In particular, the "subject" class is analyzed into the "persons", "systems"
and "medical devices" sub-classes that represent the main subject categories that
can add/view citizen information to/from PHR. The "persons" class is further analyzed to "citizen", "professionals" and "non-professionals". Under the "citizen"
class, sub-classes like "temperature", "heartrate", "healthproblem" exist that are
used to capture basic citizen health information. The "object" class is analyzed into
the four information categories of virtual PHR in the form of sub-classes and those
are further analyzed into other sub-classes that represent the main categories of

citizen documents (e.g. medications). The "environment" class is analyzed into the "location" and "time" main subclasses that describe the location and time (situational environment) where an access request is occurred.

Ontology classes are also accompanied by a set of ontology object properties that are used to create (e.g. proximity) relationships among class individuals or to capture subjects/objects status (e.g. citizen health status). For example, the property "myPhysicians" creates a proximity relationship between individuals of classes *physician* and *citizen*. Thus, it is represented in the ontology that a physician is the citizen's therapist physician. Moreover, the property "hasHealthProblem" links individuals of classes *citizen* and *healthproblem* in order to capture citizen (health) status. Thus it is represented in the ontology that the citizen has currently a health problem like a heart attack that is received by providers' EMR system and inserted into the ontology as fact.

To facilitate semantic interoperability among the virtual PHR and local authorization systems, semantic mappings among internally used security concepts (subject, object and environment attribute information) in authorization rules and the ones defined in the authorization ontology are created in each social and health care provider connected to the virtual PHR service. Thus, subject access requests for virtual PHR information is transformed into subject requests to the local systems which, in turn, are evaluated by the local authorization mechanisms.

The rule base contains ontology rules, defined in Semantic Web Rule Language (SWRL) that are expressed through the typical logic expression "antecedent ⇒ consequent" indicating that if all atoms in antecedent are true the consequent must also be true. Those are divided into reasoning and policy rules that are triggered by the inference engine based on the ontology facts. Reasoning rules are used to derive high-level attribute information that only implicitly can be inferred by other attribute information. For example, a reasoning rule can be used to derive that two persons are co-located. This rule can be used to derive that an "ambulance staff" (specialty) and the "citizen", individuals of class "persons", are co-located at the "ambulance", individual of class "location". Other reasoning rules, derive high-level attribute information for the citizen health status by combining citizen health information. For example, if citizen "healthproblem" is *heart attack* as received by a provider EMR system, a reasoning rule will derive that the citizen health status is "critical". This high-level derived attribute information can be then used in authorization policy rules.

Ontology policy rules, based on the RABAC model, are subject-to-role and role-to-permission assignments rules, as well as, permission filtering rules. Policy rules reasoning through the inference engine is conducted recursively, which means that a rule use the results of another rule as input data. In particular, a subject-to-role rule results to an activated role that is inserted into the ontology as fact and in turn triggers the execution of role-to-permission assignment rules that result to a list of permitted objects that are inserted into ontology as facts and in turn trigger the execution of relevant permission filtering rules.

In Fig. 4.4, a small portion of the authorization ontology is shown.

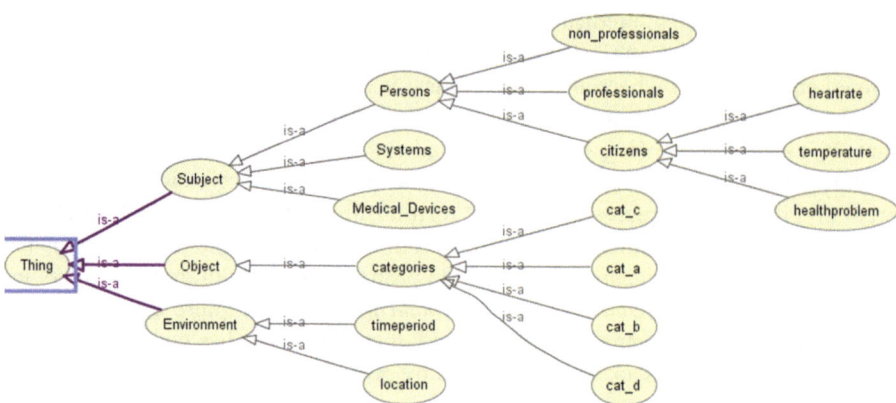

Fig. 4.4 The PHR authorization ontology

4.7.2 Authorization Policy Administration

The authorization policy administration consists of two web services that are called through the web portal of the virtual PHR service in order (a) to update authorization ontology with new subjects and to create relationships among those subjects, and b) to update the rule base with new ontology rules. In particular, those web services are the following:

- *Update Ontology:* This web service updates ontology information with subjects that can add citizen information into the information categories of virtual PHR. This is achieved through the use of relevant ontology object properties. For example, an EMR system which is added to the ontology as an individual of the class "systems" is linked to a citizen through the "myEMR" property. Thus, it is represented into the ontology that this particular EMR contains health information for this citizen. In case of removing subjects from the virtual PHR, relevant links among the citizen and those subjects through the use of object properties are deleted from the ontology.
- *Update rule base:* This web service uses the subject, object and environment attribute information from the ontology, the desired action (e.g. read/write) on objects and the decision result (e.g. permit/deny) to create or update certain ontology policy rules that are stored into the rule base of the knowledge repository. For example, a policy rule might impose that write access is granted to users connected with citizen through the ontology property "myFamily" (subject) for the XML element representing "medications" (object) category under the (a) information category of PHR (object). Another policy rule might impose that a medical device with a specified IP address (subject) can write health information to the (b) information category of PHR (object). In case of read/write access revocation from subjects corresponding ontology policy rules are deleted.

4.7.3   Authorization Enforcement Mechanism

The authorization mechanism consists of the Policy Information Point (PIP), the Policy Enforcement Point (PEP) and the Policy Decision Point (PDP).

PIP receives subject and environment attribute information from a variety of sources (e.g. sensors, medical devices and applications) and inserts it into the authorization ontology as facts. Based on these facts relevant reasoning rules are triggered into the ontology that result to high-level attribute information.

Based on the requesting subject attribute information, relevant subject-to-role assignment rules are triggered to activate certain roles. On a subject request for data access, PEP creates an authorization request, including subject roles and citizen identification information and sends it to PDP. PDP combines the authorization request information with ontology information (current subject, object and environment attribute information) and the inference engine triggers relevant authorization rules. In particular, authorization rules:

1. Specify the authorized (portion of) citizen information in information categories (a) and (b) of the virtual PHR for the subject.
2. Specify if the requesting subject is authorized to access the citizen social and health information of information categories (c) and (d), accordingly. If the result is yes, the PEP consults the authorization ontology in order to retrieve a list of social care providers and disparate EMRs for the citizen and then forms and sends authorization requests including subject roles, citizen identification information and current subject and environment attribute information to those providers' authorization systems. Those requests are transformed at the provider side into requests to local authorization mechanisms (based on the semantic mappings) and are evaluated to decide whether access should be permitted or denied. Then, authorized citizen information is retrieved from each social care provider and disparate EMR system, transformed into a common format (XML CCD document) and sent to the virtual PHR.

4.8   Prototype Implementation

In the proposed cloud-based virtual PHR service, the virtual PHR authorization system is also considered to be implemented as a cloud service. The virtual PHR concept is based on the assumption that the participating providers have implemented interacting services that enable extracting authorized social and health information on the fly from the local systems (e.g. EMRs) upon subject requests through the virtual PHR service. Moreover, subject, object and environment information is recorded and relevant authorization rules are created through the web services of authorization policy administration module.

The core of the virtual PHR authorization system is the knowledge repository as it enables a) the modeling of (subject, object and environment) attributes, b) the modeling of authorization rules, according to the RABAC model, and c) semantic transformation of virtual PHR's authorization requests into local system requests that, in turn, are handled by the local authorization mechanisms. Hence, the virtual PHR authorization mechanism interacts with the knowledge repository to identify requesting subject permissions, based on the current subject attribute information, and to determine whether an attempted access to citizen information should be permitted or denied.

Currently, work is in progress on developing a prototype implementation of the PHR authorization system that is intended to be incorporated into an experimental, cloud-based virtual PHR service. For this system implementation, the Oracle SOA suite is used for the web services of the authorization policy administration module, the Protégé Ontology Editor for modeling the PHR authorization ontology in OWL and the Jess rule engine for inferring ontology rules in SWRL. Moreover, the Sun's XML access control language (XACML) implementation is used for forming the authorization requests and implementing the authorization mechanism. A java-based web interface is also under implementation through which users will interact to view authorization rules and specify their sharing preferences. Usability has been identified as a major asset since citizens are non technology and security experts.

4.8.1 System Functionality

Consider a healthcare scenario, where an emergency physician, while on duty at the emergency department of a hospital, requires access to citizen information at hand from the virtual PHR service. To this end, the following process is followed:

- The emergency physician connects to the virtual PHR service through the web portal and requests access to citizen information. Then, the PIP of the authorization mechanism obtains the attribute information required for making authorization decisions including user specialty, duty hours, time and location of access request, citizen identification information, citizen assignment to the requesting physician and citizen health problem. This attribute information is inserted into the authorization ontology that results in inferring high-level information. For example, if the time of requested access is within duty hours, the location is hospital emergency department, user specialty is physician and citizen health problem is heart attack, the ontology inference results that "*the requesting user is an on duty emergency physician at hospital emergency department and is the treating physician of the citizen with health problem heart attack and health status critical*". In addition, the general role "hospital physician on duty" is assigned to the user.
- The PEP of the authorization mechanism creates XACML authorization requests to the PDP including activated role and citizen identification information. The PDP consults the authorization ontology that is inferred to retrieve the permissible citizen information on virtual PHR for the requesting user with activated role "hospital physician on duty" and current attribute information "*the request-*

ing user is an on duty emergency physician at hospital emergency department and is the treating physician of the citizen with health problem heart attack and health status critical".

- XACML authorization requests are also sent by the PEP to the social care providers and EMR systems for citizen information, if access to citizen information of information categories (c) and (d) is permitted by the PHR authorization policy. At the provider site, this request is transformed to a local access request in order to retrieve the permissible citizen information. For example, a healthcare provider's local authorization policy might imply that an on duty emergency physician is granted access to a pre-specified set of citizen information that contain the "allergies", "medications", "adverse reactions", "short citizen history" and latest "medical exams and operations".
- The permissible citizen information from the virtual PHR is aggregated and transformed into a common format (XML CCD document) and is presented to the requesting user through the virtual PHR web portal.

4.9   Concluding Remarks

Currently, several million people around the world have access to some kind of PHR, however problems with the privacy and security of citizen sensitive information could pose a serious impediment to PHR development. In addition, a more personalized and user-centric healthcare has been a pressing goal of the scientific community for many years (Baird et al. 2012; Rostad and Nytro 2008). In this chapter, a virtual PHR information structure is considered and a PHR authorization and access control service is provided which takes into account the fact that PHR both stores citizen information to the data repository and retrieves citizen information on the fly from social care providers and EMR systems through the use of relevant services after an explicit user request. Emphasis in the proposed authorization system is on citizen sharing preferences that are taken into account without violating the security policies of health and social care providers and current legislation and ethical guidelines. This authorization system is based on ontology-driven authorization policies where ontologies are used for semantic interoperability among provider local authorization policies and the PHR authorization policy that communicate and exchange authorization requests in order to create a global, PHR level, authorization policy.

The main objective of the proposed authorization system is to provide authorization and access control services to the proposed virtual PHR service according to a global PHR authorization policy (Calvillo et al. 2013; Carrion et al. 2011). The proposed system presented in this chapter, can support various authorization policies (as determined by relevant regulations and ethical rules) by simply altering the ontology information and rules so that current legislation is obeyed at the moment of use (Ciuciu et al. 2011).

4.10   Future Research Directions

Recent advancements in Information and Communication Technologies (ICT) like IOT and big data analytics can support a new generation of virtual PHRs that integrate large amount of citizen information from many sources and provide valuable information to citizens through the analysis of the collected big data (Giusto et al. 2010; Said and Tolba 2012). In the near future, various network-connected objects (e.g. sensors, devices, applications) will populate citizen health and environment information and this information will be transferred through Internet to PHRs and appropriate added-value context-aware services will be activated to analyze all this citizen information in order to provide valuable health information to citizen according to his/her health concerns (Giusto et al. 2010). Protecting citizen personal information is recognized among the fundamental human rights and, as the pervasiveness of communication technology increases, new efforts are focusing on privacy problem from both a legislative and technical point of view.

In such a virtual PHR environment, security and privacy become even more critical as their support becomes more difficult. The reasons lay in both the increase of network-connected objects which will be connected to PHR that in turn increases the vulnerability to all kind of security and privacy attacks and to the large amount of personal sensitive information that will flow through the network (from these objects) and will be stored to the PHR that its disclosure will result in revealing citizen habits, actions and health related problems (Giusto et al. 2010). Hence, it is important to guarantee that citizen personal information is securely transferred and accessed only by authorized subjects or for the purposes of PHR context-aware services. Control on the possession and the flow of such information is a must to guarantee an acceptable level of privacy and suggest directions for further work.

References

Baird A, Raghu T-S, Tulledge-Scheitel S (2012) The role of policy in the prevention of Personal Health Record (PHR) market failure. J Inf Technol Politics 9:117–132

Bairs A, North F, Raghu T-S (2011) Personal health records (PHR) and the future of the physician-patient relationship, In the Proceedings of the 2011 iConference, New York, USA

Barua M, Liang X, Lu R, Shen X (2011) PEACE: an efficient and secure patient-centric access control scheme for eHealth care system. In the First International Workshop on Security in Computers, Networking and Communications, pp 987–992

Berwick D (2009) What 'patient-centered' should mean: confessions of an extremist. Health Aff 28(4):555–565

Blobel B (2011) Ontology driven health information systems architectures enable pHealth for empowered patients. Int J Med Inform 80:e17–e25

Calvillo J, Roman I, Roa L-M (2013) Empowering citizens with access control mechanisms to their personal health resources. Int J Med Inf 82:58–72

Carrion I, Aleman J, Toval A (2011) Accessing the HIPAA standard in practice: PHR privacy policies. In the Proceedings of the 33rd Annual International Conference of the IEEE EMBS, Boston, Massachusetts, USA

Chen TS, Liu CH, Chen TL, Chen CS, Bau JG, Lin TC (2012) Secure dynamic access control scheme of PHR in cloud computing. J Med Syst 36(6):4005–4020

Ciuciu I, Claerhout B, Schilders L, Meersman R (2011) Ontology-based matching of security attributes for personal data access in e-health. Lect Notes Comput Sci (On the move to meaningful Internet syst) 7045:605–616

Cushman R, Froomkin M, Cava A, Abril P, Goodman K (2010) Ethical, legal and social issues for personal health records and applications. J Biomed Inf 43:S51–S55

Gajanayake R, Iannella R, Sahama T (2011) Sharing with care: an information accountability perspective. IEEE Comput Soc 15(4):31–38

Gearon C (2007) Perspectives on the future of personal health records. iHealthReports. California Healthcare Foundation. http://www.chcf.org/~/media/MEDIA%20LIBRARY%20Files/PDF/P/PDF%20PHRPerspectives.pdf. Accessed 12 Dec. 2013

Giusto D, Iera A, Morabito G, Atzori L (2010) The Internet of Things, 20th Tyrrhenian Workshop on Digital Communications

Heinze O, Birkle M, Köster L, Bergh B (2011) Architecture of a consent management suite and integration into IHE-based regional health information networks. BMC Med Inf Decis Mak 11(58). doi:10.1186/1472-6947-11-58

Jin X, Sandhu R, Krishman R (2012) RABAC: role-centric attribute-based access control. Lect Notes Comput Sci (Comput Netw Secur) 7531:84–96

Kahn J, Aulakh V, Bosworth A (2009) What it takes: characteristics of the ideal personal health record, Health Aff 28(2):369–376

Kayes A-S-M, Han J, Colman A (2013) OntCAAC: an ontology-based approach to context-aware access control for software services. Technical Report, Melbourne, Australia. Swinburne University of Technology

Kim J, Jung H, Bates D (2011) History and trends of "Personal Health Record" research in PubMed. Health Inf Res 17(1):3–17

King G, Donnell C, Boddy D, Smith F, Heaney D, Mair F (2012) Boundaries and e-health implementation in health and social care. BMC Med Inf Decis Mak 12(100). doi:10.1186/1472-6947-12-100

Kuhn D, Richard D (2010) Adding attributes to role-based access control. IEEE Comput Soc 43(6):79–81

Li M, Yu S, Ren K, Lou W (2010) Securing personal health records in cloud computing: patient-centric and fine-grained data access control in multi-owner settings. Lect Notes Inst Comput Sci (Social Inf Telecom Eng) 50:89–106

Li M, Yu S, Zheng Y, Ren K, Lou W (2012) Scalable and secure sharing of personal health records in cloud computing using attribute-based encryption. IEEE Trans Parallel Distrib Syst 24(1):131–143

Mahajan A, Patel Y (2012) Enhancing PHR services in cloud computing: patient-centric and fine grained data access using ABE. Int J Comput Sci Inf Technol Secur (IJCSITS) 2(6):1130–1135

Malamateniou F, Vassilacopoulos G, Tsanakas P (1998) A workflow-based approach to virtual patient record security. IEEE Trans Inf Technol Biomed 2(3)

Martino L, Ahuja S (2010) Privacy policies of personal health records: an evaluation of their effectiveness in protecting patient information, In the Proceedings of the 1st ACM International Heath Informatics Symposium, New York, USA

Mohan A, Bauer D, Blough D, Ahamad M, Bamba B, Krishnan R, Liu L, Mashima D, Palanisamy B (2009) A patient-centric, attribute-based, source-verifiable framework for health record sharing, In GIT CERCS Technical Report No. GIT-CERCS-09-11

Mori A, Mazzeo M, Mercurio G, Verbicaro R (2012) Holistic health: predicting our data future (from inter-operability among system to co-operability among people). Int J Med Inf 82(4):e14–28

Pirtle B, Chandra A (2011) An overview of consumers perceptions and acceptance as well as barriers and potential of electronic personal health records. Am J Health Sci 2(2):45–52

Poulymenopoulou M, Papakonstantinou D, Malamateniou F, Vassilacopoulos G (2012) Enhancing patient information sharing through social networks. In the Proceedings of the International Conference on Health Informatics—HEALTHINF, Vilamoura, Algarve, Portugal, pp 378–381

Rigbya M, Hill P, Kochc S, Keelingd D (2011) Social care informatics as an essential part of holistic health care: a call for action. Int J Med Inform 80:544–554

Rostad L, Nytro O (2008) Personalized access control for a personally controlled health record. In the Proceedings of the 2nd ACM workshop on Computer security architectures, New York, USA, pp 9–16

Ruotsalainen P, Blobel B, Seppala A, Sorvari H, Nykanen P (2012) A conceptual framework and principles for trusted pervasive health. J Med Internet Res 14(2):e52

Said O, Tolba A (2012) SEAIoT: scalable e-health architecture based on Internet of things. Int J Comput App 59(13):44–48

Shen H, Cheng U (2011) A semantic context-based model for mobile web services access control. Int J Comput Netw Inf Secur 1:18–25

Shine S-G (2012) A hybrid level access control mechanism for secure medical data sharing in cloud platform. International. J Adv Res Comput Sci Softw Eng 2(10):272–277

Steele R, Min K, Lo A (2012) Personal health record architectures: technology infrastructure implications and dependencies. J Am Soc Inf Sci Technol 63(6):1079–1091

Sujansky W, Faus S, Stone E, Brennan P (2010) A method to implement fine-grained access control for personal health records through standard relational database queries. J Biomed Inform 43:46–50

Trojer T, Katt B, Schabetsberger T, Breu R, Mair R (2012) Considering privacy and effectiveness of authorization policies for shared electronic health records. In Proceedings of the 2nd ACM SIGHIT International Health Informatics Symposium, New York, USA, pp 553–562

Weitzman E-R, Kaci L, Quinn M, Mandl K-D (2011) Helping high risk youth move through high-risk periods: personally controlled health records for improving social and health care transitions. J Diabetes Sci Technol 5(1):47–54

Wickramasinghe N, Bali R, Kirn S, Suomi R (eds) (2012) Critical issues for the development of sustainable e-health solutions (Book) XXXIV:386p

Zhang R, Liu L (2010) Security models and requirements for healthcare application clouds. In Proceedings of 3rd International Conference on Cloud Computing, IEEE Cloud'10, Miami, Florida, USA, pp 268–275

Chapter 5
Privacy-Preserving Access Control for PHR-Based Emergency Medical Systems

Vassiliki Koufi, Flora Malamateniou and George Vassilacopoulos

Abstract In recent years, patient-centered care has emerged as an innovative approach to planning, delivery and evaluation of health care that is grounded in mutually beneficial partnerships among patients, families and healthcare providers. The success of this care model depends heavily on Personal Health Records (PHRs), an evolution of patient records from simple data repositories to tools that can support care across all settings by providing real-time access to relevant information, strengthen the patient-clinician relationship by accommodating direct interaction between them and enable patients to engage the health system more efficiently by equipping them with the knowledge to make more of their own decisions. Especially, when integrated with leading-edge technologies such as web services and mobile communications, PHRs can improve the quality, efficiency and effectiveness of health care by being rendered ubiquitously accessible. As momentum continues to build for the use of PHRs, some significant attention remains justifiably focused on addressing security concerns, such as privacy of sensitive personal health information. Hence, for PHR systems to achieve user consent, trust in and acceptance, appropriate safeguards should be identified that instill public confidence in the privacy of personal health information without establishing unnecessary barriers to the legitimate uses of health IT. This paper assumes a process-oriented PHR-based EMS and presents an authorization framework for achieving privacy-preserving access to patient PHR data. The proposed framework adheres to the attribute-based access control paradigm in order to achieve authorized access to patient data when and where needed while providing break glass access to critical health information when patients experience emergency situations.

Keywords Personal Health Records · ubiquitous access · privacy · attribute-based access control · emergency care

V. Koufi (✉) · F. Malamateniou · G. Vassilacopoulos
Department of Digital Systems, University of Piraeus,
Piraeus, Greece
e-mail: vassok@unipi.gr

F. Malamateniou
e-mail: flora@unipi.gr

G. Vassilacopoulos
e-mail: gvass@unipi.gr

D.-D. Koutsouris, A. A. Lazakidou (eds.), *Concepts and Trends in Healthcare Information Systems*, Annals of Information Systems 16,
DOI 10.1007/978-3-319-06844-2_5, © Springer International Publishing Switzerland 2014

5.1   Introduction

In recent years, patient-centered care has become internationally recognized as a dimension of the broader concept of high-quality health care. Personal Health Records (PHRs) are envisaged as having a key role in the realization of the patient-centered care model by facilitating, among others, availability of comprehensive and unified health information at the point of care and knowledge-based collaborations of patients with healthcare professionals (Koufi and Vassilacopoulos 2008). A PHR is a set of computer-based tools that allow people to access and coordinate their lifelong health information and make appropriate parts of it available to those who need it (Tang et al. 2006). Hence, PHR use may entail a number of benefits, such as better access to medical information, increased patient satisfaction and continuity of care (Wiljer et al. 2008). Unlike traditional EHRs that are mainly based on the "fetch and show" model, PHRs' architectures are based on the fundamental assumptions that the complete records are held on a central repository and that each patient retains authority over access to any portion of his/her record (Wiljer et al. 2008; Lauer 2009). Thus, the development of PHRs eliminates the need for interoperability among disparate and geographically dispersed legacy healthcare information systems, hosted by different healthcare providers, so that to enable integrated access to fragmented patient information where and when needed (Koufi and Vassilacopoulos 2008; Tang et al. 2006). Indeed, the lack of interoperability among these systems, as is often the case, impedes optimal care since it leads to unavailability of important patient information when this is mostly needed.

Although the patient is the primary beneficiary and user of PHRs, healthcare professionals and organizations benefit from their use as well (U.S. Department of Health and Human Services 2006). In particular, healthcare professionals, due to the high level of mobility they experience, require ubiquitous access to relevant and timely patient data in order to make critical care decisions (Tentori et al. 2006). The integration of leading-edge technologies, such as web services and mobile communications, with PHRs can meet this requirement. Hence, quality of patient care provided is enhanced while ensuring protection and confidentiality of personal data. In addition, PHRs that contain quality information can be used as a foundation for developing several healthcare applications that may benefit healthcare providers with regard to increasing the quality of care provided while containing cost. This chapter is concerned with individual applications in the broader context of emergency healthcare delivery.

One important consideration regarding the overall integration of PHRs into clinical practice is concerned with providing sound answers to the important security questions arisen, particularly those regarding prevention of unauthorized access to medical information, in order to reduce the possibility of breaching patient privacy under any circumstances (Tang et al. 2006; Wiljer et al. 2008; Win et al. 2006). Most PHR platforms currently deployed (e.g. ICW LifeSensor, Microsoft HealthVault) meet security requirements by assigning patients the responsibility of granting access to their medical information at their own discretion or by enabling patients to delegate their doctors to set authorization rules and enforce access controls on their behalf (ICW eHealth Framework 2009; Microsoft HealthVault 2013). However, such security policies presume that patients are in a health state that allows them granting appropriate authorizations to attending physicians. Hence, PHRs may not be accessible by Emergency Department (ED) physicians when needed and, yet, emergency patient life may hinge on the instant availability and accuracy of his/ her medical information. This leads to the need for developing an effective authorization mechanism that enables ED physicians gain access to PHRs without being explicitly authorized by the patients concerned (break glass access).

In the PHR literature, most emergency case approaches proposed for providing access to integrated patient information are based on emergency cards. Examples of such systems are My Personal Health Record (myPHR) and In Case of Emergency Personal Health Record (icePHR) (My Personal Health Record 2010; Metavante 2010. Since these approaches require that patients will carry their emergency cards at all times, which may not be feasible in practice, this chapter proposes a pervasive authorization framework whereby authorizations for access to a patient's PHR are automatically granted to ambulance paramedics at the site of the incident or en route to the hospital and, also, to physicians on duty in the ED upon patient arrival. This framework has been developed in the context of an Emergency Medical System (EMS) where cooperation among healthcare professionals participating in emergency case management is expressed in terms of cross-organizational healthcare processes, where information support is provided by means of PHR systems.

The proposed authorization framework is based on the attribute-based access control (ABAC) paradigm which is essentially a next generation authorization model that can provide dynamic, context-aware and risk-intelligent access control. In particular, it consults a set of context-based authorization rules in order to specify whether a certain access mode of a given subject (e.g. healthcare professional) to a given object (e.g. healthcare processes, healthcare process tasks, web services accessing PHR system) should be permitted or denied. The contextual information is determined by a pre-defined set of attributes related to the subject (e.g. user certificate, user/patient relationship), the object (e.g.), the action (e.g. select, update) and the environment (e.g. location and time of attempted access). Our framework is intended to complement the authorization mechanism incorporated in the underlying PHR system rather than substitute it.Moreover, it does not incur any significant administrative overhead, is self-administering to a great extent and meets strong requirements in terms of scalability and flexibility.

5.2   Motivating Scenario

The basic motivation for this research stems from our involvement in a recent project concerned with developing a PHR system in the context of a prototype e-prescribing service. One aspect of the system concerned physician access to a PHR in order to retrieve useful patient information (e.g. drug allergies and chronic diseases)

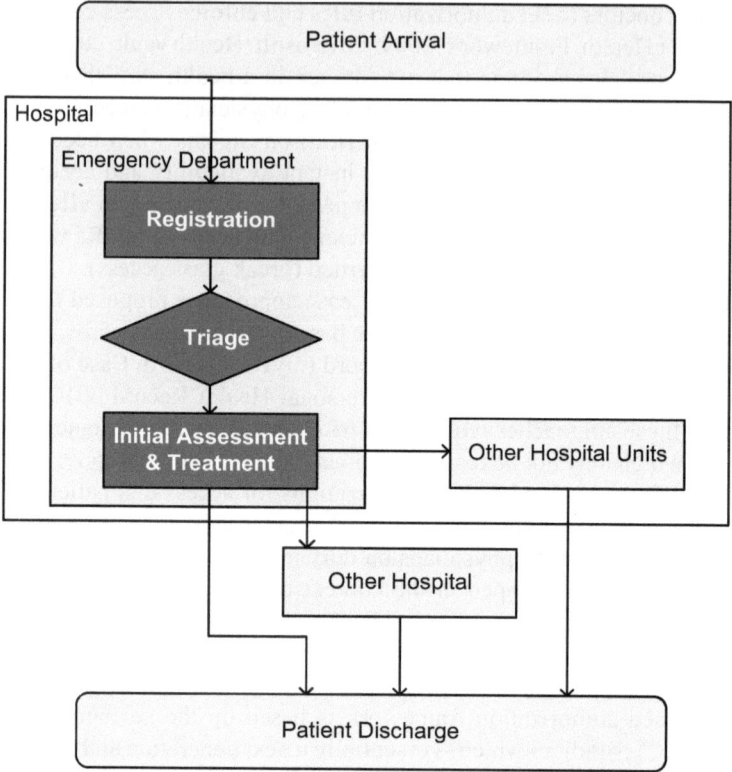

Fig. 5.1 Emergency patient flow

so that to prescribe the right drugs at the right dose for a patient. This application provided an impetus for developing another application, namely emergency health-care application, that includes ePrescribing as one of the important components since emergency patients may not be able to provide any medical information about themselves while drug administration may be imperative. Hence, ED physicians need to be granted access to integrated patient information without patient's inter-vention. In turn, this requires an effective authorization and access control mecha-nism that enforces the healthcare organization's security policy at the point of care.

Suppose a healthcare delivery situation that takes place in an ED of a hospital. Patient arrival is normally followed by his/her reception and triage, to determine the nature and severity of his/her case, and by the provision of appropriate emer-gency medical care. Figure 5.1 shows a high-level view of the patient flow from arrival to discharge from a hospital's ED. During emergency case management, ED physicians often need to have immediate access to the patient's health information even without the patient's consent. Moreover, the hospital's security policy may dictate that access permissions to emergency case information are granted to ED physicians only (a) during their working hours; (b) when they are located within

ED premises; and (c) during the time interval specified by the times of patient arrival to and departure from the ED. Hence, an effective security mechanism needs to be flexible enough to enforce the least privilege principle by allowing users, such as ED physicians, with certain attributes to have fast access to patient health information subject to contextual constraints such as time and location of attempted access. Thus, contextual information related to ED personnel (doctors, nurses, etc), resources (PHR data, etc) and the environment (time, location, etc) need to be collected at run time as they can influence authorization decisions on health information comprising a patient's PHR.

In emergency healthcare delivery, a typical security policy may dictate that: "In order to perform the medical treatment in time under emergency situation, any physician closed to patient can access his/her medical record. However, in normal situation, only the patient's attending physician can access his/her medical record". Thus, a context aware access control policy provides privacy and security protection on patient medical record without delaying patient rescue in severe cases. In addition, in order to handle sensitive medical data and compliance requirements, there is a need for granular authorization capabilities that can be persistent throughout the data's lifecycle. However, healthcare applications usually provide strong authentication that enables access control based on user identity, but few, if any, are equipped with authorization mechanisms that provide more granular authorizations which are based on contextual information. This automation capability is very important in emergency care since patients may not be in a health condition to delegate authorization for accessing their own data while more granular authorization may be dictated by the organization's security policy.

5.3 A PHR-Based Emergency System Architecture

Figure 5.2 shows a high-level architectural view of the proposed healthcare system supporting emergency case management. In essence, this architecture refers to PHR and emergency care applications delivered as services over the Internet and the hardware and systems software in the data centres that provide these services. Thus, central to the architecture is the PHR component which is accompanied by a number of peripheral applications such as the emergency care application that incorporates as sub-applications all emergency healthcare process activities including patient referrals and ePrescribing. All of these applications are licensed for use as services and are provided to authorized users on demand. The application software of the PHR and the emergency care components consist of a number of web services which are deployed and orchestrated by means of the Business Process Execution Language (BPEL). The functionality of the resultant BPEL processes is also exposed by means of web services. Authorized users interact with the system through a portal which is accessible by either a desktop workstation or any mobile device that runs an HTTP(S)-based client.

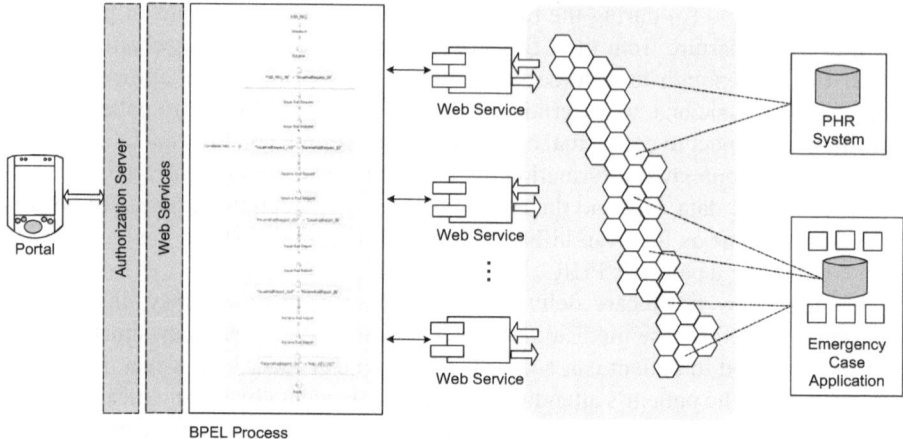

Fig. 5.2 Architecture of a PHR-based system supporting emergency care

In broad terms, the architecture of the prototype system consists of the following main components:

Portal The portal component provides a web-based front end to PHR and emergency care processes. Authorized users enter the portal to interact with the PHR and the emergency care service. The portal is flexibly sized so that to fit in PDA or mobile phone screen, which is particularly useful in cases where there is a need for remote access to these applications (e.g. in cases where a member of the paramedical staff needs to access a patient's PHR form within an ambulance en-route to a hospital's ED).

PHR system The architecture of the PHR System is based on the fundamental assumptions that the complete patient records are centrally stored and that each patient retains authority over access to any portion of his/her record. Hence, the PHR platform consists of a data repository which stores patient data and a user interface which allows patients to access their own information and authorized healthcare professionals to access appropriate parts of patient information.

Emergency care application The emergency care application consists of a data repository which stores emergency case data and the application software comprised by a number of BPEL-orchestrated web services that are accessed by authorized physicians, nurses and paramedics. Users which are authorized to use the emergency care application for some patients are also authorized to access certain portions of the PHR of these patients. Part of the emergency care application (main service) is the ePrescribing sub-application that consists of a data repository which stores drug information (e.g. interactions, indications) and drug prescriptions and the application software comprised by a number of BPEL-orchestrated web services that are accessed by authorized physicians. Users which are authorized to use the emergency care application for some patients are also authorized to access certain portions of the PHR of these patients.

5.4 Authorization Architecture

Authorization is a significant issue in any healthcare application since it is of primary importance to ensure the privacy and security of sensitive patient health information. When mobile technology is widely used in this field, the dynamically changing environment makes the issue more complicated, but also gives us the opportunity to import context awareness into this kind of applications to provide more advanced and valuable usage. Moreover, as the number of users and shared resources increase, there is a need for extra labour in order to manage permissions and there is extra risk of inappropriate data release, due to having more users who may misunderstand policy or be careless or malicious. Hence, a security system must be implemented that reduces the possibility of breaching patient privacy under any circumstances. In order to meet this requirement, the authorization mechanism proposed in this chapter adheres to the attribute-based access control paradigm which allows for the specification of more flexible, precise and fine grained authorization policies in applications operating under dynamically changing situations. A detailed description of the proposed authorization mechanism is provided in the following sections.

5.4.1 Authorization Model

As mentioned earlier, the authorization model incorporated in the proposed mechanism adheres to the attribute-based access control paradigm, according to which access permissions to resources and information are associated with a set of rules (i.e. policies) expressed through measurable attributes for users, systems and information resources and are granted to users who meet the matching policy. A detailed description of all the elements of the authorization model, namely entities involved in access control process, entity attributes and authorization policies, are provided in the next few sections.

Entities

In the proposed authorization model, four elements are participating in each access control decision: requestor (*Req*), resource (*Res*), action (*Act*) and environment (Env).

Definition 1 Requestor *Req* is the entity that requests access to an information or service asset, i.e. sends requests to a web service and invokes methods of this service.

Definition 2 Resource *Res* is the service or information asset impacted by the action requested by *Req*. *Res* is essentially a web service with a network-addressable interface containing a number of well-defined operations which may act upon:

a. a healthcare process *Pr*,
b. a task *T* of a healthcare process, or
c. a data resource *DRes*, i.e. the PHR repository (rows in relational database)

Definition 3 Action *Act* is the action a Requestor *Req* wishes to perform on a Resource *Res*. It essentially refers to an operation provided by a web service that can be invoked by a requestor.

Definition 4 Environment *Env* is the context in which access is requested, i.e. the context related to an invocation of a web service.

Entity Attributes

Each one of the above elements is described by a set of attributes which define the identity and characteristics of the corresponding element.

Definition 5 Requestor attributes $Attr_{Req} = \left\{ Attr_{Req,i} \mid i \in [1, I] \right\}$ are general attributes describing the requestor (e.g. user ID, the department of a hospital to which the user belongs, user roles, group memberships etc.), which can be retrieved from the user's certificate and/or a hospital information system.

Definition 6 Resource attributes $Attr_{Res} = \left\{ Attr_{Res,j} \mid j \in [1, J] \right\}$ are the attributes rendering the characteristics that identify the information or service asset.

Definition 7 Action attributes $Attr_{Act} = \left\{ Attr_{Act,k} \mid k \in [1, K] \right\}$ in authorization requests mainly identify the type of request issued (i.e. "read" in case of a web service resource which acts upon PHR data objects). However, in more complex scenarios, the action may be described by a combination of attributes. For example, when a new blood glucose measurement needs to be inserted in the patient's PHR, the action needs to be described by multiple attributes, such as "action type = insert", "data type = blood glucose measurement" and "measurement value = 149".

Definition 8 Environment attributes $Attr_{Env} = \left\{ Attr_{Env,l} \mid k \in [1, L] \right\}$ describe the operational, technical, or situational environment or context in which access to a resource is requested. For example, an environment attribute may refer to the current time and location of attempted access, the type of communication channel, such as protocol or encryption strength, or the client type (e.g. desktop computer, smart phone, etc).

Authorization Policy Formulation

In the proposed framework policies are formulated as follows:

Definition 9 An attribute-based authorization policy P for performing an Action Act on an asset Res is a 4-tuple $(Req, Act, Res, \{p - Attr_{Req}, p - Attr_{Act}, p - Attr_{Res}, p - Attr_{Env}\})$ stating that a requestor Req is allowed to perform action Act to an asset Res subject to constraints $\{p - Attr_{Req}, p - Attr_{Act}, p - Attr_{Res}, p - Attr_{Env}\}$ imposed by the attributes of Req, Act, Res and Env. Res is always a web service WS that may correspond to a process Pr, a process task T or a data resource $DRes$. These are represented as $Pr, \{Pr, T\}$ and $\{Pr, T, Dres\}$ respectively. In each one of these cases the respective policy is formed as follows:

Definition 9.1 (BPEL process web service invocation) An attribute-based authorization policy P_{Pr} for performing an Action Act on a BPEL process Pr is a 4-tuple $(Req, Act, Pr, \{p - Attr_{Req}, p - Attr_{Act}, p - Attr_{Pr}, p - Attr_{Env}\})$ stating that a requestor Req is allowed to perform action Act to the web service acting upon process Pr subject to constraints $\{p - Attr_{Req}, p - Attr_{Act}, p - Attr_{Pr}, p - Attr_{Env}\}$ imposed by the attributes of Req, Act, Pr and Env.

Definition 9.2 (web service task execution) Given an authorization to a requestor Req identified by attributes $Attr_{Req}$ for performing an Action Act on a BPEL process Pr, an attribute-based authorization policy P_T for process task execution T is a 4-tuple $(Req, Act, \{Pr, T\}, \{p - Attr_{Req}, p - Attr_{Act}, p - Attr_{\{Pr,T\}}, p - Attr_{Env}\})$ stating that Req is allowed to perform action Act to the web service acting upon process task $\{Pr, T\}$ subject to constraints $\{p - Attr_{Req}, p - Attr_{Act}, p - Attr_{\{Pr,T\}}, p - Attr_{Env}\}$ imposed by the attributes of $Req, Act, \{Pr, T\}$ and Env. Since each task is linked to a single application-specific web service, granting access to the task amounts to granting access to this web service. Therefore, no explicit policy needs to be defined for this web service.

Definition 9.3 (web service invocation) Given an authorization for invoking web service WS acting upon a process task by a requestor Req identified by attributes $Attr_{Req}$, an attribute-based authorization policy P_{Dres} for accessing an information asset $DRes$ is a 5-tuple $(Req, Act, \{Pr, T, DRes\}, \{p - Attr_{Req}, p - Attr_{Act}, p - Attr_{DRes}, p - Attr_{Env}\}, \{p_u\})$ stating that Req is allowed to perform action Act to the web service acting upon a data resource $\{Pr, T, Dres\}$ subject to constraints $\{p\text{-}Attr_{Req}, p\text{-}Attr_{Act}, p\text{-}Attr_{DRes}, p\text{-}Attr_{Env}\}$ imposed by the attributes of $Req, Act, DRes$ and Env and also constraints $\{p_u\}$ imposed by the PHR owner. In case of an emergency, $\{p_u\}$ constraints are bypassed.

For example, an authorization requirement may specify that "An ED physician can issue prescriptions from within a hospital, while on duty and only for patients treated by him in the ED of the hospital". This requirement contains (a) the contextual constraint "only for patients treated by him in the ED of the hospital" which describes a physician-to-patient "proximity" relationship between a physician and a patient that can be expressed as a requestor attribute and is related to the resource attribute identifying the patient for whom the action is requested, and (b) two contextual constraints "from within a hospital" (location) and "while on duty" (temporal) that can be expressed as environmental attributes.

Definition 10 The authorization policy base $Policy_{base} = \{P_m\} \mid m \in [1, M]\} = P_{pr} \cup P_T \cup P_{Dres}$ is a union of all the aforementioned policies on web services acting upon processes, process tasks and/or data resources where each policy P_i may be either a single policy or a set of other policies.

Authorization Policy Evaluation

Upon request for a web service invocation, the access control decision process is initiated which triggers the evaluation of all applicable policies in the policy base. The function used for this purpose (Fig. 5.3) receives as input the set of attributes identifying the requestor, action, resource and environment involved in the access request and evaluates the relevant, applicable policies against these attributes' values.

5.4.2 Authorization System

Authorization Architecture

As shown in Fig. 5.4, the proposed authorization architecture consists of the following main components that are important actors during the authorization process. These components submit, accept, and/or act upon information from other components.

- **Requestor:** It refers to the staff treating the patient (i.e. physicians, nurses and paramedics) or to processes acting on their behalf. The service consumer is authenticated my means of a cryptographically protected credential (i.e. X.509 certificate) issued by an Authentication Authority.
- **Policy Enforcement Point (PEP):** It refers to the trusted entity that enforces the decisions made by a Policy Decision Point (PDP) regarding access over protected resources (web services and PHR data). It is placed as an interceptor in front of the application server that hosts the protected resource. Upon a request for access to a protected resource, PEP:
  - Intercepts access request and translates it to an XML request
  - Sends the request to the Policy Decision Point (PDP) for evaluation
  - Enforces the response PDP sends back, i.e. "Permit" or "Deny" by forwarding the request to the protected resource.
- **Policy Information Point (PIP):** It refers to an attribute store where all the information that is required for policy evaluation are collected. Attribute values are retrieved during policy evaluation and, often, from different information systems within the infrastructure which are used as trusted attribute stores. There are two PIP connectors created in the proposed system, one for attributes than can

1	**ISSUE** access_request(*Req*, *Act*, *Res*)
2	**BEGIN** attribute_collection
3	**FOR each** Entity in {*Req*, *Act*, *Res*, *Env*}
4	**FOR each** $Attr_{Entity,I}$ in $Attr_{Entity}$
5	Acquire attribute value
6	Add attribute to the Entity attribute set
7	**END FOR**
8	**END FOR**
9	**END** attribute_collection
10	**BEGIN** make access control decision based on attribute vales and user-defined policies
11	PDPdecision = PDP_make_access_decision(request of *Req* to *Act* on *Res* under *Env*)
12	PHRSysPolicy= retrieve user-defined policies related to *Req*
13	**IF** (PDPdecision = 'permit' and PHRSysPolicy = 'permit') **THEN**
14	Forward the request to the relevant Web Service
15	**ELSE**
16	Deny the request
17	**END IF**
18	**END** make access control decision based on attribute vales and user-defined policies
19	**FUNCTION** PDP_make_access_decision(request of *Req* to *Act* on *Res* under *Env*)
20	retrieve policies(*Req*, *Act*, *Res*)
21	evaluate policies (*Req*, *Act*, *Res*, *Env*)
22	return decision
23	**END FUNCTION**

Fig. 5.3 Function for authorization policy evaluation

be reached via LDAP and a second for attributes than can be reached via SQL queries. For example, attributes relevant to the requestor, such as the hospital where he is occupied and his specialty, may be retrieved by means of an LDAP query while attributes relevant to the patients he is treating may be retrieved by means of an SQL query to the PHR system.

- **Policy Decision Point (PDP):** It refers to the entity that reaches an access control decision regarding an access request to a protected resource after evaluating the request against all the relevant policies. If PDP reaches a decision as expected it responds with Permit or Deny. If no matching policy is found or an error occurs the response is "Indeterminate". It is implemented as a service on

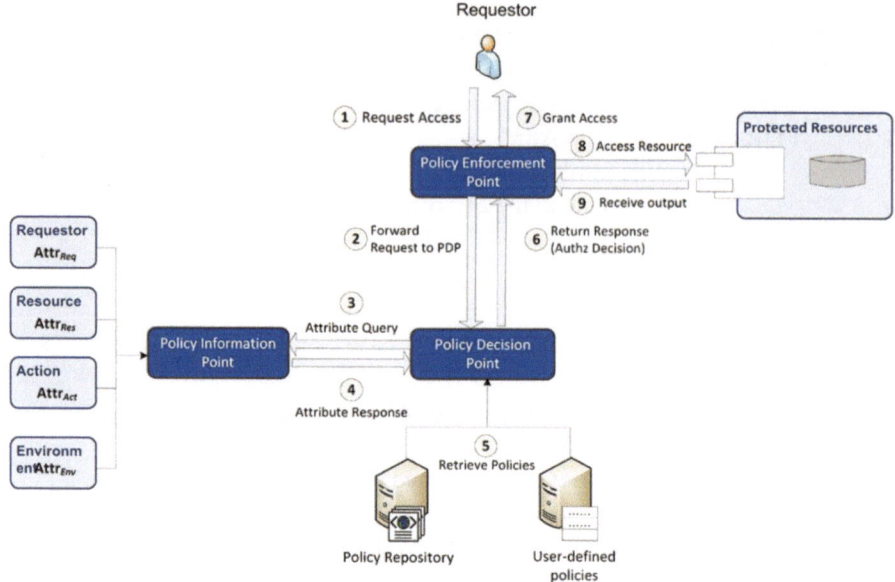

Fig. 5.4 Authorization architecture

the same application server where PIP is deployed and is configured with the two kinds of PIP connectors mentioned above, i.e. PIP connectors for LDAP and SQL.

- **Policy Repository:** It is the repository storing all access control policies with regard to healthcare process execution, process task execution and PHR data access.
- **User-defined Policies:** It is the set of policies defined by the citizen through the PHR system GUI and are stored at the PHR System Policies.
- **Protected Resources:** It refers to all the resources protected by the proposed authorization framework, as they are described in Definition 2 above.

According to Fig. 5.4, each request for gaining access to a resource is received by the PEP protecting it. The PEP makes an authorization call to the PDP, which in turn queries for additional subject, resource, action and environment attributes from the appropriate PIP. After acquiring the requested attributes, the PDP retrieves the relevant policies from the policy repository and the policies created by the PHR owner, evaluates the request against these policies and returns a response (and applicable obligations) to the PEP in the form of an authorization decision to grant or deny access. An obligation is information returned with the decision upon which the PEP may or may not act (e.g. an obligation may contain additional information concerning a decision to deny). If access is permitted, the PEP grants the requester access to the resource; otherwise, access is denied. The PEP fulfills any obligations, if applicable.

Fig. 5.5 A high level model
of an ePrescribing process

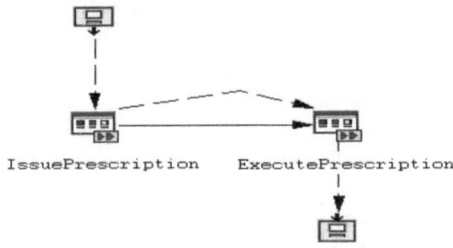

5.5 **Implementation Issues**

To illustrate the functionality of the proposed authorization architecture, a prototype
system was implemented that draws on the ePrescribing healthcare process depicted
in Fig. 5.5. Prototype system implementation was based on the Oracle 11g SOA
(Oracle 11g SOA suite 2013). In particular, the following components of this Suite
have been used: (i) Integrated Service Environment (ISE) for developing the web
services; (ii) a services registry for discovering and managing the lifecycle of services; (iii) a BPEL-based orchestration engine for tying the services into business
processes which are also exposed as web services; and, (iv) an enterprise portal for
healthcare professionals, patients and collaborating healthcare organizations to access content, collaborate and take actions via interaction with healthcare processes.

With regard to the healthcare process illustrated in Fig. 5.5, three interconnected
web services have been developed: the prescription request enabler (Pr-ISS), the
prescription execution enabler (Pr-EXEC) and the PHR access enabler (PHRE).
The higher level tasks depicted in Fig. 5.5 belong to Pr-ISS and Pr-EXEC, while the
lower level sub-tasks that are concerned with physician and pharmacist accesses to
patient record data (not shown in Fig. 5.5) belong to PHRE. The sample patient records containing these data were generated in Microsoft Healthvault, where access
control policies defined by the patient are also incorporated (Microsoft HealthVault
2013). These policies are defined explicitly by the patient or by an authorized person via the Graphical User Interface provided by the vendor. Moreover, the authorization policies defined in an earlier section, which are stored in the policy repository, are expressed as XML constructs using the vocabulary defined by the XAC-
ML profile for web services (OASIS eXtensible Access Control Markup Language
(XACML) TC 2013). These policies are segregated in two main types depending
on the web services they refer to, namely in policies concerning access rights on
the web services used for exposing BPEL processes and process tasks and policies
concerning access rights on web services querying the PHR System database. Since
both processes and databases constitute resources which are organized as a hierarchy, when specifying policies on them the hierarchical resource profile of XACML
can be used for the representation of these components (OASIS eXtensible Access
Control Markup Language (XACML) TC 2013). This profile specifies how XAC-
ML provides access control for resources that are organized as a hierarchy, such as
file systems, XML documents and databases. We consider this profile suitable for

specifying access control policies on BPEL process tasks as well. According to this profile, non-XML data can be represented by a URI of the following form:
    <scheme>://<authority>/<pathname>
    where:

- <scheme> identifies the namespace of the URI and can be either a protocol (e.g. "ftp", "http", "https") or a file system resource declared as "file".
- <authority> is typically defined by an Internet-based server or a scheme-specific registry of naming authorities, such as DNS, and
- <pathname> is of the form <root name>{/<node name>}. The sequence of <root name> and <node name> values should correspond to the components in a hierarchical resource.

Suppose that the process illustrated in Fig. 5.5 is named "PrescrProcProcess". Then the task "IssuePrescription" of this process would be represented as follows:
    "https://localhost:8443/active-bpel/services/PrescrProcProcess/IssuePrescription"

In turn, suppose that the types of health information contained in a PHR are medical history, conditions, medications, measurements and fitness with medical history information being subdivided in family history, immunization and procedures. The web service which should be invoked in order to retrieve the family history of the patient may be represented as follows:
    "https://localhost:8443/PHRE/getFamilyHistory"

An example of a task-related policy and in particular a policy that constitutes the realization of authorization requirement mentioned in Section "Authorization Policy Formulation" is illustrated in Fig. 5.6. It specifies that an ED physician has the permission to perform the operation "execute" (specified within <Action>) on the resource identified by the URI "http://localhost/active-bpel/services/PrescrProcProcess/IssuePrescription" (specified within <Resource>) only for patients admitted in ED, when he is on duty and within hospital premises (specified within <Condition>). A policy regarding access to the PHR web service mentioned above has the same form as the one illustrated in Fig. 5.6 with the following two differences:

- DataType of Resource (line 3) would be https://localhost:8443/PHRE/getFamilyHistory
- The DataType of Action (line 11) would be "invoke"

Finally, in achieving the robust privacy preserving access control framework envisaged, additional security features have been incorporated. In particular, users are authenticated via an LDAP server and all subsequent web transactions are executed under the Secure Socket Layer (SSL) via HTTPS.

When a physician attempts to invoke Pr-ISS in order to issue a prescription for drug administration to one of the patients in the ED, a request for a web service invocation is issued which is identified by the PEP and is passed to the policy decision service which, as mentioned earlier, plays the role of PDP. With the assistance of PIP, which is incorporated in the PDP service, attributes relevant to the requestor (physician), the action requested (issue a prescription for drug adinistration), the re-

```
1    <Resource>
2     <ResourceMatch MatchId="&function;string-equal">
3      <AttributeValue DataType="&xml;string">http://localhost/active-bpel/services/
            PrescrProcess/IssuePrescription
4      </AttributeValue>
5                     <ResourceAttributeDesignator   AttributeId="&resource;resource-id"
DataType="&xml;string"/>
6     </ResourceMatch>
7    </Resource>
8    …
9    <Action>
10    <ActionMatch MatchId="&function;string-equal">
11     <AttributeValue DataType="&xml;string">execute</AttributeValue>
12                    <ActionAttributeDesignator   AttributeId="&action;action-id"
DataType="&xml;string"/>
13    </ActionMatch>
14      </Action>
15    …
16   <Condition>
17    <Apply FunctionId="&function;and">
18    <Apply FunctionId="&function;string-equal">
19    <EnvironmentAttributeDesignator
          AttributeId="urn:oasis:names:tc:xacml:2.0:environment:userPatientRelationship"
DataType="&xml;string"/>
20     <AttributeValue DataType="&xml;string">currentPatient</AttributeValue>
25    </Apply>
26    <Apply FunctionId="&function;string-equal">
27     <EnvironmentAttributeDesignator
          AttributeId=" urn:oasis:name
DataType="&xml;string"/>
28     <AttributeValue DataType="&xml;yes">onDuty</AttributeValue>
29    </Apply>
30    <Apply FunctionId="&function;string-equal">
31     <EnvironmentAttributeDesignator
          AttributeId="urn:oasis:names:tc:xacml:2.0:environment:patAdmissDept"
DataType="&xml;string"/>
32     <AttributeValue DataType="&xml;string">ED</AttributeValue>
33    </Apply>
34     <Apply FunctionId="&function;string-equal">
35     <EnvironmentAttributeDesignator
          AttributeId="urn:oasis:names:tc:xacml:2.0:environment:location"
DataType="&xml;string"/>
36     <AttributeValue DataType="&xml;string">inPremises</AttributeValue>
37    </Apply>
38    </Apply>
39    </Condition>
```

Fig. 5.6 Sample policy

source (instantiate BPEL process of Fig. 5.5 and execute the IssuePrescription task) are retrieved along with information regarding the conditions under which the request has been issued (e.g. time of attempted access, location of attempted access). In turn, the PDP evaluates the contextual constraints (e.g. the "proximity" relationship between physician and patient, time and location of attempted web service invocation) of the relevant policies which it retrieves from the policy repositories (XACML policies and Microsoft Healthvault policies) in order to reach a decision on whether to permit or deny the requested web service invocation.

5.6 Results and Discussion

The privacy preserving access control framework proposed in this paper contributes to the information security state of the art by providing fine-grained access control over healthcare processes and through these to PHR data. Under certain circumstances (e.g. emergency cases) break glass access to critical PHI is provided. According to HIPAA, break glass refers to a quick means of granting emergency access on critical PHI to people who, under any other circumstances, are not authorized to access these data. In the proposed framework, incidents requiring break glass access to PHI are indicated by certain combinations of values assigned to the attributes of requestors, resources, actions and environment.

In addition, the proposed framework does not incur any significant administrative overhead since any changes in the access control policies are immediately reflected to the access control decisions during policy evaluation process resulting in either granting additional permissions or revoking assigned permissions as appropriate. Hence, the proposed framework meets strong requirements in terms of scalability and flexibility while it can be considered self-administering to a great extent. With regard to its performance, this depends mainly on the time required for the PDP to reach a decision regarding an access request. Thus, system performance evaluation amounts to the evaluation of the algorithm incorporated in PDP (Fig. 5.3). When it comes to algorithm performance measurement, the adoption of an empirical approach with certain metrics presents significant drawbacks since the results depend heavily on the infrastructure where the experiment will be carried out. Since algorithms are platform-independent (i.e. a given algorithm can be implemented in an arbitrary programming language on an arbitrary computer running an arbitrary operating system) the evaluation of the algorithm can be performed by evaluating the algorithm's run-time complexity. In this case, the worst-case scenario of a given algorithm is often evaluated by examining the structure of the algorithm and making some simplifying assumptions. In the case of our algorithm the complexity is $O(n^2)$ which is not considered as prohibitively high. However, the instruction in line 11 may cause some delay since the time required for its execution depends heavily on the number of policies stored in the policy repository, which, in a multi-owner and multi-user environment such as the proposed cloud PHR system, is expected to be high. Currently, the retrieval of relevant policies from the policy repository is performed by using the Sun XACML API. However, a number of approaches have been proposed for improving the performance of policy decision points (e.g. XACMLight, XACML Enterprise, XEngine)(Turkmen and Crispo 2008; Liu et al. 2011). A comparative analysis of these approaches is a task to be undertaken in the near future in order to identify the solution that will best suit the needs of our system.

5.7   Concluding Remarks

Healthcare organizations are faced with the challenge to improve healthcare quality, preventing medical errors, reducing healthcare costs, improving administrative efficiencies, reducing paper work and increasing access to affordable healthcare. Patient-centered care is being increasingly recognized as a care model that can meet the aforementioned requirements. This emerging care model depends on technology and, more specifically, on the availability of electronic patient health records and IT systems that can support care across all settings and accommodate direct interaction with consumers. PHRs can provide, among others, online access to global patient information and not only to certain pieces collected by individual healthcare providers and also can activate the patient in knowledge-based collaborations with healthcare professionals. As such, they can be used as basic infrastructures for building and operating several important systems, such as EMS systems. In these systems, a suitable authorization and access control mechanism needs to be in place, which will provide fine-grained access control over sensitive personal health information under normal circumstances but will facilitate overriding of normal access control rules in emergency situations so that healthcare delivery not be delayed or baulked. This chapter presents such an authorization framework for process-oriented PHR-based EMS systems. The proposed framework adheres to the attribute-based access control (ABAC) paradigm which is considered suitable for multi-owner and multi-user environments such as PHRs. ABAC is essentially a next generation authorization model that can provide dynamic, context-aware and risk-intelligent access control. Moreover, it can help achieve efficient regulatory compliance, effective services and a top-down approach to governance through transparency in policy enforcement.

References

ICW eHealth Framework, Lifesensor (2009) http://idn.icw-global.com/solutions/lifesensor/lifesensor.html. Accessed 10 Dec. 2013

Koufi V, Vassilacopoulos G (2008) HDGPortal: a grid portal application for pervasive access to process-based healthcare systems. In: Proceedings of the 2nd International Conference in Pervasive Computing Technologies in Healthcare, Tampere, Finland, 31 January–2 February 2008

Lauer G (2009) Health record banks gaining traction in regional projects. http://www.ihealthbeat.org/features/2009/health-record-banks-gaining-traction-in-regional-projects.aspx. Accessed 10 Dec. 2013

Liu A, Chen AF, Hwang J, Xie T (2011) Designing fast and scalable XACML policy evaluation engines. IEEE Trans Comput 60:1802–1817. doi:10.1109/TC.2010.274

Metavante (2010) In case of emergency personal health record. https://www.icephr.com/. Accessed 10 July 2010

Microsoft HealthVault (2013) https://www.healthvault.com/gr/el. Accessed 15 Dec. 2013

My Personal Health Record (MyPHR) (2010) http://myphr.ca/. Accessed 10 July 2010

OASIS eXtensible Access Control Markup Language (XACML) TC (2013) https://www.oasis-open.org/committees/tc_home.php?wg_abbrev=xacml. Accessed 15 Dec. 2013

Oracle 11gSOAsuite (2013) http://www.oracle.com/us/products/middleware/soa/suite/overview/index.html. Accessed 15 Dec. 2013

Tang PC, Ash JS, Bates DW, Overhage JM, Sands DZ (2006) Personal health records: definitions, benefits, and strategies for overcoming barriers to adoption. J Am Med Inf Assoc 13(2):121–126

Tentori M, Favela J, Rodriguez MD (2006) Privacy-aware autonomous agents for pervasive healthcare. IEEE Intell Syst 21(6):55–62

Turkmen F, Crispo B (2008) Performance evaluation of XACML PDP implementations. In: Proceedings of the 2008 ACM workshop on secure web services, ACM, New York, USA, 27–31 October 2008

U.S. Department of Health and Human Services (2006) Personal health records and personal health record systems. A report and recommendations from the National Committee on Vital and Health Statistics. http://www.ncvhs.hhs.gov/0602nhiirpt.pdf. Accessed 10 Dec. 2013

Wiljer D, Urowitz S, Apatu E, DeLenardo C, Eysenbach G, Harth T, Pai H, Leonard KJ (2008) Patient accessible electronic health records: exploring recommendations for successful implementation strategies. J Med Internet Res 10(4):e34

Win KT, Susilo W, Mu Y (2006) Personal health record systems and their security protection. J Med Syst 30:309–315

Chapter 6
Monitoring Patients in a Comorbid Condition with the Aid of Computerized Decision Support System

Di Lin and Fabrice Labeau

Abstract In this chapter, we present the detailed process to design a telecommunication and computer technology based platform for monitoring patients in the presence of a comorbid condition. Specifically, we take the monitoring of patients with both atrial fibrillation (AF) and Wolff Parkinsons White (WPW) as an example to clarify this process. As the core of this monitoring platform, a decision support system performs combining of guidelines for different diseases in view of the potential conflict occurring. We present the detailed process of designing this decision support system as well as its implementation. Finally, we analyze the system performance, including both system accuracy and the ability of a system to detect conflicts between different clinical guidelines. Specifically, we take into account the impact of both sensing errors and data entry errors on system performance.

Keywords E-health · Patient monitoring · Decision support system · Constraint logic programming · System performance

6.1 Introduction

Consider an emergency department with a 70-year-old man complaining of dizziness, a sensation of fluttering in the chest, shortness of breath, and fainting. At the time of presentation he had a rapid irregular pulse and his blood pressure is around

D. Lin (✉)
Department of Electrical and Computer Engineering, McGill University, Montréal, Canada
e-mail: di.lin2@mail.mcgill.ca

D. Lin
School of Information and Software Engineering, University of Electronic Science and Technology of China, Chengdu, China
e-mail: di.lin2@mail.mcgill.ca

F. Labeau
Department of Electrical and Computer Engineering, McGill University, Montréal, Canada
e-mail: fabrice.labeau@mcgill.ca

D.-D. Koutsouris, A. A. Lazakidou (eds.), *Concepts and Trends in Healthcare Information Systems,* Annals of Information Systems 16,
DOI 10.1007/978-3-319-06844-2_6, © Springer International Publishing Switzerland 2014

135/95, respiratory rate of 20, and heart rate of 230. A 12-lead ECG showed an irregular, wide complex QRS tachycardia. The ECG findings match atrial fibrillation (AF) in the setting of Wolff Parkinsons White (WPW) syndrome.

6.1.1   Clinical Guideline

This patient has both a chronic disease (WPW) and an acute disease (AF). The clinical guidelines for WPW and that for AF are shown in Fig. 6.1. According to the guideline for WPW, the patient will probably be first given the drug flecainide (F) at a low level of dosage, and then checked to determine if this patient's WPW is stable. If not, the guideline suggests one of two actions, either increasing the level of F if the F level is below a threshold (the maximal dosage of F that causes no risk to this patient, *DF_risk*) or taking another treatment. Afterwards, this patient will be released home either when he/she is stabilized or when he/she takes another treatment. In our following model, we assume that the level of F will be adjusted at most three times, if the patient is still not stablized, he/she will receive another treatment. Following the guideline for AF, the patient will receive electrical cardioversion (EC) treatment if hemodynamic instability (HI) is present. Otherwise, the patient is given intravascular injection of flecainide (FIV) or amiodarone (AIV), depending on the presence of structured heart disease (HD). The patient is given oral amiodarone (A) in cases of a recurring AF episode (RAE). Finally, the patient is discharged.

An adverse interaction between guidelines for WPW and AF stating that amiodarone and a certain or above dosage of flecainide cannot be administered to the patient at the same time. Amiodarone increases the toxicity of Flecainide in the blood and when combined with a certain or above oral dosage of Flecainide would result in a toxicity level higher than 1.0 mg/L which is harmful to a patient. In this case, doctors will reduce the dosage of flecainide used to stabilize WPW when amiodarone is administered as part of the AF therapy.

6.1.2   ECG Features to Diagnose WPW and AF

ECG is a transthoracic interpretation of the cardiac activity over a period of time, and an ECG signal can be detected by electrodes attached to the skin of a human body and recorded by a device external to the body. Generally, an ECG signal is composed of a P wave, a QRS complex, a T wave, and a U wave. Diagnosis on both WPW and AF is dependent on a few ECG features of a patient.

We summarize WPW related ECG features as (I) widened QRS complex (QRS complex width > 0.12 s), (II) Shortened PR intervals (PR width < 0.12 s), (III) ST changes seen in the form of delta waves (Fengler et al. 2007). Also we summarize the AF related ECG features as (I) Replacement of P waves with oscillatory or fibrilatory waves of different sizes, amplitudes and timing, (II) QRS complex

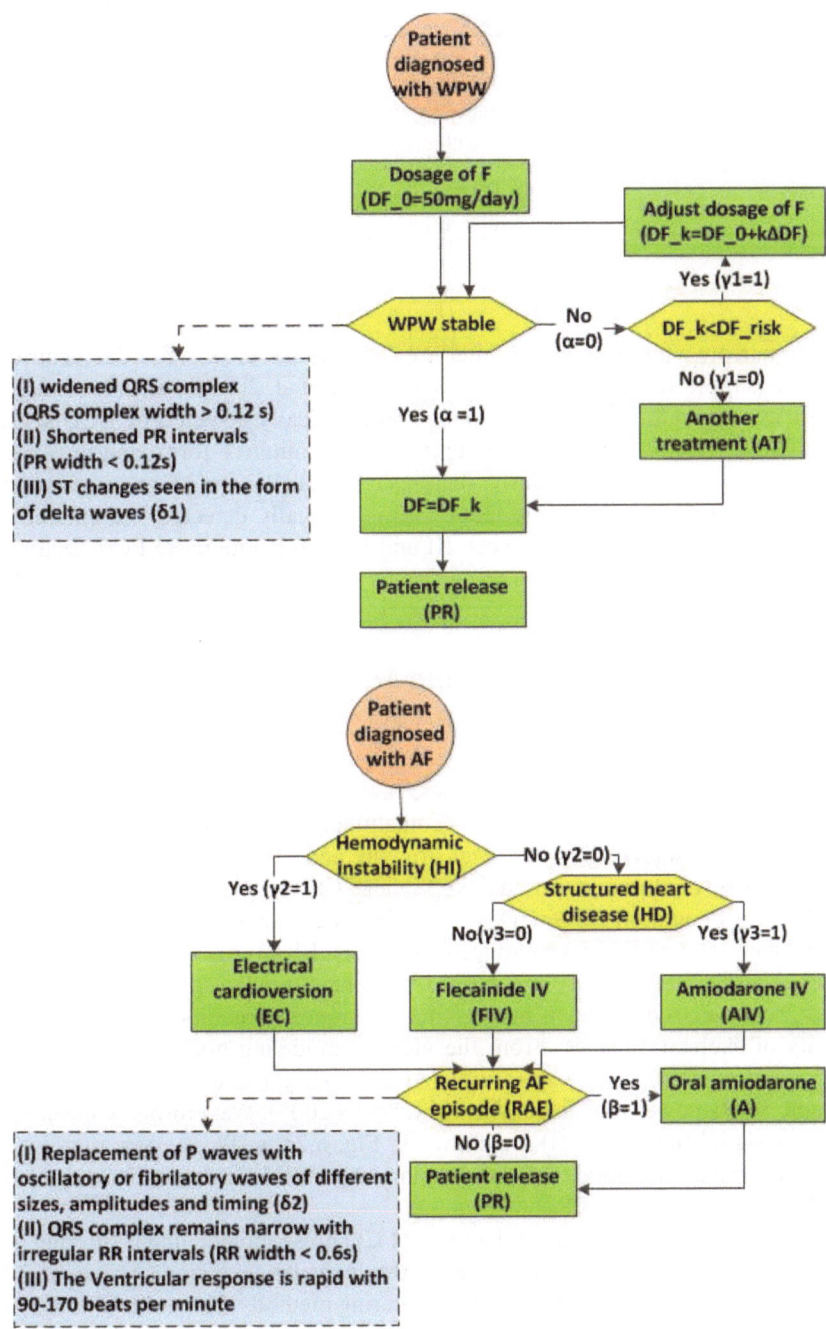

Fig. 6.1 Clinical guidelines for WPW and AF (Allan et al. 2012)

Table 6.1 Representation of ECG features

ECG features	Symbols
Width of QRS wave	*QRSW*
Width of PR wave	*PRW*
ST changes seen in the form of delta wave	$\delta 1$
Replacement of P waves with oscillatory or fibrilatory waves	$\delta 2$
Width of RR wave	*RRW*
Ventricular response	*VR*

remains narrow with irregular RR intervals (RR width < 0.6 s), (III) The Ventricular response is rapid with 90–170 beats/min (Fengler et al. 2007). Features (I) and (II) for WPW are quantitative, so they can be automatically detected by ECG sensors, while feature (III) is hard to be presented in a quantitative form, and thus the result is manually entered. Similarly, features (II) and (III) for AF are automatically detected by ECG sensors, while feature (I) is manually detected and entered. For the convenience of analysis in Sects. III and IV, we denote these ECG features as symbols, shown in Table 6.1.

6.1.3 Sources of ECG Noise and Methods of Denoising ECG Signals

Due to technical or physiological issues, raw ECG data, which are directed collected from human bodies, are always contaminated by noise and artifact, altering the trace of ECG signals from an ideal structure and rendering any interpretation of wave features (duration, amplitude, etc.) in an ECG signal inaccurate and misleading. The most common ECG noise sources include baseline wander, electrode motion artifacts, Power line interference (50/60 Hz), Electromyographic noise (EMG noise). These types of noise are caused by perspiration, respiration, body movements, poor electrode contact, interferences from nearby equipments, the electrical activity of skeletal muscles. From the view of modeling noise, the impact of all these types of noise can be approximated by a white noise source as well as the periodic 50 Hz power line noise (Amit and Willis 2007). Waveforms of clean signal plus raw signal (noisy signal) are shown in Fig. 6.2a, b. Please note that the data of clean signals are collected from the standard MIT-BIH database 2000 and the standard PTB database 2008.

The most popular methods of denoising ECG noise include linear filtering (Paul et al. 2000), adaptive filtering (Lu et al. 2009), wavelet denoising (Ayat et al. 2009; Sayadi and Shamsollahi 2006), Bayesian filtering methods (Sameni et al. 2007), and Empirical Mode Decomposition (EMD) based techniques (Amit and Willis 2007; Deering and Kaiser 2005; Wu and Rangayyan 2007; Jinseok et al. 2012). In view of our scenario in which constantly monitoring a patient's ECG signal is required, we need a real-time denoising method with fairly high sensitivity and specificity.

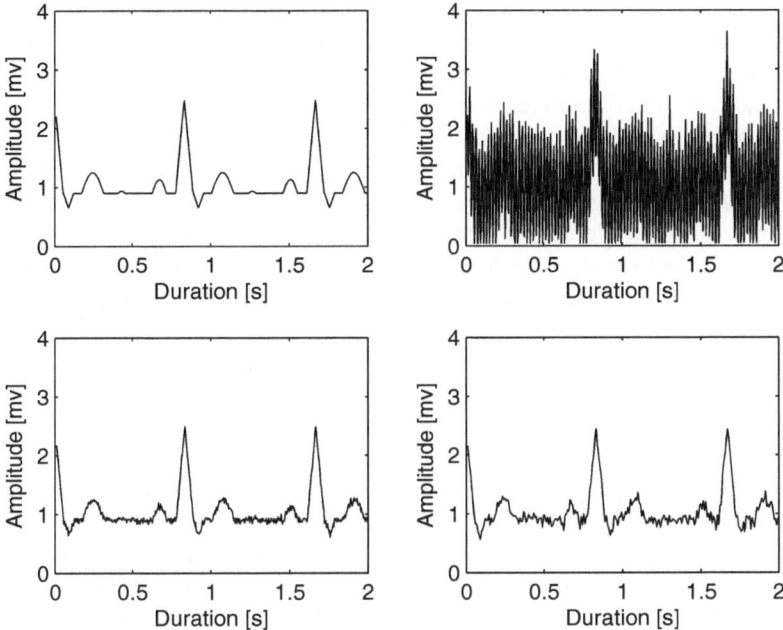

Fig. 6.2 Waveforms of ECG signals (*Top-left*: clean signal; *Top-right*: noisy signal; *Bottom-left*: denoised signal with enhanced EMD; *Bottom-right*: denoised signal with wavelet)

Among these denoising methods, we finally choose a wavelet method (Ayat et al. 2009) and an enhanced EMD method (Jinseok et al. 2012) in our following analysis. Both methods can attain sensitivity and specificity above 95 % and computation time less than 0.5 s (using MATLAB version 2010a on a 2.40 GHz Intel Core i7 processor, the computational time is 0.18–0.47 s for a 2 s data segment).

6.1.4   Related Work on Monitoring Patients in a Comorbid Condition

The related work on analyzing clinical guidelines falls under two main streams: (1) Processing a single clinical guideline (Boyd et al. 2005; Latoszek-Berendsen et al. 2010; Fox et al. 2010), (2) Combining multiple clinical guidelines for a patient in a comorbid condition (Hing et al. 2010; Wilk et al. 2011). The first stream is composed of verifying semantic errors and inconsistent definitions in a guideline in order to improve its quality (Boyd et al. 2005; Latoszek-Berendsen et al. 2010) as well as using a clinical guideline to critique actual actions (Fox et al. 2010). Research in the second stream, despite its importance, seems to be in its infancy. In (Hing et al. 2010; Wilk et al. 2011), the authors propose a methodology as well as its specific implementation for combining multiple clinical guidelines. However, it requires participation of clinicians and manual construction of the resulting guideline. Riano et al. in (Riano et al. 2012) advocate using an ontological model for guideline personalization. Unfortunately, it needs to be conducted manually by physicians using a specialized clinical guideline editor instead of automatically by a computer.

Similarly to other approaches in stream two, our decision support system employs medical sensors for semi-automated data collection (a few contexts of patients are hard to be collected by sensors and need to be manually entered by health staff) and employs logical model based algorithms to make diagnosis on patient conditions as well as detect conflicts between guidelines. Unlike other approaches, we focus on how to analyze the accuracy of a decision support system as well as the ability of this system to detect a conflict between clinical guidelines.

6.2 Design of Monitoring System

Following the ideas proposed in (Wilk et al. 2011; Hing et al. 2010) for the design of decision support units, we developed a monitoring system for patients with both WPW and AF. This system is designed to deliver patients related services and information via telecommunications and computing technologies. In this system, ECG features of a particular patient are partially collected by a device, which contains a group of sensors, and partially entered manually by health staff. Via wireless networks and internet, the patient's ECG data are transferred to a data server, which can be accessed by clinicians or doctors for online diagnosis or filing. Also a decision support unit at the data server would make initial decisions on patient condition as well as potential treatment plans. By referring to these initial decisions and treatment plans, doctors would make the final diagnosis as well as the corresponding treatment plan and send them to patients through a reverse link, denoted as *diagnosis feedback* in Fig. 6.3.

As shown in Fig. 6.3, our monitoring system is composed of three domains, namely, User domain, Service domain, and Data domain. The details of first two domains are presented in our previous chapter (Lin et al. 2012). We summarize them for completeness, and then we emphasize the data domain, which is the core for diagnosis on patient conditions. The user domain mainly includes a patient device responsible for collecting data and sending these data to the data server in a hospital. By and large, our patient device is mainly composed of three parts, namely, data acquisition module, cellular communication module, micro control unit (MCU). The data acquisition module (shown in Fig. 6.4) is modified from an off-the-shelf compact module that runs data acquisition algorithms, and this module consists of a gas-pump unit and a gas pressure sensor. The cellular communication module (shown in Fig. 6.5) takes charge of transmitting the acquired data to a remote data server via wireless networks. The core component of this module is a Subscriber Identity Model (SIM300C), which enables the data to access both GSM and GPRS communication networks. As the core of our patient device, MCU would store and run communication protocols and control signal processing programs (shown in

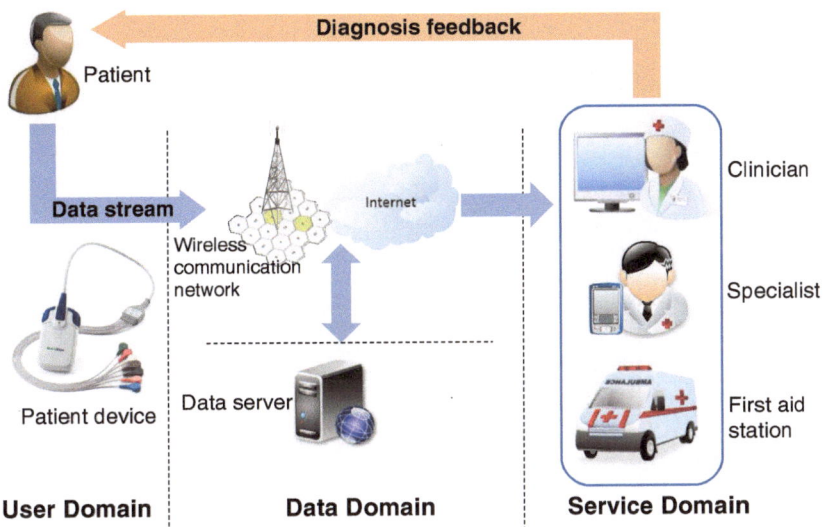

Fig. 6.3 Architecture of patient monitoring system

Fig. 6.4 Data acquisitior
module of a patient device

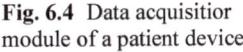

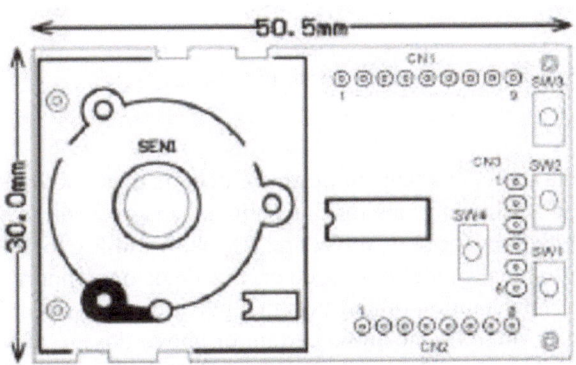

Fig. 6.6). The service domain of our system are composed of three types of service, namely, clinician service, specialist service, and first-aid service. Clinical service is for regular diagnosis, and specialist service is for the cases when making a decision is difficult or even beyond the scope of regular clinical guidelines. If the relevant data show that a patient is in emergency condition, alarms would be sent to the first-aid station for emergent treatment, either to an ambulance when this patient is outside a hospital or to some healthcare staff when this patient is in hospital.

The data domain is mainly composed of a data server, which is in charge of analyzing patient data and storing them for filing. Also a decision support unit at

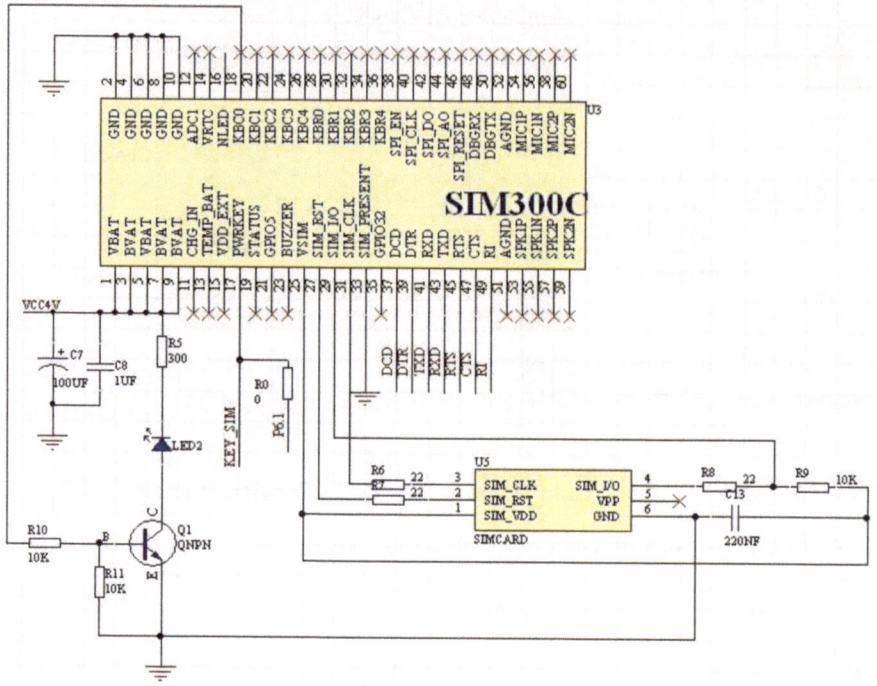

Fig. 6.5 Communication module of a patient device

data server can help clinicians or doctors make both diagnosis on patient conditions and treatment plans for this patient. This decision is made building on the clinical guidelines for both WPW and AF, shown in Fig. 6.1. Instead of simply adding two individual guidelines together, our decision support unit merges these guidelines in consideration of conflicts that may occur between these two guidelines. Specifically, amiodarone and a certain or above dosage of flecainide cannot be administered to the patient at the same time. Thus, the general process of making decisions on patient conditions is composed of two steps: (1) detecting the possible conflicts between these two guidelines; (2) mitigating these conflicts. In our specific case, either increasing the level of F if the F level is below a threshold (the maximal dosage of F that causes no risk to this patient) or taking another treatment.

6.3   Design of Decision Support System in the Patient Device

In this section, we will present the detailed process of designing a support decision system, which is embedded in the patient device. As the core of patient device, a decision support system is designed building on clinical guidelines and is in charge

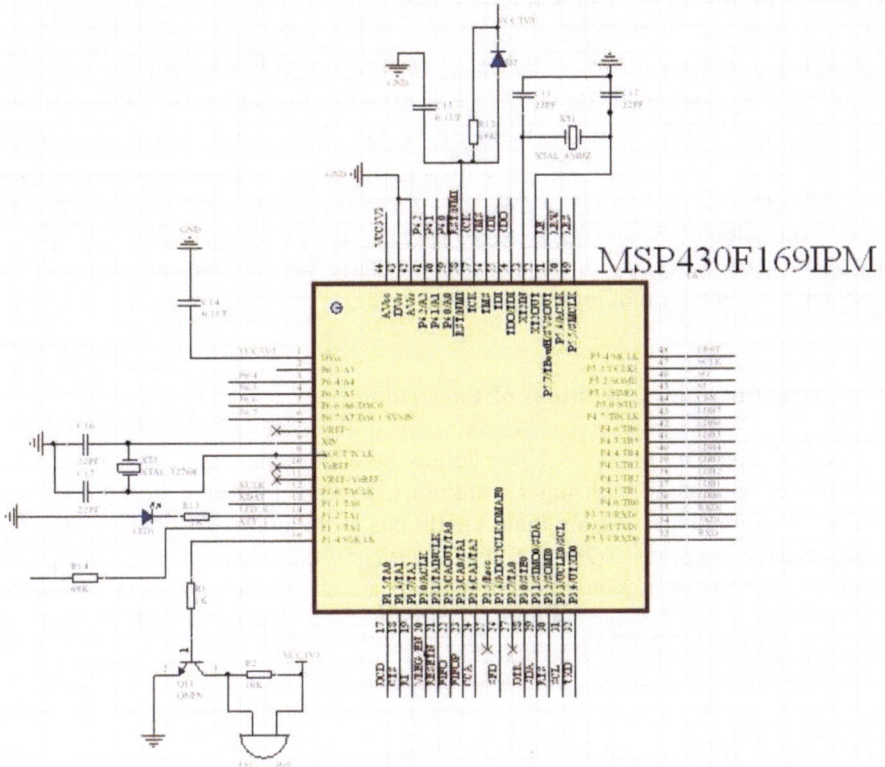

Fig. 6.6 Micro control unit of a patient device

of making diagnosis on patient conditions. In the following, we will present the detailed design of a support decision system.

6.3.1 Translate Clinical Guidelines into Logic Expressions

The first step of designing a support decision system for combining multiple guidelines is translating each clinical guideline into a logic expression. This step is composed of three substeps: (1) transform paths in the clinical guidelines into logic expressions; (2) transform the inner conditions of each node (in the dashed, blue area of Fig. 6.1) into logic expressions; (3) transform constraints between guidelines into logic expressions.

Transform Paths in the Clinical Guidelines

For each path in the clinical guidelines, we can represent it in the form of logic expressions. For example, the path $DF\_0 = 50 \rightarrow \alpha = 1 \rightarrow DF = DF\_0 \rightarrow PR$ can be transformed into the following logic expression: $(DF\_0 = 50) \wedge (\alpha = 1) \wedge (DF = DF\_0) \wedge PR$. The path $DF\_0 = 50 \rightarrow \alpha = 0 \rightarrow DF\_0 < DF\_risk \rightarrow DF\_1 = DF\_0 + \Delta DF \rightarrow \alpha = 1 \rightarrow DF = DF\_1 \rightarrow PR$ can be transformed into the following logic expression: $(DF\_0 = 50) \wedge (\alpha = 0) \wedge (DF\_0 < DF\_risk) \wedge (DF\_1 = DF\_0 + \Delta DF) \wedge (\alpha = 1) \wedge (DF = DF\_1) \wedge PR$. Similarly, we can transform all paths in guidelines into the form of logic expression.

Transform the Inner Conditions of Each Node

For each dashed box of Fig. 6.1, we define the conditions within it as inner conditions. For each node with inner conditions, we can transform these conditions into logic expressions. For the inner conditions at the node of 'WPW stable', we can represent them as $(QRSW > 0.12) \wedge (PRW < 0.12) \wedge (\delta 1 = 1)$ (Corresponding ECG features to aforementioned symbols are shown in Table 6.1). Similarly, we can represent the inner conditions at the node of 'Recurring AF episode' as $(\delta 2 = 1) \wedge (RRW < 0.6) \wedge (VR > 90)$.

Transform Constraints Between Guidelines

As mentioned in Sect. I.A., When combined with a certain or above oral dosage of flecainide, amiodarone would result in a toxicity level higher than 1.0 mg/L which is harmful to a patient. We denote the dosage of flecainide that causes harm to the patient as DF_toxic, which might be lower than DF_risk, the maximal dosage of F that causes no risk to this patient in the individual guideline for WPW. Thus, we must guarantee $DF\_k \leq DF\_toxic$, and this constraint does not exist in any individual guideline, but apprears when two guidelines are combined together. In the logic form, we can express this constraint as $not((DF\_k > DF\_toxic) \wedge A)$. Also once this constraint is violated, namely, $(DF\_k > DF\_toxic) \wedge A$ occurs, a few actions must be taken by clinicians to lower down the dosage of flecainide to DF_toxic or below.

6.3.2 Establish a Constraint Logic Programming Model

In view of transforming paths, inner conditions, as well as constraints between guidelines, we can establish a constraint logic programming (CLP) model. Building

Table 6.2 CLP model for combining clinical guidelines

Transform	CLP expression
Paths (WPW)	$(DF\_0 = 50) \wedge (\alpha\_0 = 1) \wedge (DF = DF\_0) \wedge PR$,
	$(DF\_0 = 50) \wedge (\alpha\_0 = 0) \wedge (\gamma1\_0 = 0) \wedge AT \wedge (DF = DF\_0) \wedge PR$,
	$(DF\_0 = 50) \wedge (\alpha\_0 = 0) \wedge (\gamma1\_0 = 1) \wedge (DF\_1 = DF\_0 + \Delta DF) \wedge$
	$(\alpha\_1 = 1) \wedge (DF = DF\_1) \wedge PR$,
	$(DF\_0 = 50) \wedge (\alpha\_0 = 0) \wedge (\gamma1\_0 = 1) \wedge (DF\_0 = DF\_0 + \Delta DF) \wedge$
	$(\alpha\_1 = 0) \wedge (\gamma1\_1 = 0) \wedge AT \wedge (DF = DF\_1) \wedge PR$,
	$(DF\_0 = 50) \wedge (\alpha\_0 = 0) \wedge (\gamma1\_0 = 1) \wedge (DF\_1 = DF\_0 + \Delta DF) \wedge$
	$(\alpha\_1 = 0) \wedge (\gamma1\_1 = 1) \wedge (DF\_2 = DF\_0 + 2\Delta DF) \wedge (\alpha\_2 = 1) \wedge$
	$(DF = DF\_2) \wedge PR$,
	$(DF\_0 = 50) \wedge (\alpha\_0 = 0) \wedge (\gamma1\_0 = 1) \wedge (DF\_1 = DF\_0 + \Delta DF) \wedge$
	$(\alpha\_1 = 0) \wedge (\gamma1\_1 = 1) \wedge (DF\_2 = DF\_0 + 2\Delta DF) \wedge (\alpha\_2 = 0) \wedge$
	$(\gamma1\_2 = 0) \wedge AT \wedge (DF = DF\_2) \wedge PR$,
Paths (AF)	$(\gamma2 = 1) \wedge EC \wedge (\beta = 0) \wedge PR$,
	$(\gamma2 = 0) \wedge (\gamma3 = 0) \wedge FIV \wedge (\beta = 0) \wedge PR$,
	$(\gamma2 = 0) \wedge (\gamma3 = 1) \wedge AIV \wedge (\beta = 0) \wedge PR$,
	$(\gamma2 = 1) \wedge EC \wedge (\beta = 1) \wedge A \wedge PR$,
	$(\gamma2 = 0) \wedge (\gamma3 = 0) \wedge FIV \wedge (\beta = 1) \wedge A \wedge PR$,
	$(\gamma2 = 0) \wedge (\gamma3 = 1) \wedge AIV \wedge (\beta = 1) \wedge A \wedge PR$
Inner conditions	$(\alpha = 1) \wedge (QRSW > 0.12) \wedge (PRW < 0.12) \wedge (\delta1 = 1)$,
	$(\alpha = 0) \wedge not((QRSW > 0.12) \wedge (PRW < 0.12) \wedge (\delta1 = 1))$,
	$(\beta = 1) \wedge (\delta2 = 1) \wedge (RRW < 0.6) \wedge (VR > 90)$,
	$(\beta = 0) \wedge not((\delta2 = 1) \wedge (RRW < 0.6) \wedge (VR > 90))$
Constraints	$not((DF\_k > DF\_risk) \wedge A)$

on this model, the problem of diagnosing patient conditions can be described as a constraint logic programming problem, and a solution to this problem is a diagnosis on patient conditions. Specifically, the model is shown as Table 6.2. The CLP model is exactly to ensure that all logic expressions for inner conditions and for constraints between guidelines are 'true', while at least one logic expression for WPW paths as well as at least one logic expression for AF paths are 'true'.

6.3.3   Implement a CLP Model on the ECLiPSe Platform

We employ the ECLiPSe system (Cattafi et al. 2011) to represent and solve a CLP model created from the combined logical model (see Table 6.2), and to identify violated constraints in the CLP model if no solution exists. ECLiPSe is a platform which supports Zinc, which is a medium level CLP modelling language. It is high-level enough to express most CLP problems easily and in a largely solver-independent way, and it is also low-level enough to be easily mapped onto many solvers. Also ECLiPSe provides a special library (called repair) to monitor constraints and to retrieve a set of conflicting ones. When a constraint falls into a conflict (i.e. when it is violated given the tentative assignment of variables), it appears in this conflict set.

In the following, we show sample ECLiPSe code for monitoring constraints between guidelines:

```
Constraint1(A, DF, DF_toxic) r_conflict cs,
conflict_constraints (cs, Conflicts),
Constraint1 (A, DF, DF_toxic): -(A and (DF $ >
DF_toxic)) $ = 0.
```

To clarify how this code runs on the platform of ECLiPSe, we assume the following scenario: a patient takes Oral Amiodarone ($A = 1$), and at the same time he takes 150 mg/day of flecainide (DF = 150) while the maximal dosage of F without toxicity is 130 mg/day ($DF\_toxic = 130$), then ECLiPSe will return

```
Conflicts = [Constraint1 (1, 150, 130)].
```

As expected, ECLiPSe can capture the constraint $Constraint1(A, DF, DF\_toxic)$, and shows the result in the conflict set.

6.4   Analysis on System Performance

In this section, we will analyze the performance of our decision support system. Specifically, the performance is evaluated by both the system accuracy as well as the conflict detecting ability of our system, namely the ability of detecting the conflicts between clinical guidelines.

6.4.1   System Accuracy Analysis

The system accuracy (ACC) is defined as the probability that the decision results for both AF and WPW are correct, and its value is equal to the multiplication of $PrAF$ and $PrWPW$:

$$ACC = PrAF \times PrWPW \tag{6.1}$$

where $PrAF$ denotes the probability of a correct decision for AF, while $PrWPW$ denotes the probability of a correct decision for WPW. Given that

$$PrWPW = Pr(\alpha = 1, \hat{\alpha} = 1)$$
$$+Pr(\alpha = 0, \hat{\alpha} = 0)Pr(\gamma 1 = 0, \hat{\gamma} 1 = 0)$$
$$+Pr(\alpha = 0, \hat{\alpha} = 0)Pr(\gamma 1 = 1, \hat{\gamma} 1 = 1)Pr(\alpha = 1, \hat{\alpha} = 1)$$
$$+Pr^2(\alpha = 0, \hat{\alpha} = 0)Pr(\gamma 1 = 1, \hat{\gamma} 1 = 1)Pr(\gamma 1 = 0, \hat{\gamma} 1 = 0)$$
$$+Pr^2(\alpha = 0, \hat{\alpha} = 0)Pr^2(\gamma 1 = 1, \hat{\gamma} 1 = 1)Pr(\alpha = 1, \hat{\alpha} = 1)$$
$$+Pr^3(\alpha = 0, \hat{\alpha} = 0)Pr^2(\gamma 1 = 1, \hat{\gamma} 1 = 1)Pr(\gamma 1 = 0, \hat{\gamma} 1 = 0) \qquad (6.2)$$

where $\alpha = 1$ and $\alpha = 0$ represents stabilized WPW in truth (refer to Fig. 6.1), respectively, while $\hat{\alpha} = 1$ and $\hat{\alpha} = 0$ represent the estimation result of AF recurring and AF not recurring, respectively. Similarly, $\gamma 1 = 1$ and $\gamma 1 = 0$ represents the truth of F dosage reaching below and above the maximal dosage of F without risk to patients (refer to Fig. 6.1), respectively, while $\hat{\gamma} 1 = 1$ and $\hat{\gamma} 1 = 0$ represent estimating F dosage to reach below and above the dosage of F with risk.

$$PrAF = Pr(\gamma 2 = 1, \hat{\gamma} 2 = 1)Pr(\beta = 0, \hat{\beta} = 0)$$
$$+Pr(\gamma 2 = 0, \hat{\gamma} 2 = 0)Pr(\gamma 3 = 0, \hat{\gamma} 3 = 0)Pr(\beta = 0, \hat{\beta} = 0)$$
$$+Pr(\gamma 2 = 0, \hat{\gamma} 2 = 0)Pr(\gamma 3 = 1, \hat{\gamma} 3 = 1)Pr(\beta = 0, \hat{\beta} = 0)$$
$$+Pr(\gamma 2 = 1, \hat{\gamma} 2 = 1)Pr(\beta = 1, \hat{\beta} = 1)$$
$$+Pr(\gamma 2 = 0, \hat{\gamma} 2 = 0)Pr(\gamma 3 = 0, \hat{\gamma} 3 = 0)Pr(\beta = 1, \hat{\beta} = 1)$$
$$+Pr(\gamma 2 = 0, \hat{\gamma} 2 = 0)Pr(\gamma 3 = 1, \hat{\gamma} 3 = 1)Pr(\beta = 1, \hat{\beta} = 1) \qquad (6.3)$$

where $\beta = 1$ represents non-stablized WPW and $\beta = 0$ represents the truth of AF recurring and AF not recurring (refer to Fig. 6.1), while $\hat{\beta} = 1$ represents non-stabilized WPW and $\hat{\beta} = 0$ represents stabilized WPW in estimation. Similarly, $\gamma 2 = 1$ and $\gamma 2 = 0$ represent HI occurring and not occurring in truth (refer to Fig. 6.1), respectively, while $\hat{\gamma} 2 = 1$ and $\hat{\gamma} 2 = 0$ represent HI occurring and not occurring in estimation. $\gamma 3 = 1$ and $\gamma 3 = 0$ represent HD occurring and not occurring in truth (refer to Fig. 6.1), respectively, while $\hat{\gamma} 3 = 1$ and $\hat{\gamma} 3 = 0$ represent HD occurring and not occurring in estimation.

The rationale for Eqs. (6.2) and (6.3) is to calculate the probability of correct decisions when flowing in each path shown in Table 6.2. For example, for the path $(DF\_0 = 50) \wedge (\alpha\_0 = 0) \wedge (\gamma1\_0 = 0) \wedge AT \wedge (DF = DF\_0) \wedge PR$, the correct decision is made when and only when both $\alpha = \hat{\alpha} = 0$ and $\gamma 1 = \hat{\gamma} 1 = 1$. Thus, the probability of correct decisions when the case falling in this path is $Pr(\alpha = 0, \hat{\alpha} = 0)Pr(\gamma1 = 0, \hat{\gamma}1 = 0)$. The probability of correct decisions for other paths can be similarly calculated, and then the average system accuracy can be calculated when summing up the probability for each path.

Equations (6.1), (6.2) and (6.3) show that the system accuracy depends on a few specific probabilities, and these probabilities can be classified into two groups building on whether these probabilities are linked with ECG features. $Pr(\beta = 0, \hat{\beta} = 0)$,

$Pr(\beta = 1, \hat{\beta} = 1)$, $Pr(\alpha = 1, \hat{\alpha} = 1)$, $Pr(\alpha = 0, \hat{\alpha} = 0)$, can be categorized into the first group, because they can be presented as functions of ECG features, building on the conditions of both WPW and AF from ECG in Section I.B. Also $Pr(\gamma 1 = 0, \hat{\gamma} 1 = 0)$, $Pr(\gamma 2 = 1, \hat{\gamma} 1 = 1)$, $Pr(\gamma 2 = 0, \hat{\gamma} 2 = 0)$, $Pr(\gamma 2 = 1, \hat{\gamma} 2 = 1)$, $Pr(\gamma 3 = 0, \hat{\gamma} 3 = 0)$, $Pr(\gamma 3 = 1, \hat{\gamma} 3 = 1)$, which are not linked with ECG features, can be categorized into the second group.

The first group of probabilities can be shown as

$$
\begin{aligned}
Pr(\beta = 1, \hat{\beta} = 1) &= Pr(RR < 0.6, RR + \Delta RR < 0.6) \\
&\times Pr(VR > 90, VR + \Delta VR > 90) \times Pr(\delta 2 = 1, \hat{\delta 2} = 1) \\
Pr(\beta = 0, \hat{\beta} = 0) &= Pr(RR > 0.6, RR + \Delta RR > 0.6) \\
&\times Pr(VR > 90, VR + \Delta VR > 90) \times Pr(\delta 2 = 1, \hat{\delta 2} = 1) \\
&+ Pr(RR \leq 0.6, RR + \Delta RR \leq 0.6) \\
&\times Pr(VR \leq 90, VR + \Delta VR \leq 90) \times Pr(\delta 2 = 1, \hat{\delta 2} = 1) \\
&+ Pr(RR > 0.6, RR + \Delta RR > 0.6) \\
&\times Pr(VR \leq 90, VR + \Delta VR \leq 90) \times Pr(\delta 2 = 1, \hat{\delta 2} = 1) \\
&+ Pr(RR > 0.6, RR + \Delta RR \leq 0.6) \\
&\times Pr(VR > 90, VR + \Delta VR \leq 90) \times Pr(\delta 2 = 1, \hat{\delta 2} = 1) \\
Pr(\alpha = 1, \hat{\alpha} = 1) \\
&= Pr(QRS > 0.12, QRS + \Delta QRS > 0.12) \\
&\times Pr(PR < 0.12, PR + \Delta PR < 0.12) \\
&\times Pr(\delta 1 = 1, \hat{\delta 1} = 1) \\
Pr(\alpha = 0, \hat{\alpha} = 0) \\
&= Pr(QRS > 0.12, QRS + \Delta QRS > 0.12) \\
&\times Pr(PR \geq 0.12, PR + \Delta PR \geq 0.12) \\
&\times Pr(\delta 1 = 1, \hat{\delta 1} = 1) \\
&+ Pr(QRS \leq 0.12, QRS + \Delta QRS \leq 0.12) \\
&\times Pr(PR < 0.12, PR + \Delta PR < 0.12) \\
&\times Pr(\delta 1 = 1, \hat{\delta 1} = 1) \\
&+ Pr(QRS \leq 0.12, QRS + \Delta QRS \leq 0.12) \\
&\times Pr(PR \geq 0.12, PR + \Delta PR \geq 0.12) \\
&\times Pr(\delta 1 = 1, \hat{\delta 1} = 1)
\end{aligned}
\tag{6.4}
$$

where RR represents the width of RR interval, PR represents the width of PR interval, QRS represents the width of QRS interval, VR represents the ventricular response. Also ΔRR denotes the difference of RR interval between a clean data (data from PTB standard database) and a noisy data (clean data contaminated by noise) or a denoised data (noisy data processed by denoising methods). ΔPR denotes the difference of PR interval between a clean data and a noisy data or denoised data. ΔQRS denotes the difference of QRS interval between a clean data and a noisy data or denoised data. ΔVR denotes the difference of VR interval between a clean data and a noisy data or denoised data.

For the second group of probabilities, assume that events $\gamma i = 1$ and $\gamma i = 0$ occurs with an equal probability, and γi are independent and identically distributed (i.i.d.) (for $i = 1, 2, 3$). Also the probability of $Pr(\hat{\gamma} i | \gamma i)$ for $i = 1, 2, 3$ is assumed to be

$$Pr(\hat{\gamma} i | \gamma i) = \begin{cases} 1 - P_e & \gamma i = \hat{\gamma} i \\ P_e & \gamma i \neq \hat{\gamma} i \end{cases} \tag{6.5}$$

where P_e is the probability of entry errors occurring at the decision node of paths.

Building on these assumptions, the second group of probabilities can be shown as

$$Pr(\gamma_i = j, \hat{\gamma}_i = j) = 0.5(1 - P_e) \quad for \, i = 1, 2, 3 \, and \, j = 0, 1 \tag{6.6}$$

Similarly, we assume $Pr(\delta i = j, \hat{\delta} i = j) = 0.5(1 - P_d)$ for $i = 1$, 2 and $j = 0$, 1, where P_d is the probability of entry errors occurring within inner conditions.

6.4.2   Conflict-Detecting Ability of Our System

As presented in Sect. I.A., the conflict should be detected if a patient is supposed to take amiodarone and a certain or above dosage of flecainide at the same time. Also the ability of our system to detect conflicts between guidelines is evaluated by the probability of successfully detecting conflicts, namely, the probability of conflicts being detected given these conflicts occurring. Mathematically, the probability of successfully detecting conflicts (SDC) can be shown as:

$$SDC = Pr(Conflicts \, being \, detected \, | \, Conflicts \, occuring)$$
$$= \frac{Pr^2(\alpha = 0, \hat{\alpha} = 0)Pr^2(\gamma 1 = 1, \hat{\gamma} 1 = 1)Pr^2(\beta = 1, \hat{\beta} = 1)}{Pr^2(\alpha = 0)Pr^2(\gamma 1 = 1)Pr(\beta = 1)} \tag{6.7}$$

given $Pr(\alpha = 0) = \sum_{j,=0,1} Pr(\alpha = 0, \hat{\alpha} = j)$, $Pr(\gamma 1 = 1) = \sum_{j=0,1} Pr(\gamma 1 = 1, \hat{\gamma} 1 = j)$,

$Pr(\beta = 0) = \sum_{j=0,1} Pr(\beta = 0, \hat{\beta} = j)$, where $Pr(\alpha = 0, \hat{\alpha} = 0)$, $Pr(\beta = 1, \hat{\beta} = 1)$,

$Pr(\gamma 1 = 1, \hat{\gamma} 1 = 1)$ are shown in Eq. (6.4), while $Pr(\alpha = 0, \hat{\alpha} = 1)$, $Pr(\beta = 1, \hat{\beta} = 0)$, $Pr(\gamma 1 = 1, \hat{\gamma} 1 = 0)$ can be similarly calculated as Eq. (6.4). The rational for equation Eq. (6.7) is that we assume a conflict being detected when and only when the dosage of F increases twice to reach the level that causes toxicity to patients. Thus, the probability of conflicts occurring is exactly the probability of going through the last path in the guideline for WPW as well as one of the last three paths in the guideline for AF (shown in Table 6.2).

6.4.3 Distribution of ECG Parameters

As shown in Eqs. (6.4) and (6.7), both ACC and SDC are determined by EGC parameters, particularly dependent on four groups of probability, shown as

$$Pr(Q > Q_1, Q + \Delta Q > Q_2)$$
$$= \int_{Q_1}^{+\infty} \int_{Q_2-Q}^{+\infty} pdf_Q(x) pdf_{\Delta Q}(y) \, dxdy$$
$$Pr(Q > Q_1, Q + \Delta Q < Q_2)$$
$$= \int_{Q_1}^{+\infty} \int_{-\infty}^{Q_2-Q} pdf_Q(x) pdf_{\Delta Q}(y) \, dxdy$$
$$Pr(Q < Q_1, Q + \Delta Q > Q_2)$$
$$= \int_{-\infty}^{Q_1} \int_{Q_2-Q}^{+\infty} pdf_Q(x) pdf_{\Delta Q}(y) \, dxdy$$
$$Pr(Q < Q_1, Q + \Delta Q < Q_2)$$
$$= \int_{-\infty}^{Q_1} \int_{-\infty}^{Q_2-Q} pdf_Q(x) pdf_{\Delta Q}(y) \, dxdy$$

$$(6.8)$$

where $Q = RR, VR, QRS, PR$.

It is shown that RR, PR, QRS of ECG in PTB database 2008 are in skew normal distribution, and VR is uniformly distributed (Miyamoto et al. 2012), namely, the probability density functions (pdf) of these parameters are shown as Eqs. (6.9) and (6.10).

$$pdf_Q(x) = \frac{1}{w_Q \pi} e^{-\frac{(x-\epsilon_Q)^2}{2 w_Q^2}} \int_{-\infty}^{a_Q \left(\frac{x-\epsilon_Q}{w_Q}\right)} e^{-\frac{t^2}{2}} \, dt \qquad (6.9)$$

where $Q = RR, PR, QRS$. ϵ_Q determines the location, α_Q determines the shape, w_Q determines the scale and should be positive.

$$pdf_{VR}(x) = \begin{cases} 1/(2x_{max}) & if \ x \in [-x_{max}, x_{max}] \\ 0 & otherwise \end{cases} \qquad (6.10)$$

In the following, we focus on the distribution of ΔRR, ΔVR, ΔQRS, ΔPR. To the best of our knowledge, no concurrent publication has presented the distribution of these parameters. Thus, we will estimate their distribution by measurement, and the measurement process is detailed as follows: We first generate AWGN noise given the signal and SNR, and add this AWGN noise into ECG signal (clean data) to simulate noisy ECG signal (raw data). Then, we denoise the raw data by employing wavelet and enhanced EMD methods, respectively (shown in Fig. 6.2). Next, we collect ΔRR, ΔVR, ΔQRS, ΔPR by comparing the clean ECG signal and the noisy signa (or denoised data) as well as recording the difference of their RR, VR, QRS, PR values. By repeating the aforementioned procedures quite a few times (e.g. 10,000), we can draw the histogram of ΔRR, ΔVR, ΔQRS, ΔPR. Finally, we can match the histograms with off-the-shelf distribution to determine the distribution of ΔRR, ΔVR, ΔQRS, ΔPR.

In the measurement process, we assume that the noise in ECG is AWGN plus periodic 50 Hz power line noise. Also the data presented in the process of measurement are provided by a standard database (PTB database) which contains ECG signals of 294 subjects, both healthy and diagnosed with a variety of clinical conditions 2008. The histogram of these parameters as well as their estimated distributions are shown in Figs. 6.7, 6.8, 6.9: the distributions of ΔRR, ΔPR, ΔQRS are estimated as Gaussian, while the distribution of ΔVR is estimated as Double-exponential. Please note that we try to fit these data (for minimum mean square error, MMSE) with common distributions, including Beta, Binomial, Birnbaum–Saunders, Double-exponential, Exponential, Extreme value, Gamma, Gaussian, Generalized extreme value, Generalized Pareto, Inverse Gaussian, Logistic, Log-logistic, Lognormal, Nakagami, Negative binomial, Poisson, Rayleigh, Rician, t-location-scale, Weibull with varying parameters. Also we employ the fitting toolbox of Matlab for the aforementioned fitting process.

6.5   Simulation and Results

Building on the distribution of ECG features, we demonstrate the issue with respect to average system accuracy as well as the probability of our system successfully detecting the occurrence of conflicts between clinical guidelines. In view of Eqs. (6.1) and (6.7), we can analytically compute the average system accuracy as well as the probability of detecting conflicts, respectively. On the other hand, we run Monte Carlo simulations by Matlab to verify our theoretical results based on Eqs. (6.1) and (6.7). In the Monte Carlo simulation, we use Matlab to generate both the exact ECG signal and the noisy ECG signal. Then, we employ both wavelet method and enhanced EMD method (shown in Fig. 6.2) to denoise ECG signal contaminated by AWGN. Next, we compare the diagnosis result with the exact ECG features and that with the denoised ECG features. Specifically, if these two decisions are the same, then, the number of correct diagnosis increases by 1; otherwise, the number of incorrect diagnosis increases by 1. This process is repeated 10^4 times. Finally, we record the number of both correct and incorrect diagnosis after repeating the above-mentioned process thousands of times. Additionally, we can calculate the system accuracy by dividing the number of correct diagnosis by that of all diagnosis (both correct and incorrect diagnosis).

For both analytical and simulation scenarios, the parameters are as follows: both the probability of entering errors for regular paths in the clinical guidelines and the probability of entering errors for inner conditions are 10% (Becher and Chassin 2001), namely, $P_e = P_d = 10\%$ in Eqs. (6.5) and (6.6).

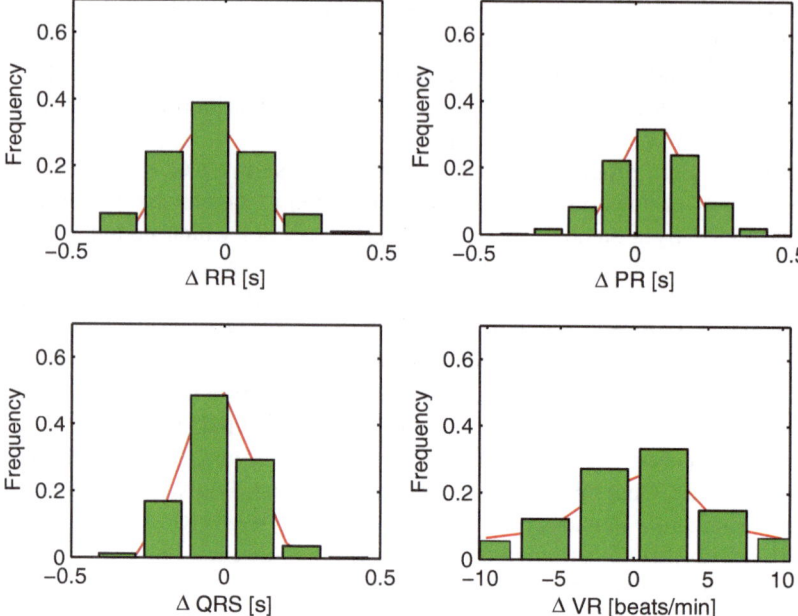

Fig. 6.7 Histogram of ECG features (raw signal)

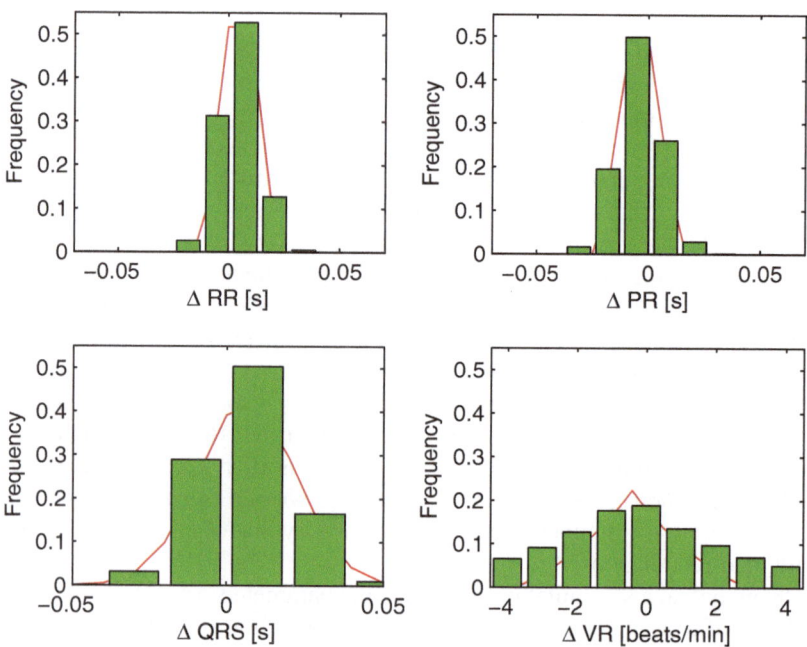

Fig. 6.8 Histogram of ECG features (denoised signal with wavelet)

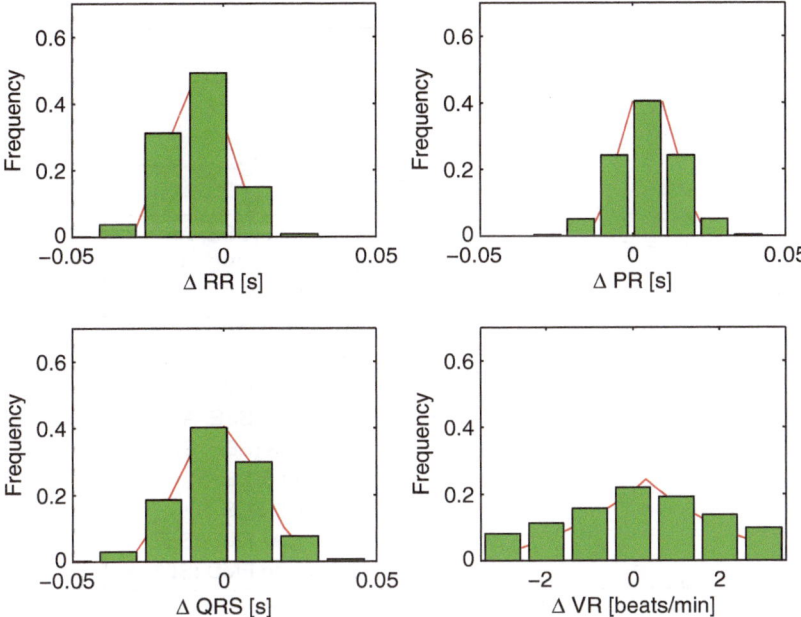

Fig. 6.9 Histogram of ECG features (denoised signal with enhanced EMD)

Figure 6.10 shows that both the analytical result and the simulation result of the average system accuracy match well, proving the accuracy of our analytical results. The slight difference comes from calculating the distribution of ECG features. We employ pdf of ECG features to analytically calculate system accuracy, while we employ probability mass function (PMF) of ECG features (as shown in Figs. 6.7, 6.8, 6.9) to simulate. Thus, the analytical calculation slightly underestimate the system accuracy. Also Fig. 6.10 shows that denoising methods, both wavelet and enhanced EMD, can increase the system accuracy by around 20 % than without using them. The enhanced EMD can attain a slightly higher system accuracy than wavelet method, and both methods can attain a system accuracy above 90 % when SNR is above 18 dB. Also Fig. 6.10 shows the proportion of contributions made by these two types of errors to lowering down system accuracy: 5–15 % decrease of system accuracy is caused by sensing errors, while only around 5 % decrease of system accuracy is caused by manual entry errors.

Figure 6.11 shows that the probability of detecting conflicts will increase with the rise of SNR. Similar to the scenario of calculating system accuracy, denoising methods, both wavelet and enhanced EMD, can increase the probability of detecting conflicts by around 20 % than without using them. However, unlike the scenario of calculating system accuracy, both wavelet and enhanced EMD methods can attain a probability of detecting conflicts above 90 % when SNR reaches 18 dB or above. Also Fig. 6.11 shows the proportion of contributions made by these two

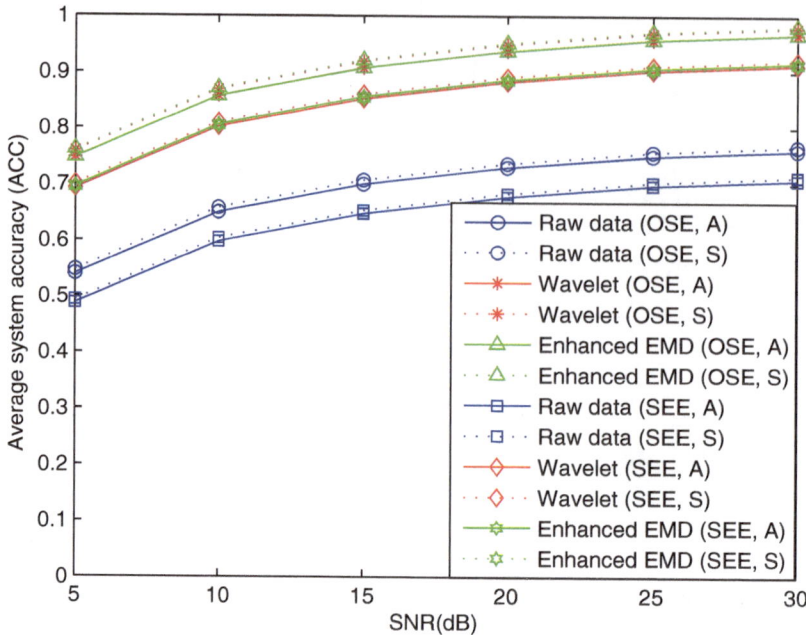

Fig. 6.10 Average system accuracy vs. SNR (*OSE* represents only sensing errors, *SEE* represents both sensing errors and entry errors, *A* represents analytical result, *S* represents simulation result)

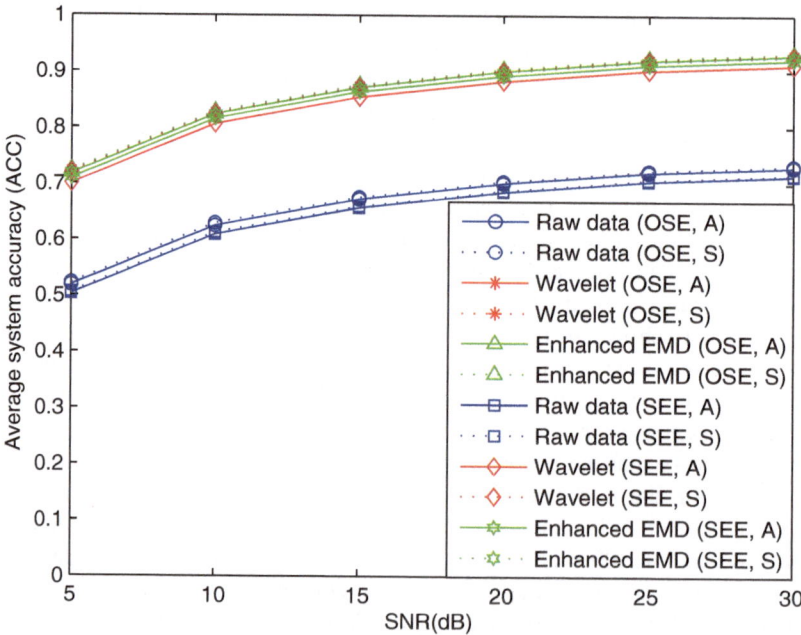

Fig. 6.11 Probability of successfully detecting conflicts vs. SNR (*OSE* represents only sensing errors, *SEE* represents both sensing errors and entry errors, *A* represents analytical result, *S* represents simulation result)

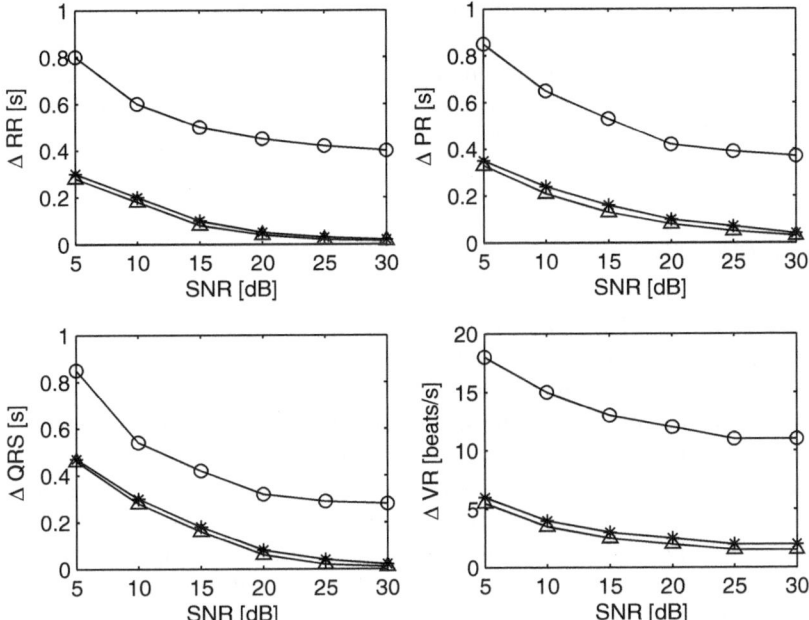

Fig. 6.12 Sensitivity of ECG features vs. SNR (*Circled line*: raw data; *Triangular line*: enhanced EMD; *Starred line*: wavelet)

types of errors to lowering down system accuracy: 5–20 % decrease of system accuracy is caused by sensing errors, while only around 1 % decrease of system accuracy is caused by manual entry errors. The reason why manual entry errors contribute less to the decrease of conflict detecting probability than to the system accuracy is: only an entry error occurring on the paths leading to conflicts will impact the probability of detecting conflicts, while the other entry errors have no impact on this probability.

Both the system accuracy and the probability of detecting conflicts are dependent on the ECG features. When a signal is contaminated by noise, the ECG features will not be exactly extracted, and errors in ECG features will lead to the decrease of both system accuracy and the probability of detecting conflicts. Figure 6.12 shows how sensitive the ECG features will be with the change of SNR, in other word, how the errors of ECG features will change with SNR. Figure 6.12 illustrates that ΔQRS changes slightly faster than ΔRR and ΔPR, and much faster than ΔVR, while ΔRR and ΔPR change almost at the same speed.

As expected, both the average system accuracy and the probability of successfully detecting conflicts increase with SNR. At the same time, however, system cost may decrease, since a sensor with advanced sensing circuits, which can lower down noise, may be at a higher price. In practice, we should take into account both the system performance and the system cost. Given the acceptable system performance, we can find the necessary SNR to guarantee the performance. For example, given the acceptable system accuracy as 90% and the acceptable probability of detecting conflicts 90%, then, the SNR should be higher than 18 dB. This can offer some information to select sensors in the design of a wireless healthcare system. Thus, our analysis on system accuracy not only helps healthcare staff evaluate the system accuracy, but enables the designer of wireless healthcare system to select proper sensors.

6.6   Conclusion

In this chapter, we develop a telecommunication and computer aided system to monitor the patients in a comorbid condition, with both WPW and AF, and originally integrate a decision support unit, in view of combining clinical guidelines of multiple diseases, into our monitoring system. This decision support unit can make diagnosis on patient conditions as well as detect conflicts between clinical guidelines, and the detailed process of this decision unit is presented in our chapter. Also we present the issues about system performance in consideration of potential error sources: both ECG sensing errors and manual entry errors. Specifically, we propose an analytical method to evaluate the performance of our monitoring system by linking both system accuracy and the ability of detecting conflicts with the distribution of ECG features. To proof the reliability of our analytical analysis, we show the result of our analysis matching that of Monte Carlo simulation well. Both analytical and simulation results show that sensing errors have more impacts on system performance (both system accuracy and the probability of detecting errors) than manual entry errors do. Also the results show that the SNR of ECG should be higher than 18 dB to achieve both the system accuracy and the probability of detecting conflicts above 90%. The methodology and analysis in this chapter can help healthcare staff and system designers evaluate the system performance or select appropriate sensors for a healthcare monitoring system.

Acknowledgements Thanks to Prof. Guixia Kang, Prof. Wojtek Michalowski, Ms. Hoda Daou, Mr. Subhra Mohapatra who worked with us and offered us quite a few fantastic ideas to finish this draft.

This work was partially supported by the Natural Sciences and Engineering Research Council (NSERC) and industrial and government partners, through the Healthcare Support through Information Technology Enhancements (hSITE) Strategic Research Network, and was partially supported by Quebec MDEIE PSR-SiiRi program.

References

Ayat M, Shamsollahi MB, Mozaffari B, Kharabian S (2009) ECG denoising using modulus maxima of wavelet transform. Conf Proc IEEE Eng Med Biol Soc 2009:416–419

Becher C, Chassin M (2001) Improving quality, minimizing error: making it happen. Health Aff 20:68–81

Boyd CM, Darer J, Boult C, Fried LP, Boult L, Wu AW (2005) Clinical practice guidelines and quality of care for older patients with multiple comorbid diseases: implications for pay for performance. J Am Med Assoc 294:716–724

Cattafi M, Gavanelli M, Nonato M, Alvisi S, Franchini M (2011) Optimal placement of valves in a water distribution network with CLP(FD). Theory Pract Log Program 11:731–747

Deering R, Kaiser J (2005) The use of a masking signal to improve empirical mode decomposition. IEEE International conference on acoustics, speech, and signal processing, Durham, 485–488, 2005

Fengler BT, Brady WJ et al (2007) Atrial fibrillation in the Wolff-Parkinson-White syndrome: ECG recognition and treatment in the ED. Am J Emerg Med 25(5):576–583

Fox J, Glasspool D, Patkar V, Austin M, Black L, South M, Robertson D, Vincent C. (2010) Delivering clinical decision support services: there is nothing as practical as a good theory. J Biomed Inform 43:831–843

Hing MM, Michalowski M, Wilk S, Michalowski W, Farion K (2010) Identifying in- consistencies in multiple clinical practice guidelines for a patient with co-morbidity. In: Proceedings of KEDDH-10, Hong Kong, pp 447–452, 2010

Jinseok L, McManus DD et al (2012) Automatic motion and noise artifact detection in Holter ECG data using empirical mode decomposition and statistical approaches. IEEE Trans Biomed Eng 59(6):1499–1506

Latoszek-Berendsen A, Tange H, van denHerik HJ, Hasman A (2010) From clinical practice guidelines to computer-interpretable guidelines. A literature overview. Methods Inf Med 49:550–570

Lin Di, Xidong Z, Fabrice L, GuiXia K (2012) Analysis on the accuracy of a decision support system for hypertension monitoring. VTC Spring, 1–5

Lu G, Brittain JS, Holland P, Yianni J, Green AL, Stein JF, Aziz TZ, Wang S (2009) Removing ECG noise from surface EMG signals using adaptive filtering. Neurosci Lett 462(1):14–19

Miyamoto A, Hayashi H et al (2012) Clinical and electrocardiographic characteristics of patients with short QT interval in a large hospital-based population. Heart Rhythm 9(1):66–74

Nimunkar AJ, Tompkins WJ (2007) EMD-based 60-Hz noise filtering of the ECG. Conf Proc IEEE Eng Med Biol Soc 2007:1904–1907

Paul JS, Reddy MR, Kumar VJ (2000) A transform domain SVD filter for suppression of muscle noise artefacts in exercise ECGs. IEEE Trans Biomed Eng 47(5):654–663

Riano D, Real F, Lopez-Vallverdu JA, Campana F, Ercolani S, Mecocci P, Annicchiarico R, Caltagirone C (2012) An ontology-based personalization of health-care knowledge to support clinical decisions for chronically ill patients. J Biomed Inform 45:429–446

Sameni R, Shamsollahi MB, Jutten C, Clifford GD (2007) A nonlinear Bayesian filtering framework for ECG denoising. IEEE Trans Biomed Eng 54(12):2172–2185

Sayadi O, Shamsollahi MB (2006) ECG denoising with adaptive bionic wavelet transform. Conf Proc IEEE Eng Med Biol Soc Suppl:6597–6600

Skanes AC, Healey JS, Cairns JA, Dorian P, Gillis AM, McMurtry MS, Mitchell LB, Verma A, Nattel S (2012) Canadian cardiovascular society atrial fibrillation guidelines: recommendations for stroke prevention and rate/rhythm control. Can J Cardiol 28(2):25–136

The MIT-BIH Sinus Rhythm database (2002) The MIT-BIH Sinus Rhythm database. http://www.physionet.org/physiobank/database/nsrdb/. Accessed 01 June 2013

The PTB diagnostic ECG database (2008) National metrology institute of germany. http://www.physionet.org/physiobank/datab ase/ptb db/. Accessed 01 June 2013

Wilk S, Michalowski M, Michalowski W, Mainegra Hing M, Farion K (2011) Reconciling pairs of concurrently used clinical practice guidelines using constraint logic programming. AMIA Annu Symp Proc 2011:944–953

Wu YF, Rangayyan RM (2007) An unbiased linear artificial neural network with normalized adaptive coefficients for filtering noisy ECG signals. Proceedings of 20th Canadian conference on electrical and computer engineering, Vancouver, 2007

Chapter 7
Critical Success Factors in the Implementation of Integrated Healthcare Information Systems

Anna Paidi and Dimitra Iliopoulou

Abstract Health care organisations require, without a doubt, highly effective Integrated Information Systems. The vast amounts of data they handle, the pressures of life-and-death contingencies, and the need for uninterruptible operation shape a framework of highly specialized implementation. The implementation, therefore, of a large scale IT systems in public health care organisations can be daunting. In fact, there have been many implementation failures, because of either: (a) poor identification of Critical Success Factors (CSFs), or (b) inadequate linking and monitoring of the CSFs to the relevant project management activities.

In this chapter, it will be described a novel method of tracking the Critical Success Factors during the implementation of an Integrated Health Information System. Identifying the Critical Success Factors and pursuing the relevant activities steer the project in the right direction, avoids and corrects problems, and instils a proactive mentality that breeds success. This methodology has already been applied to the Implementation of the Integrated Healthcare Information System of a large Regional Healthcare Authority of Attica (Athens), Greece.

Keywords Healthcare information systems · Critical success factors · Management activities · Implementation

7.1 Introduction

Health care organizations require highly effective Integrated Information Systems. The implementation of Integrated Information Systems in hospitals is a challenging problem due to the requirements and demands imposed on such systems, including the ability to:

- Handle vast amounts of data
- Be installed in healthcare units that have rudimentary information systems only

A. Paidi (✉)
1st Regional Health Authority of Attica, 3 Zacharof str., 11521 Athens, Greece
e-mail: paidi.anna@gmail.com

D. Iliopoulou
Biomedical Engineering Laboratory, School of Electrical and Computer Engineering,
National Technical University of Athens, 15780 Zografou, Athens, Greece

D.-D. Koutsouris, A. A. Lazakidou (eds.), *Concepts and Trends in Healthcare Information Systems,* Annals of Information Systems 16,
DOI 10.1007/978-3-319-06844-2_7, © Springer International Publishing Switzerland 2014

- Operate efficiently and effectively
- Provide services continuously (i.e. in an uninterrupted manner; Paidi et al. 2006).
- Face the strongly people-centered healthcare sector (Berler et al. 2005)

Inevitably the design of such parameters makes the implementation of Healthcare Information Systems a complex process. A further problem is that complex information system implementation does not readily lend themselves to textbook project management approaches, and frequently results in failure. There have been many well-published implementation failures. This means that increasingly large sums of money are being invested in new health information systems but a substantial proportion of this will go to waste on unimplemented or ineffective systems (Heeks 2006). Many issues are listed in the health-care informatics bibliography that have to be dealt with, in order to implement any type of information system in health care sector (Berler et al. 2005).

The success of a Healthcare Information System implementation is achieved when most stakeholders groups attain their major goals and do not experience significant undesirable outcomes. Mainly the success is dependent on careful identification and monitoring of critical quantitative and qualitative factors that influence the outcome (Rockhart and Bullen 1981; Boynton and Zmud 1984; Leidecker and Bruno 1984; Shank et al. 1985; Sumner 1999; Poon and Wagner 2001).

A Critical Success Factor (CSF) is defined as action—process—state, which is necessary for the successful implementation of Healthcare Information Systems. The satisfaction of all CSFs is considered a necessary and sufficient condition to achieve the successful implementation of Healthcare Information Systems.

However, the Critical Success Factors (CSFs) are frequently only superficially identified and are often not linked to the essential project management and administrative activities of the implementation. In order to improve the success of implementing integrated information systems it is necessary to define a clear process that identifies the CSFs unambiguously, and translates them into a plan of action, comprising measurable goals that can be monitored and acted upon throughout the implementation process.

In this chapter, it will be described a novel method of tracking the CSFs during the implementation of an Integrated Healthcare Information System. Identifying the CSFs and pursuing the relevant activities steers the project in the right direction, avoids and corrects problems, and instils a proactive mentality that brings success.

7.2 Methods

7.2.1 Selections, Data Collection and Analysis of CSFs

CSFs can be systematically identified, using several tools and techniques, including document review, interviews, and brainstorming sessions (Leideckerand Bruno 1984; Shank et al. 1985; Sumner 1999). The first step is defining the scope of CSFs, the organisation levels involved and any implementation constraints identified. In addition, the selection of participants should be identified. Several considerations influence the list of participants in the CSF derivation activity. The type of CSF (enterprise or operational unit) determines strongly whom to include in the relevant discussions. The specific nature of the CSFs sought (strategic versus tactical and technological versus organisational) can also affect the selection of participants. Finally, the selection of participants should reflect their various roles in the organisation, to ensure that they can provide the proper information in the required quality and quantity.

To identify CSFs we examined factors across the whole enterprise. To ensure we identified all CSFs, we traced through the hierarchy of the organisation and involved both the executive managers and operational units' managers. The Central Offices and representative users were included in the scope as a part of the total system.

The next step is the collection of data relating to the CSFs. There are two main means of data collection, and these are by reviewing critical documents and by conducting interviews. Document review can provide a thorough understanding of the strategy and the direction of an organisation, as well as its focus and values. One limitation is that although some organisations have clearly documented strategies, goals and objectives, there are others do not have such. Another drawback is that documentation reviews may provide information on the intentions and plans of an organisation rather than the actual status of the organisation.

A better instrument for data collection is by conducting formal interviews with participants. Previous attempts have been made to codify the interview process, and although this is not straightforward, some basic rules and guidance can be applied to all interviews. In addition thorough preparation is necessary before conducting an interview. Questions should be adaptable to the level of the person being interviewed and all information should be obtained without requiring follow up interviews. Another important consideration is the order of interviews. Starting the interview process from the higher levels gives a better view of the organisation, and continuing with lower level interviews clarifies the details. On the other hand adopting a bottom up approach may result in the collected information not being as useful.

Data analysis is the next fundamental step. This requires the data collected from interviews and documents to be categorised, assimilated and interpreted to produce useful information that accurately describes the organisation's procedures and intentions. This information must relate to the supporting business processes and activities that are relevant to the CSFs.

To perform the analysis of the CSFs we chose to use affinity analysis. Affinity refers to the similarity between different things and by using such analysis we can understand not only relationships among CSFs but also the relevant processes that affect CSFs. This is illustrated in Table 7.1 which shows how CSFs are related to individual processes and also how many CSFs are related to a single process.

To construct this table it is necessary to:

- Determine the comparison criteria
- Develop a comparison matrix
- Determine the affected CSFs
- Analyse the relationships

Table 7.1 CSF and critical processes

CRITICAL PROCESSES		CSFs						Number of influenced CFSs
		CSF 1	CSF 2	CSF 3	CSF 4	CSF 5	CSF 6	
1	Process 1	■	■		■	■	■	5
2	Process 2	■	■		■	■	■	5
3	Process 3	■	■	■			■	3

7.2.2 Quantification

In order to monitor effectively the achievement of CSFs, a formal methodology for quantification is required. Due to the complex nature of the variables (hierarchical structure, limited resources and priorities, qualitative judgments, semi-structured decision-making processes) we have chosen to do this using the Analytic Hierarchy Process (AHP) (Saaty 1986).

The analytic hierarchy process is a systematic method for quantifying important factors that affect final outcomes (Saaty 1986, 1987, 1990; Mustaf and Al-Bahar 1991; Salmeron and Herrero 2005; Labib and Shah 2001). It is especially useful in situations where important qualitative aspects must be considered in conjunction with measurable quantitative factors.

AHP reduces complexity by:

- Decomposing a problem into a hierarchical structure
- Making pairwise comparisons based on the relative importance (or priorities) of each element at every level of the hierarchy
- Applying an algorithmic method to calculate the results
- Checking the results for consistency and sensitivity

7.2.3 Hierarchical Decomposition

In the field of technology management there have been several studies on the use of AHP (Saaty 1990; Mustaf and Al-Bahar 1991; Salmeron and Herrero 2005). In these studies, the hierarchical models been employed are functional, rather than structural, and encompass either 3 levels (Objective—Criteria—Factors), or 4 levels (Objective—Criteria—Sub-criteria—Factors). In this implementation, a 4-level hierarchy is employed with the following semantics:

Level 0: Overall objective (the successful implementation of the integrated information system)

Level 1: The identified critical success factors

Level 2: The business processes that are essential for the achievement of the CSFs

Level 3: The detailed activities that are carried out collectively during the above business processes

7.2.4 *Pairwise Comparison*

All comparisons are carried out at the same level of the hierarchy. This is a judgment process of the relative significance of each element, in affecting its immediate superordinate. A linear scale from 1 to 9 is applied representing with 1 a weak contribution and 9 an extreme contribution to the superordinate level. Although this scale is arbitrary, empirical evidence has shown that it fits in well with the human psychology of judgment.

7.2.5 *Monitoring*

During the implementation phases, the percentage of successful execution of each activity is estimated, and this is used in order to estimate the degree of satisfaction of the critical success factors, and hence, of the overall objective.

7.3 Results

This methodology has already been applied to the Implementation of the Integrated Healthcare Information System of a large Regional Health Authority of Attica (Athens), Greece. The project encompasses the full implementation of an Integrated Healthcare Information System (IHIS). The project focused on the implementation of two basic layers: a patient administration system and an Enterprise Resource Planning (ERP) in 10 hospitals of Attica. Additional to these two basic layers in the IHIS a Biomedical Technology Management system and a Business Intelligence System are included (Paidi et al. 2006).

The Critical Success Factors, identified using the methods described above, included the following (Paidi et al. 2006):

1. The consistent management commitment by the governing bodies and the managers of both the Regional Authority and the hospitals. This commitment involves the appropriate and sufficient management support, in order to achieve the successful implementation and operation of the System.
2. The alignment of project goals and objectives with the strategic and business goals of the Regional Authority and the hospitals.
3. The effective project management, using suitable methods, which ensure the quality and functionality of project deliverables within a specified time frame and budget.
4. The essential user involvement in all phases and activities of the project.
5. The planning, organization, implementation and monitoring of an effective training program for all users of the system.

6. The effective management of organizational change, (an integral part of the implementation of Information Systems in complex organizations, such as hospitals).

The critical business processes for the achievement of the above Critical Success Factors are analysed. A complete analysis of each Critical Success Factor is illustrated here below, by describing:

- the purpose of achieving
- the critical processes that are essential for the achievement of the CSF
- the duration of their project lifecycle
- a measurable effect, and
- how to measure the effect

1st Critical Success Factor (CSF) *The consistent management commitment by the governing bodies and the managers of both the Regional Authority and the hospitals. This commitment involves the appropriate and sufficient management support, in order to achieve the successful implementation and operation of the System.*

Purpose The consistent management commitment contributes to the achievement of the effective change management, the alignment of the project with the strategic and business objectives of the Regional Authority and hospitals and the successful implementation and completion of the Project.

Critical Processes

A. Involvement of Management of the Regional Authority

Activities

- *Constitution of a steering committee, consisting of: Chairman of Governing Body (Board of Directors)—Manager of the Regional Authority, Vice-chairman of Regional Authority, Project Manager of the Regional Authority and Director of consultants.*
- *Quarterly ordinary meetings of the Steering Committee (and additional extraordinary meetings whenever necessary).*
- *Development of trust and partnership among vendors, consultants, management and personnel of hospitals and the Regional Authority.*
- *Quick decision process by the management of the Regional Authority concerning issue resolution and change requests in strategic and business matters.*

B. Involvement of the Hospital Managers

Activities

- *Participation of the managers of hospitals in the Steering Committee meetings, when it is necessary, and commitment by them to perform the decided upon activities*
- *Quick decision process by management of the hospitals concerning issue resolution and change requests.*

C. Constant communication and update of the management of the Regional Authority and the hospital managers

Activities

- *Initial meeting of Steering Committee in order to discuss the importance, the specific issues and the risks of the project.*
- *Unscheduled meetings of the management of Regional Authority with Project Manager of Regional Authority in order to discuss and decide about every immediate problem of the problem.*
- *Progress reporting by the Project Manager of the Regional Authority to the management of Regional Authority.*
- *Progress reporting by the Project Manager of the Regional Authority to the managers of the hospitals.*

Duration Throughout the duration of project implementation

Measurable effect
- Updated management of the Regional Authority and the hospital managers,
- Project progress,
- Effective decision making and
- Available resources required

Method of Monitoring
- Meetings reporting
- Minutes of Meetings/decisions
- Measurement of the frequency of the submitted progress reports

2nd Critical Success Factor (CSF) *The alignment of project goals and objectives with the strategic and business goals of the Regional Authority and the hospitals.*

Purpose The maximum possible service of the strategic and operational objectives of the Regional Authority, through the implementation of best practices and consistent operation, achieved with properly designed Information Systems.

Critical Processes

A. Involvement of Management of the Regional Authority

Activities

- *Meetings of the Project Manager of Regional Authority with the Steering Committee and the management of regional authority during the planned update of the Business Plan of Regional Authority.*
- *Meetings of the Project Manager of Regional Authority with the management of Regional Authority during the implementation of the Project Implementation Study.*

B. Involvement of the Hospital Managers

Activities

- *Meetings of the management of regional authority with the Hospital Managers during the implementation of the Project Implementation Study.*

C. Constant communication and update of the management of the Regional Authority and the hospital managers

Activities

- *Meetings of the Steering Committee with the management of Regional Authority in order to discuss and decide about strategic and specific issues of the project, particularly on matters of alignment of project goals and objectives with the strategic and business goals*
- *Unscheduled meetings of the management of Regional Authority with the Project Manager of Regional Authority whenever necessary in order to discuss about matters of business processes and specifics of implementation of the project.*
- *Progress reporting by the Project Manager of the Regional Authority to the management of regional authority.*
- *Progress reporting by the Project Manager of the Regional Authority to the managers of the hospitals.*

D. Tracking of the legislative and organizational changes in Health.

Activities

- *Continuous monitoring of the legislative and organizational changes by the Project Manager of Regional Authority and the managers of hospitals, and assessment of their impact on the Project implementation*
- *Meeting of the Steering Committee whenever required to take decisions relating to change business goals of Regional Authority and hospitals.*

E. Requirements assessment updating

Activities

- *Requirements assessment updating of the Project Implementation Study (within the conventional framework of the project) whenever required in cooperation with the Contractor's Project and the technical consultants.*

Duration Throughout the duration of project implementation.

Measurable effect The Integrated Information System will meet the strategic, business and operational objectives of the Regional Authority and hospitals. The Project Implementation Study will incorporate and ensure this alignment.

Method of Monitoring
- Quick convergence cycles of the Project Implementation Study up to its completion
- Adequate documentation of the strategic choices of the Project Implementation Study
- Meetings reporting
- Minutes of Meetings/decisions

3rd Critical Success Factor (CSF) *The effective project management, using suitable methods, which ensure the quality and functionality of project deliverables within a specified time frame and budget.*

Purpose The identification and address of all those factors and risks which make the implementation of Healthcare Information Systems a difficult undertaking with significant risk of failure during implementation. Moreover, the effective project management methods ensure the quality of 'products', within specified time frames and budget.

Critical Processes

A. Project Management and Implementation methodology

Activities

- *Determination of the methodology of the project, taking into consideration the proposed implementation methodology by the Contractor Project, in cooperation with Project Manager of Regional Authority and the technical consultants.*
- *Defining monitoring processes apply the project methodology throughout the duration of the Project by all stakeholders.*
- *Updating Deliverables "Project Management System—User Roles and Responsibilities Management of IT Projects of Regional Authority" and "Project Management System—Projects Management and Monitoring Design of Regional Authority" by technical consultants after signing the Contract with the Contractor project of Regional Authority (those required by the Contracting Authority- Regional Authority, within the conventional framework of the project).*
- *Expert technical support during the process of signing of contracts and clarification the obligations of the Contractor, particularly on service provision customization and interoperability.*
- *Intensify the involvement of staff of Informatics of Regional Authority in the stages of implementation and installation of hardware.*
- *Education of all involved in the Project Management in the use of monitoring and management tools used.*
- *Determination of preconditions of infrastructure adequacy.*

B. Adequate partnership between vendor, consultants and personnel of Hospitals and Regional Authority

Activities

- *Determination of an effective communication framework of all involved in the project, executives of the Working Groups of Hospitals and Regional Authority (the Working Groups), the Contractor Project and Technical Consultants.*

C. Change request management

Activities

- *Determination of a methodological framework to manage change request (in relevance with Critical Success Factor #6), taking into account—but not limited to it— the proposed methodology Change Request Management by the Contractor Project.*

The methodological framework will be determined in cooperation with Project Manager of Regional Authority, Technical Consultants, and senior members of the Working Groups of Hospitals and Regional Authority and Contractor Project.

D. Project Quality Management

Activities

– *Determination of a methodological framework to manage Project quality, taking into account—but not limited to it—the proposed methodology Project quality management by the Contractor Project. The methodological framework will be determined in cooperation with Project Manager of Regional Authority, Technical Consultants, senior members of the Working Groups of Hospitals and Regional Authority and Contractor Project.*

Duration Throughout the duration of project implementation.

Measurable effect The successful implementation of the project within a specified time frame, budget and product quality.

Method of Monitoring
• Constant updated measurement of the implementation progress
• Constant updated measurement of the budgetary progress
• Identification of measurable risk assessment factors and the ways of timely corrections

4th Critical Success Factor (CSF) *The essential user involvement in all phases and activities of the project.*

Purpose Increase the awareness of the users concerning the benefits provided by Information System and their participation in the phases of planning and implementation, in order to treat it as their "own" that meets their "own" needs.

Critical Processes

A. User involvement and participation

Activities

– *Constitution of Working Groups consisting of doctors, nurses and administrative personnel of hospitals and Regional Authority. The Technical Consultants have the duty to inform and educate the Working Groups members about the Project.*
– *Frequent meetings of executives of the Contractor with end users of hospitals in requirement analysis.*
– *Strict implementation of the communication framework to be determined for information and communication of all involved users.*

B. Project Publicity and Promotion

Activities

– *Workshops to inform all users.*

C. *Involvement of Management of the Regional Authority*

Activities

– *Involvement in the selection and approval of employees of Regional Authority that will participate in the Working Groups for the implementation of the Project.*

D. Involvement of the Hospital Managers

Activities

– *Involvement in the selection and approval of employees of hospitals that will participate in the Working Groups for the implementation of the Project.*

Duration Throughout the duration of project implementation.

Measurable effect Increased user involvement in project implementation, initiatives and accelerate decision-making.

Method of Monitoring
- Measurement rate of participation of users in meetings and information days—compared to the calls for meetings and the initial estimation
- Percentage contribution to shape the requirements of the Study Implementation (estimated)
- Percentage of degree and quality of participation in testing and pilot operation of the system, taking into account the availability planned for each user group (estimated)

5th Critical Success Factor (CSF) *The planning, organization, implementation and monitoring of an effective training program for all users of the system.*

Purpose An effective educational process connected with the implementation that produces knowledgeable and technically skilled users, within the constraints posed by the operation of the hospital and the Regional Authority.

Critical Processes

A. Training program organization

Activities

– *Organization of a training program for trainers in cooperation with the Project Manager of Regional Authority, Working Groups, the Contractor and technical consultants.*
– *Organization of a training program for users in cooperation with the Project Manager of Regional Authority, Working Groups, the Contractor and technical consultants.*
– *Review training material for trainers and users prepared by the Contractor*
– *Determination of the training certification method both trainers and users.*
– *Schedule training program.*

B. Training program implementation

Activities

- *Determination of a framework to monitor the implementation of the training program for trainers and users.*
- *Monitoring and audit the certification process of the training program according to the determined certification method.*
- *Measuring user satisfaction with assessment questionnaire for the training program, the training materials, and the trainers.*

C. Involvement of Management of the Regional Authority

Activities

- *Involvement in the selection and approval of employees of Regional Authority that will be the trainers of the users of the Project.*

D. Involvement of the Hospital Managers

Activities

- *Involvement in the selection and approval of employees of hospitals that will be the trainers of the Project.*

Duration Throughout the duration of project implementation.

Measurable effect Effective training for all trainers and users involved in the project, acceptance of systems by users and successful transition to productive functioning of Information System.

Method of Monitoring
- Percentage of presence and participation of trainers/users in the educational process
- Rating satisfaction of trainers/users
- Confined cycles re-education
- Effective use of electronic educational material during the pilot operation

6th Critical Success Factor (CSF) *The effective management of organizational change, (an integral part of the implementation of Information Systems in complex organizations, such as hospitals).*

Purpose Address and eliminate resistance (at the lowest possible cost) presented by users in the implementation of Healthcare Information Systems

Critical Processes

A. User involvement and participation

Activities

- *Constitution of Working Groups consisting of doctors, nurses and administrative personnel of hospitals and Regional Authority. The members of the Working*

Groups act as catalyst for management of organizational and technological change.

- *Effective training program for users and especially for trainers.*
- *Support users during the transition to the operation in the productive phase with the presence of the Contractor's instructors and the trainers of each hospital and Regional Authority in the workplace.*

B. Adequate partnership between vendor, consultants and personnel of hospitals and Regional Authority

Activities

- *Determination of an effective program of management organizational change in cooperation with Contractor of the Project, the executives of Regional Authority and the Working Groups of hospitals.*

C. Involvement of Management of the Regional Authority

Activities

- *Involvement in the selection and approval of employees of Regional Authority that that will participate in the Working Groups for the implementation of the Project.*
- *Participation in the kick-off workshop for the information of users of the Project.*
- *Decision making by the management of Regional Authority about change requests in business matters.*
- *Adoption by the management of Regional Authority incentives for the users.*

D. Involvement of the Hospital Managers

Activities

- *Involvement in the selection and approval of employees of Regional Authority that that will participate in the Working Groups for the implementation of the Project.*
- *Participation in the kick-off workshop for the information of users of the Project.*
- *Decision making by the managers of hospitals about change requests in business matters.*
- *Submit suggestions by the managers of hospitals about incentives for the users.*

E. Constant communication and briefing of the Management of the Regional Authority and hospitals Managers

Activities

- *Kick-off meeting of Steering Committee in order to discuss the organizational and management changes of the project.*
- *Meetings of Steering Committee in order to inform the Management of Regional Authority about the project.*

- *Unscheduled meetings of the Management of Regional Authority with Project Manager of Regional Authority in order to discuss and decide about every change request of the project.*
- *Progress reporting by the Project Manager of the Regional Authority to the Management of Regional Authority.*
- *Progress reporting by the Project Manager of the Regional Authority to the Managers of the hospitals.*

F. Project Publicity and Promotion

Activities

- *Workshops to inform all users.*
- *Implementation of publicity actions that are defined in a Study of Publicity Actions for the IT Projects of Regional Authority designed by the Technical Consultants.*

Duration Throughout the duration of project implementation.

Measurable effect Effective change management will be essential to successful implementation—operation and maximizing the benefits of the Project.

Method of Monitoring
- Record the time and financial parameters of the projects
- Meetings reporting
- Minutes of Meetings/decisions
- Measurement of the frequency and quality of content submitted progress reports

The CSFs are organised and structured in a matrix that clarifies the relationship between CSFs and individual critical business processes and shows also the number of CSFs influenced by each critical process. The number of CSFs influenced by each critical process, is drawn in the last column of the Table 7.2.

The critical processes influence more than one Critical Success Factor, as shown in detail in Table 7.2. The number influenced of CSFs can be used as a useful variable. From the above correlation is evident that critical processes can be grouped into three groups:

High influence CSF group included the following critical processes
- Involvement of Management of the Regional Authority
- Involvement of the hospital Managers

Medium influence CSF group included the following critical processes
- Constant communication and briefing of the Management of the Regional Authority and hospitals Managers
- User involvement and participation
- Adequate partnership between vendor, consultants and personnel of hospitals and Regional Authority
- Project Publicity and Promotion

Table 7.2 Correlation between CSFs and critical processes

CRITICAL PROCESSES	CRITICAL SUCCESS FACTORS						Number of influenced CFSs
	CRITICAL SUCCESS FACTOR 1	CRITICAL SUCCESS FACTOR 2	CRITICAL SUCCESS FACTOR 3	CRITICAL SUCCESS FACTOR 4	CRITICAL SUCCESS FACTOR 5	CRITICAL SUCCESS FACTOR 6	
1 Involvement of Management of the Regional Authority	■	■		■	■	■	5
2 Involvement Hospitals Managers	■	■		■	■	■	5
3 Constant communication and briefing of the Management of the Regional Authority and Hospitals Managers	■	■				■	3
4 User involvement and participation				■	■		2
5 Adequate partnershipbetweenvendor, consultants andpersonnelofHospitals and Regional Authority.			■			■	2
6 Project Publicity and Promotion				■		■	2
7 Tracking of thelegislativeand organizational changes inHealth		■					1
8 Project ManagementandImplementation methodology			■				1
9 Requirements assessment updating		■					1
10 Change request management			■				1
11 Project quality management			■				1
12 Training program organization					■		1
13 Training program implementation					■		1

Low influence CSF group included the following critical processes
- Tracking of the legislative and organizational changes in Health
- Requirements assessment updating
- Project Management and Implementation methodology
- Change Request Management
- Project Quality Management
- Training program organization
- Training program implementation

So the most critical processes concern the involvement of Management of the Regional Authority and hospitals. It should however be noted that the successful execution of all critical processes is a necessary and sufficient condition for the successful implementation of Healthcare Information Systems.

7.4 Conclusion

The methodology described in this chapter and its application have served a valuable function in clarifying and quantifying the crucial parameters of implementation of Integrated Healthcare Information Systems and its risk. The identification and analysis of the CSFs, their quantification, the monitoring and the evaluation of this methodology are crucial for quantifying the complexity of the project and for preparing the hospital for successful implementation.

The monitoring of CFSs can be achieved by estimating the percentage of successful execution of each activity and this can be used (together with the preassigned weights of the AHP method) in order to estimate the degree of satisfaction of the critical success factors, and hence, of the overall objective. The Project Manager of the Regional Authority has been chosen as the most appropriate person to be put in charge of monitoring the CFSs.

During the life cycle of implementation, the quantification process has to be re-evaluated as based on actual data, and on the degree of achievement of each critical success factor. This accomplished by estimating the percentage of successful execution of each activity, and its sensitivity to the satisfaction of the critical success factors.

With this approach applied to the Integrated Healthcare Information Systems framework, the all-important management of change can be further quantified, measured and successfully accomplished.

References

Berler A, Pavlopoulos S, Koutsouris D (2005) Using key performance indicators as knowledge-management tools at a regional health-care authority level. IEEE Trans Inf Technol Biomed 9(2):184–192

Boynton AC, Zmud RW (1984) An assessment of critical success factors. Sloan Manage Rev 26:17–27

Heeks R (2006) Health information systems: failure, success and improvisation. Int J Med Inform 75(2):125–137

Labib A, Shah J (2001) Management decisions for a continuous improvement process in industry using analytical hierarchy process. Work Study (J Product Sci) 50:189–193

Leidecker JK, Bruno AV (1984) Identifying and using critical success factors. Long Range Plan 17:23–32

Mustaf MA, Al-Bahar JF (1991) Project risk assessment using the analytic hierarchy process. IEEE Trans Eng Manag 38:46–52

Paidi A, Voutsinas G, Zoulias E, Nathanail G (2006) The role of critical success factors in the implementation of integrated healthcare information systems. J Inf Technol Healthc 4(5):326–334

Poon P, Wagner C (2001) Critical success factors revisited: success and failure cases of information systems for senior executives. Decis Support Syst 30:393–418

Rockhart JF, Bullen CV (1981) A primer on critical success factors. Center for Information Systems Research, Massachusetts Institute of Technology, Cambridge

Saaty T (1986) Axiomatic foundation of the analytic hierarchy process. Manage Sci 32:841–855

Saaty TL (1987) Rank generation, preservation, and reversal in the analytic hierarchy process. Decis Sci 18:157–177

Saaty T (1990) How to make a decision: the analytic hierarchy process. Eur J Oper Res 48:9–26

Salmeron JL, Herrero I (2005) An AHP-based methodology to rank critical success factors of executive information systems. Comput Stand Interfaces 28:1–12

Shank ME, Boynton AC, Zmud RW (1985) Critical success factor analysis as a methodology for MIS planning. MIS Q 9:121–129

Sumner M (1999) Critical success factors in enterprise wide information management systems projects. Americas Conference on Information Systems. Milwaukee

Chapter 8
A Preventive Adverse Drug Events System

Zina Nakhla and Kaouther Nouira

Abstract In this paper we propose the construction of a Preventive Adverse Drug Events (PADE) system. This system is based on a well structured data derived from a standard knowledge representation so called ontology. Such ontology is defined as a formal representation of terms related to specific domain, and has the characteristic to be updated each time when a change of the knowledge occurs. The idea is to automatically map the ontology and eventual changes on database using a set of rules. To demonstrate the relevance of the proposed approach, a comparison with current approaches (single table, dual scheme and OntoDB approaches) is performed.

Key words Ontology · Adverse Drug Event

8.1 Introduction

In order to improve the performance at all levels of the healthcare system, a Preventive Adverse Drug Events (PADE) system is proposed. This new system aims to use Artificial Intelligence (AI) approach to supervise physicians when writing prescriptions and alerts them when an Adverse Drug Event (ADE) can take place. ADE is an incident which occurs in healthcare domain resulting from medical intervention related to drug (Handler et al. 2007) (i.e. adverse side effects, interaction with other medicinal products, etc…). It can cause a temporary or sustainable incapacities and extra time of hospitalisation….

As Chandrasekaran et al. in (1999) "Theories in artificial intelligence fall into two broad categories: mechanism theories and content theories". The term mechanism includes rule systems, machine learning algorithms… However, in some times we can't implement a mechanism without a suitable description of the domain. Knowing that ontologies enumerate and give specific and semantic description of domain concepts and define their attributes and various relationships between them (Noy 2003), we can conclude that ontologies are typically content theories (Chandrasekaran et al. 1999).

Z. Nakhla (✉) · K. Nouira
BESTMOD Laboratory, High Institute of Management, University of Tunis, 41, Rue de la liberte, Bouchoucha, 2000 Bardo, Tunis, Tunisia
e-mail: zinanakhla@yahoo.fr

D.-D. Koutsouris, A. A. Lazakidou (eds.), *Concepts and Trends in Healthcare Information Systems*, Annals of Information Systems 16,
DOI 10.1007/978-3-319-06844-2_8, © Springer International Publishing Switzerland 2014

Nowadays, ontologies are widely used in different domains such as Semantic Web (Ding et al. 2005), Natural Language Processing (Estival et al. 2004), Medicine (Gamberger et al. 2007), Commerce (Li and Peng 2011), etc... But ontology of the domain is not a goal in itself (Chandrasekaran et al. 1999). The target is to standardize the knowledge representation of a specific domain and to allow applications to use standard structured data. Several approaches and systems were proposed to store ontology together with individual instances of classes or concepts, so called knowledge base (Chandrasekaran et al. 1999). But for applications manipulating a large amount of ontology based data, query performance becomes a new issue (Dehainsala et al. 2007). So ontology based databases (OBDB) are required. Some trials of automatic mapping ontology to databases have been done (n. a. 2007):

- Single Table approach (McBride 2001): based on mapping ontology elements such as concepts and properties in a single table with three columns (subject, predicate, object). This triplet used to characterize each concept by a name, a comment and its super-concept.
- Dual Scheme approach (Alexaki et al. 2001; Tom 1993): based on mapping ontology concepts on a first table and instances on second table.
- OntoDB approach (n. a. 2002; n. a. 2007): depends on ontology structure. It maps each concept on a table.

These approaches are limited. In fact, for the first approach, there is no distinction between instances and concepts. Although this problem has been corrected in the second approach but the query execution remains engender a long delay. The third approach involves the creation of a huge number of tables in a database (DB) which is sometimes not reasonable. In the following, a novel approach is proposed.

The paper is organised as follows: Section 8.2 discusses the limits of medical computer application and the need of a preventive ADE system based on ontology. Section 8.3 presents ADE Ontology. Section 8.4 describes Ontology Based Data-Base (OBDB) and the mapping rules from ontology to (DB). Section 8.5 presents experiments and results. Finally, we give conclusions and perspectives.

8.2   Prevent ADE Systems

ADEs prevention can reduce health costs of $ 760,000 per year (Handler et al. 2007). In the literature, some computer systems are developed to deal with such problems (Schmidt-Schaub and Smolka 1991; Lataief et al. 2010; McDonald et al. 2005), but, unfortunately, they have several limits such as:

- A big number of irrelevant alerts (McDonald et al. 2005).
- A big number of errors in the detection of drug interactions (Bates et al. 2010).
- A very slow execution time (Hunt et al. 1998).

Fig. 8.1 PADES
infrastructure

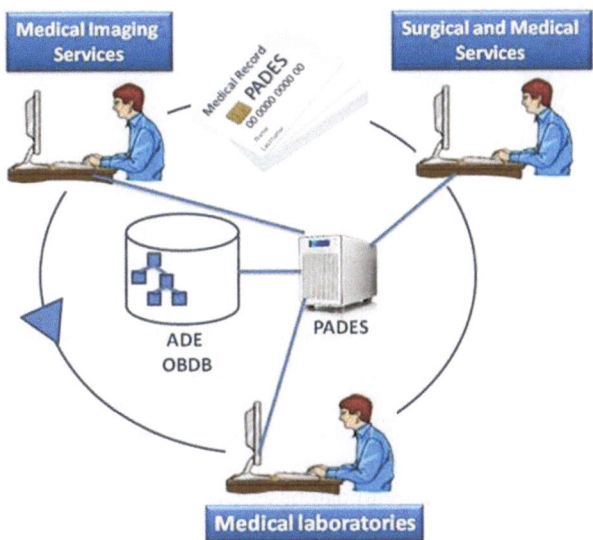

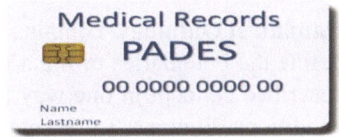

Fig. 8.2 PADES chip card

- Non privacy to patient information (McDonald et al. 2005).
- Difficulty to interpret alert (Lataief et al. 2010).

In fact, some systems are based on the voluntary and anonymous data entry by the medical staff (Oliven et al. 2010), which causes the existence of erroneous and missing data. Other systems use not suitable ontologies (i.e. Computerized Prescriber Oreder Entry (CPOE) (Koppel et al. 2005), Clinical Decision Support Systems (CDSS) (Hunt et al. 1998), Optimization Prescribing Adverse Drug Event (OPADE) (Zegher et al. 1994)...) and generate loopholes in the data structure. These low-quality data lead obviously to low-quality results.

To ensure high-quality data this work aims to develop PADES based on a specific ontology (ADE Ontology) (see Fig. 8.1). To a medical consultation or exploration (medical imaging, medical analysis, surgery,...) the patient presents his chip card (see Fig. 8.2), which contains his medical records in order to be updated. When the doctor would administer a new treatment, PADES confront the chip card data with the ADE OBDB data using some AI tools and alerts the physician whether an ADE can take place.

ADE OBDB contains well structured data based on ontology extracted from ADE domain. In the following, ADE Ontology is presented.

Fig. 8.3 Local canonical
ontology of symptom domain

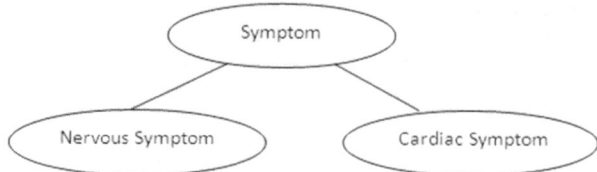

8.3 ADE Ontology

ADE ontology already defined in (Tom 1993) is the result of a team work composed
of computer scientists, experts (physicians and pharmacists) and specialists in Natural Language Processing. The aim was to clarify the structure of ADE knowledge
and to update it automatically using retrieval information tools applied on Online
Medical Research Databases.

To map ontology to database, we need, first, to define ontologies and their components. Studer in 1995 (Studer et al. 1998) presented ontology as "*Formal specification of a shared conceptualization*".

According to Jean et al. in (n. a. 2007), ontology can be classified into two types
depending on the types of concepts which contains:

Canonical Ontology contains only primitive concepts. The primitive concepts can
define the boundaries of the area conceptualized by an ontology (Gruber 1995). It
described concept in one way using a description that can include only necessary
conditions. Figure 8.3 presents a local ontology of symptom, which contains concept (*Symptom*) and two subconcept (*Nervous Symptom and Cardiac Symptom*).
These subconcept present a primitive concept.

Non Canonical Ontology contains primitive concepts and defined concepts.
These concepts extend the vocabulary of ontology and give more detail on the concept. Many ontologies models support the defined concepts as a description logics,
Frame Logic (F-Logic), Web Ontology Language (OWL)…(n. a. 2002). Figure 8.4
illustrates a non canonical local ontology contains a defined concepts (*Abnormal
heart beat and Abnormal blood pressure*).

8.4 Ontology Based DataBase

Ontology Based DataBase (OBDB) is defined as "*a database model, that allows
both ontologies and their instances to be stored and queried in a single database*"
(Jean et al. 2006). It is a data source that contains ontology, a set of data, links
between them and elements that define the ontological sense (Pierra et al. 2005;
Dehainsala et al. 2007). It aims to enable the sharing, management, integration
and querying structured data associated with large conceptual ontologies. It represents ontologies, data structure and links between them (see Fig. 8.5). It brings

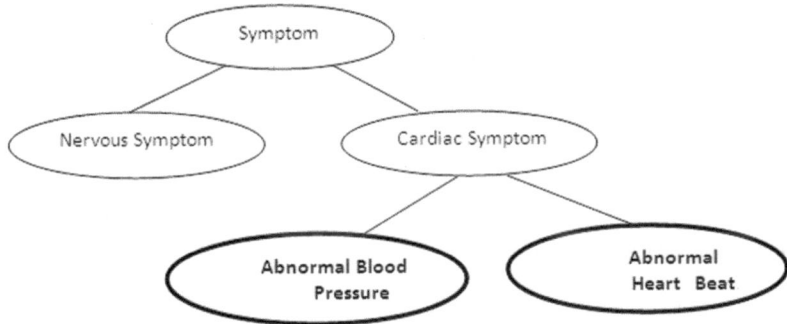

Fig. 8.4 Local non canonical ontology of symptom domain

Fig. 8.5 OBDB architecture

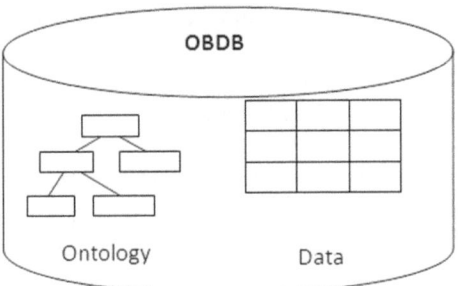

new characteristics, that we cannot find in the traditional DB as the representation of ontology and data in the same DB. And, it allows the association of each data to ontological concept, which defines the meaning. OBDB facilitates DB querying and the management of ontology and data. Ontology is the input; rules are the process to create DB, and DB is the output (See Fig. 8.5).

To construct OBDB, we must analyse the semantic of ontology components and mapped them to database. Mapping between ontology and DB is defined by Cullot et al. (2007) as "*a set of correspondences between database components and ontology components*". The mapping process starts by treating concepts, relationships and instances (Zhao et al. 2012).

Two steps for DB construction are proposed: (1) Apply rules to ontology, (2) generate DB. Ontology is the input; rules are used to create DB, and DB is the output (See Fig. 8.6).

Definition 1 (Ontology structure) An ontology structure is a quintuple (Xiao-Yong et al. 2006; Wang et al. 2006):

$$O = (C, R, A, I, F).$$

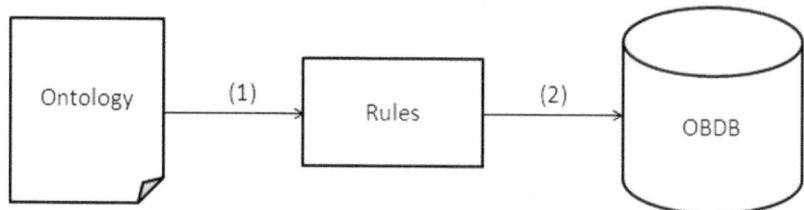

Fig. 8.6 Ontology constructing steps

Where:

C: a finite set of concepts.
R: a finite set of relations.
A: a set of finite set of axioms, which is expressed as an appropriate logical language.
I: instances.
F: a set of functions.

Definition 2 (Relational DB) Relational DB is composed of a set of tables $(T1, T2...Tn)$, and each table is composed of a set of fields $(F1,...,Fm)$ which can be primary key *(Pk)* or foreign key *(Fk)* and data $(d1,..., dn)$ (Li and Zhang 2011).

Definition 3 (Concept composition) Concept is a triplet:

$$C = (Pv, Pc, Hc).$$

Where:

- **Pv (Property value)**: is a value constraint or the values assigned to the concept properties in order to obtain an instance.
- **Pc (Property constraint)**: denotes the cardinality constraint. We have two kinds of cardinality maxCardinality and minCardinality $Pc=(minCard, maxCard)$, *minCard* is a restriction containing constraint describes the number of individuals that have at least *minCard=n* semantically distinct values; *maxCard* is a restriction containing constraint describes the number of instances that have at most *maxCard=N* semantically distinct values.
- **Hc (Hierarchical concept)**: is called concept hierarchy, which is a directed relation {C1: = H(C2)} denotes that *C2* is a subconcept of *C1* (Li and Zhang 2011). There are two kinds of hierachical relation Parent relation *C1: = P(C2)* means that *C1* is the parent of *C2* and child relation *C2: Ch(C1)* means that *C2* is the child of *C1*.

Based on general features of relational DB and ontology, we propose the specific rules which map ontology to DB:

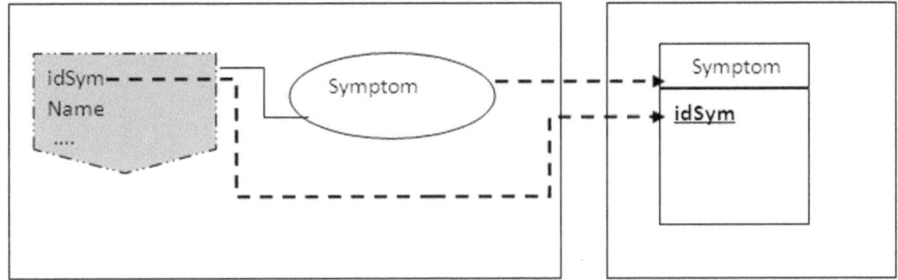

Fig. 8.7 Example of application of rule 2

Rule 1 Mapping approach converts ontology into DB tables:

$$DB := map(O).$$

Rule 2 When C is a parent concept then C is mapped to table T:

$$T := Tab(C)$$

and

$$Pk(T) := id(C).$$

Where:

Tab (X): Maps the concept X to table.
id(Y):   Returns the field of concept Y, which is not null and unique as identifier.
Pk(Z):   Refers to the primary key of concept Z.

Figure 8.7 shows an example of mapping concept to table. Concept "Symptom" and their properties map to table named "Symptom" with primary key "idSym"

Rule 3 When C1 and C2 are two concepts mapped to tables (respectively T1 and T2), and C1 = H(C2) then the primary key of the table T2 will be a foreign key in table T1.

When T1 = Tab(C1) and T2 = Tab(C2),

$$then \ Fk(T1) := PK \ (T2).$$

Where:

Fk(X):   refers foreign key of concept X.
PK(Y): returns the primary key of concept Y.

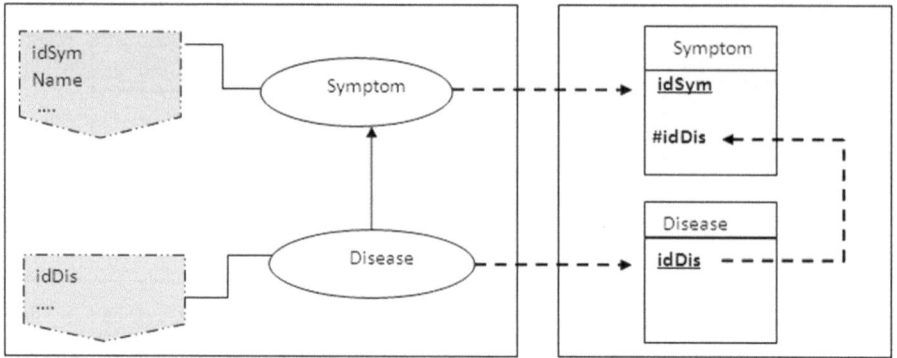

Fig. 8.8 Example of application of rule 3

Figure 8.8 shows an example of mapping field between table. "Disease" and "Symptom" two concepts map to table using rule 2. The primary key "idDis" of concept "Disease", which is the parent concept map to foreign key in the concept "Symptom".

Rule 4 When two concepts *C1* and *C2* map to tables (respectively *T1*, *T2*) in DB and *R* is a relationship between *C1* and *C2* ($R(C1, C2) = True$), then *R* maps to relationship between table *T1* and table *T2*.

$$\text{When } R\ (C1, C2) = \text{True and } T1 = \text{Tab } (C1),\ T2 = \text{Tab } (C2)$$

then R is preserved in DB.

Rule 5 When two concepts related with relationship *R* and (*C1* and/or *C2*) not mapped to tables then *R* is not preserved in DB.

Rule 6 A pure concept is mapped to field in DB table related to parent concept.

$$\text{When } C2 = Ch(C1) \text{ and } Ch(C2) = Null$$

$$\text{then } T := Tab(C1) \text{ and } T := Field(T, C2).$$

Where:

Field(X,C):   affects to table *X* the pure concept *C* as field.

Figure 8.9 presents an example which describes the relation between ontology and DB. DB contains two tables: *disease* and *symptom*. Each table has a set of fields. For example, table *symptom* has three fields: *idSym, nameSym, typeSym*. The underlined fields indicate the primary keys.

Ontology contains four concepts:

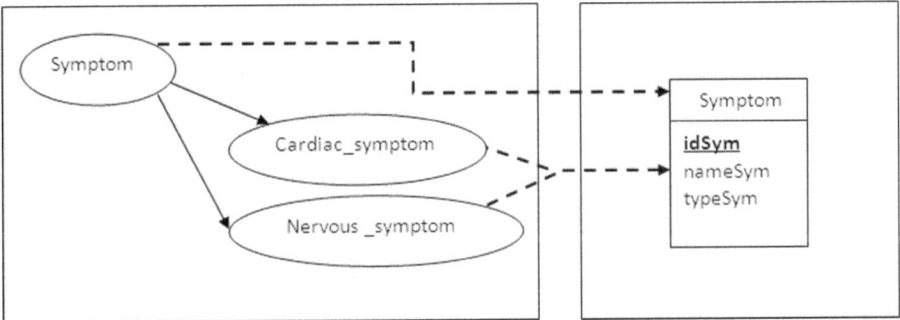

Fig. 8.9 Example of application of rule 6

Symptom, Disease, Cardiac_symptom, Nervous_symptom. Cardiac_symptom, Nervous_symptom are two subconcepts.

Some concepts in ontology are not mapped to tables, they are mapped to attributes in tables. Such as *Cardiac_symptom* and *Nervous_symptom* are mapped to *nameSym* attribute in *Symptom* table.

Rule 7 In general case, instances are mapped to records when related concepts are mapped to tables. But, when concept maps to attribute so its instances map to values of this attribute (that means: instances represent the list of values which this attribute can take).

8.5   Experiments and Results

In order to evaluate the effectiveness of our approach in ADE domain, we carried out a series of tests to compare our approach to others approaches (single table, dual scheme, OntoDB). We developed our algorithm in Java Language using Eclipse and OWLAPI (Onology Web Language API). To perform our tests, we use a real ontology of ADE domain, which has tens classes and properties. The average deep of ontology hierarchy is 4.

Figures 8.10 and 8.11 illustrate an example of mapping between ontology and DB using rules explained previously. The example presents a part of ADE ontology, which describes the different kinds of ADE problem occurred in health care domain and the resulted OBDB.

For example, *Cardiac-symptom, Adverse-drug-event-symptom, Adverse-drug-event-cause*... are concepts mapped to tables in DB (**Rule 1**). **Rule 3** is used to map the relationship between them. The subconcepts of *Adverse-Drug-Event-Cause*: *Drug-interaction, lack-information-patient,* and *miss-knowledge-drug* are pure, they are, hence, mapped to fields in *Administration-Adverse-Drug-Event-Cause* table (**Rule 6**).

Fig. 8.10 ADE ontology

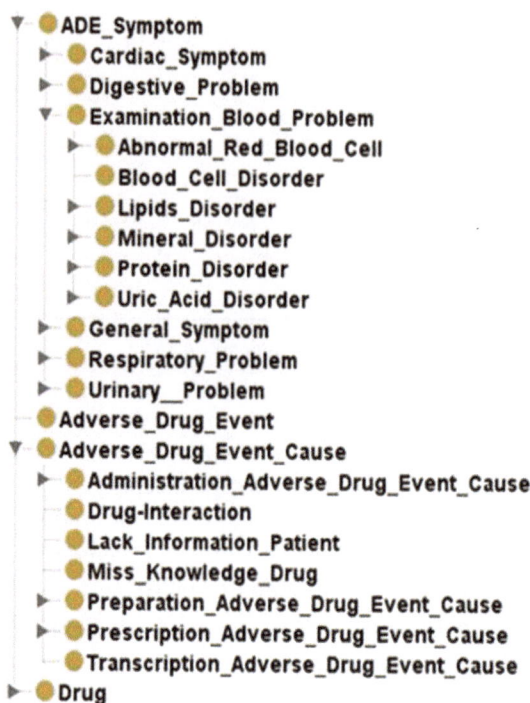

Table 8.1 resumes the mapping result of each approach. It presents the number of tables in DB and the number of records generated by each approach. Single table approach generates one table with 107 records, causing an auto join in querying. The dual scheme approach generates 102 tables increasing joint number between table in querying. OntoDB approach engenders 92 classes in DB, but we can find many unuseful classes. But our approach generates 21 tables, containing only the useful tables.

8.6 Conclusion

Aiming to improve medical computer system construction and reduce the occurrence of ADE, this paper presents a method for automatically generating relational DB from ADE ontology resources. Some mapping rules are proposed for automatically generate relational DB from ADE ontology. The paper presents a comparison between approaches depending on the number of tables and querying problem, which can be occurred. This method needs to be tested on different domains in order to confirm its effectiveness.

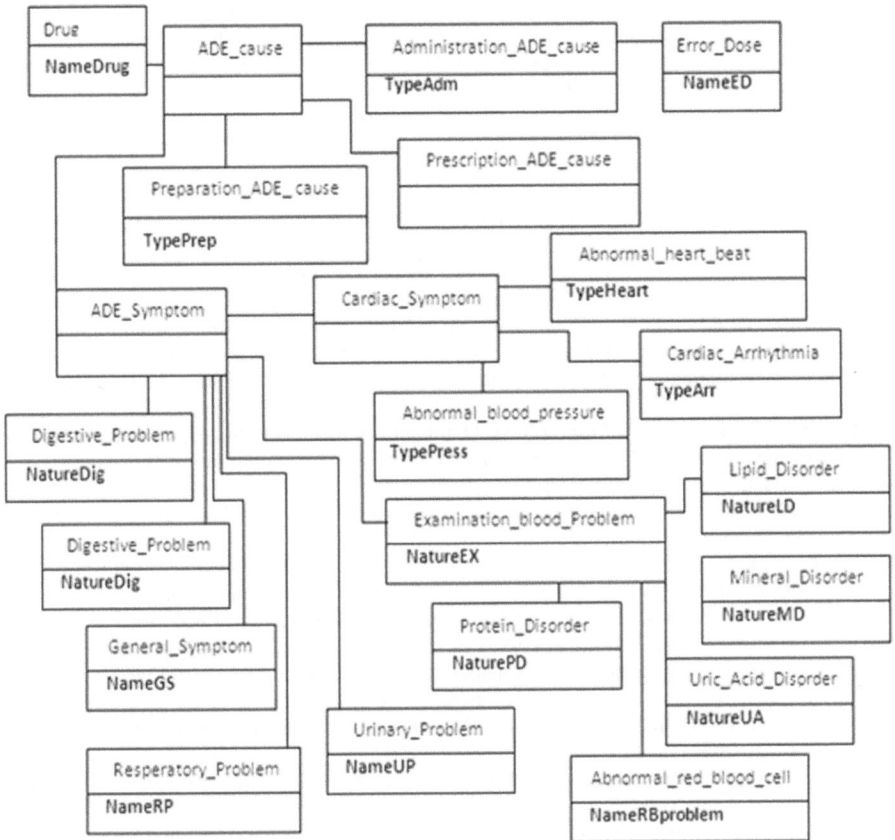

Fig. 8.11 Mapping ADE ontology

Table 8.1 Comparison between mapping approaches

	Single table	Dual scheme	OntoDB	Our approach
Number of table	1	102	92	21
Total number of record	107	15	15	15

References

n. a. (2002) Integration de bases de donnees heterogenes par articulation a priori d'ontologies: application aux catalogues de composants industriels. PhD thesis Ecole Nationale Superieure de Mecanique et d'Aerotechnique

n. a. (2007) OntoQL, un langage d'exploitation des bases de donnees a base ontologique. PhD thesis, Ecole Nationale Superieure de Mecanique et d'Aerotechnique

Alexaki S, Christophides V, Karvounarakis G, Plexousakis D, Tolle K (2001) The ICS-FORTH RDFsuite: managing voluminous RDF description bases. In Proceedings of the 2nd International Workshop on the Semantic Web (SemWeb 2001), Hongkong, China, May 1, 2001

Bates DW, Lipsitz S, Metzger J, Welebob E, Classen DC (2010) Mixed results in the safety perfor-
    mance of computerized physician order entry. Health Aff 29(4):655–663
Chandrasekaran B, Josephson JR, Benjamins VR (1999) What are ontologies, and why do we need
    them? IEEE Intell Syst Appl 14(1):20–26
Cullot N, Ghawi R, Ytongnon K (2007) DB2OWL: a tool for automatic database- to-ontology
    mapping. In Proceeding of 15th Italian Symposium on Advanced Database Systems (SEBD
    2007), pp 491–494, Torre Canne, Italy, 17–20 June 2007
Dehainsala H, Pierra G, Bellatreche L (2007) OntoDB: an ontology-based database for data inten-
    sive applications. In: In Proceedings of the 12th International Conference on Database Systems
    for Advanced Applications (DASFAA'07). LNCS, Springer, pp 497–508
Ding L, Kolari P, Ding Z, Avancha S, Joshi A (2005) Using ontologies in the semantic web: a
    survey. Technical Report -CS-05-07, UMBC, July 2005
Estival D, Nowak C, Zschorn A (2004) Towards ontology-based natural language processing. In
    Proceeedings of the Workshop on NLP and XML (NLPXML-2004): RDF/RDFS and OWL in
    Language Technology, NLPXML'04, Stroudsburg, PA, USA. Association for Computational
    Linguistics, pp 59–66
Gamberger D, Jovic A, Prcela Marin (2007) Ontologies in medical knowledge representation. In
    Proceedings of the ITI 2007 29th International Conference on Information Technology Inter-
    faces, Cavtat, Croatia, pp 535–540
Gruber T (1995) Toward principles for the design of ontologies used for knowledge sharing? Int J
    Hum-Comput Stud 43(5–6):907–928
Handler S, Altman R, Perera S, Hanlon J, Studenski S, Bost J, Saul M, Fridsma D (2007) A system-
    atic review of the performance characteristics of clinical event monitor signals used to detect
    adverse drug events in the hospital setting. J Am Med Inform Assoc 14:451–458
Hunt D, Haynes R, Hanna S, Smith K (1998) Effects of computer-based clinical decision support
    systems on physician performance and patient outcomes. JAMA 280:1339–1346
Jean S, At-Ameur Y, Pierra G (2006) Querying ontology based database using otoql (an ontology
    query language). In: In Proceedings of OTM Confeder- Ated International Conferences (OD-
    BASE06), pp 704–721
Koppel R, Metlay J, Cohen A, Abaluck B, Localio A, Kimmel S, Strom B (2005) Role of computer-
    ized physician order entry systems in facilitating medication errors. JAMA 293(10):1197–1203
Lataief M, Mhamdi S, Asady R, Siddiqi S, Abdullatif A (2010) Adverse event in a Tunisian hospi-
    tal: results of retrospective cohort study. Int J Qual Health Care 22(5):380–385
Li J, Zhang L (2011) Automatic generation of ontology based on database. J Comput Inf Syst
    7(4):1148–1154
Li G, Peng Q (2011) Using ontology and rough set building e-commerce knowledge manage-
    ment system. In: Jin D, Lin S (eds) CSISE (3), volume 106 of Advances in Soft Computing.
    Springer, pp 13–18
McBride B (2001) Jena: implementing the RDF model and syntax specification. In: Staab S (ed)
    Proceedings of the 2nd International Workshop on the Semantic Web—SemWeb'2001, vol-
    ume 40 of CEUR-WS, Hongkong, China
McDonald H, Rosas-Arellano MP, Devereaux PJ, Beyene J, Sam J, Haynes RB, Garg AX, Ad-
    hikari NK (2005) Effects of computerized clinical decision support systems on practitioner
    performance and patient outcomes. JAMA 293(10):1223–1238
Noy NF (2003) What do we need for ontology integration on the semantic web, position statement.
    In: Proceeding of the 1st semantic integration Ws., pp 175–176
Oliven A, Michalake I, Zalman D, Dorman E, Yeshurun D, Odeh M (2010) Prevention of prescrip-
    tion errors by computerized, on-line surveillance of drug order en entry. Int J Med Inform
    74(5):377–386
Pierra G, Hondjack D, Ameur Y, Bellatreche L (2005) Bases de donnes base ontologique. Principe
    et mise en oeuvre. Ing Syst Inf 10(2):91–115
Schmidt-Schaub M, Smolka G (1991) Attributive concept descriptions with com-plements. Artif
    Intell 47:1–26

Shen H, Hu J, Zhao J, Dong J (2012) Ontology-based modeling of emergency incidents and crisis management. Proceedings of the 9th international ISCRAM conference, Vancouver, Canada

Studer G, Richard B, Fensel D (1998) Knowledge engineering: principles and methods. Data Knowl Eng 25(1–2):161–197

Tom G (1993) A translation approach to portable ontologies. Knowl Acquis 2(5):199–220

Wang S, Li M, Du XY (2006) Learning ontology from relational database. In Proceedings of the Fourth International Conference on Machine Learning and Cybernetics. IEEE Press, pp 3410–3415

Xiao-Yong DU, Wang S, Li Man (2006) A survey on ontology learning research. J Softw 17(9):1837–1847

Zegher I, Venot A, Milstein C, Sene B, Carolis B, Pizzutilo S (1994) Optimization of drug prescription using advanced informatics. Comput Method Program Biomed 45(1–2):131–136

Chapter 9
Computational Modeling and Simulations in Life Sciences

Athina A. Lazakidou, Maria Petridou and Dimitra Iliopoulou

Abstract Today, the modern computer is capable of performing billions of basic math operations each second. Clearly, it would take one man a life time to perform a similar number of computations. When applied to Medicine, the revolutionary potential of the mathematical modeling approach becomes clear. In medicine, mathematical modeling can radically improve both dug development and hospital technology. Advances in technology and the development of new experimental methods have had a significant impact on the study of disease. This has led to new research directions, including: the acquisition of detailed 'molecular fingerprints' from patients containing information, for instance, on genotype, gene or protein expression, or metabolite levels; the study of intracellular processes in healthy and diseased tissue via the manipulation of gene activity within cells; and the construction of comprehensive disease-specific databases that combine patients' medical history with laboratory and clinical data as well as saving relevant tissue samples. In this chapter, the author aims at equipping the readers with a perspective on current and future applications of mathematical modeling in medicine.

Keywords Computational models · Simulation · Medical robotics · Life sciences · Medicine · Medical informatics

A. A. Lazakidou (✉)
Department of Nursing, Faculty of Human Movement and Quality of Life Sciences, University of Peloponnese, Orthias Artemidos & Plateon, 23100 Sparta, Greece
e-mail: lazakid@uop.gr

M. Petridou
School of Computer Science & IT Jubilee Campus, The University of Nottingham, Wollaton Road, NG8 1BB Nottingham, UK
e-mail: psxmp4@exmail.nottingham.ac.uk

D. Iliopoulou
Biomedical Engineering Laboratory, School of Electrical and Computer Engineering, National Technical University of Athens, Heroon Polytechneiou Str. 9, 15780 Zografou, Athens, Greece
e-mail: dilio@biomed.ntua.gr

D.-D. Koutsouris, A. A. Lazakidou (eds.), *Concepts and Trends in Healthcare Information Systems,* Annals of Information Systems 16,
DOI 10.1007/978-3-319-06844-2_9, © Springer International Publishing Switzerland 2014

9.1 Introduction

Computer modeling is the process by which a computer is used to develop a mathematical model of a complex system or process. Computer modeling is an efficient way to take into account many different factors and to simplify and organize real-world processes. Computational analysis and modeling can help make sense of the data being collected. Molecular fingerprints can be used to identify biomarkers that signal an elevated risk of acquiring a disease or to confirm diagnosis. Healthcare simulation can be extended beyond the traditional role of comparing scenarios or visualizing workflows. A simulation model can be incorporated as a component of ongoing efforts to monitor and improve performance and increase efficiency. In such a role, a simulation model is developed not only to conduct experiments, but anchored in the running information systems of the organization. A true benefit of simulation can be harvested when the simulation models are fully integrated into the routine fabric of healthcare delivery, i.e., the existing information system applications which support the daily operation of the healthcare provider. Essentially, the vision is not to treat simulation as a tool for conducting a one-time set of experiments when a major change is planned, but make the simulation models run in parallel to other applications as a routine part of the everyday work environment. Simulation has a broad application potential in healthcare, which can be classified in a few major directions, formed around different disciplines or sub-disciplines. Each direction may have its own gradients or sub-directions as well. The following is a more general classification of healthcare simulation:

- **Clinical Simulation:** simulation is mainly used to study, analyse and replicate the behavior of certain diseases including biological processes in human body.
- **Operational Simulation:** simulation is mainly used for capturing, analyzing, and studying healthcare operations, service delivery, scheduling, healthcare business processes, and patient flow.
- **Managerial Simulation:** simulation is mainly used as a tool for managerial purposes, decision making, policy implementation, and strategic planning.
- **Educational Simulation:** Simulation is used for training and educational purposes, where virtual environments and virtual and physical objects are extensively used to augment and enrich simulation experiment.

9.2 Computational Models for Medical Image Analysis

Medical Image Analysis plays a crucial role in the diagnosis, planning, control and follow-up of therapy. To be combined efficiently with medical robotics, Medical Image Analysis can be supported by the development of specific computational models of the human body operating at various levels. Medical Imaging can be used for the planning and control of the motion of medical robots. Examples include the use of pre-operative images and geometric reasoning for path planning, the combined use of pre-operative and intra-operative images to control a surgical procedure with augmented reality visualization, or the simulation of surgical interventions on virtual organs built from pre-operative images and atlases with realistic visual and force feedback. Such procedures require the use of advanced medical image analysis methods and the development of a hierarchy of computational models of the human body (Ayache 2004). These computational models aim at reproducing the geometrical, physical and physiological properties of human organs and systems at various scales. They can be used in conjunction with medical images and robotics to actually enhance the possibilities of image analysis and robot control. In this chapter has been illustrated the potential use of computational models in a number of advanced medical applications including image guided, robot-assisted and simulated medical interventions (Stasis 2003; Istepanian 2001; Giakoumaki 2005).

9.3   Computational Models for Image Guided, Robot-Assisted and Simulated Medical Interventions

Medical Imaging can be used for the planning and control of the motion of medical robots. Examples include the use of pre-operative images and geometric reasoning for path planning, the combined use of pre-operative and intra-operative images to control a surgical procedure with augmented reality visualization, or the simulation of surgical interventions on virtual organs built from pre-operative images and atlases with realistic visual and force feedback (Delingette et al. 2006).

Computational models of the human body could be used in conjunction with medical imaging techniques to assist in the preparation, simulation and control of medical interventions. A key point is the possibility offered by these models to actually fuse the geometrical, physical, and physiological information necessary to provide a thorough and reliable analysis of the complex and multimodal biomedical signals acquired on each patient, possibly at various scales.

Some research topics that open new perspectives in improving medical practice (Ayache 2004; Bourquain et al. 2002):

- **Statistical Analysis.** The development of large databases of medical images should further improve the robustness and accuracy of the previously discussed computational models, and therefore the performances of image-guided intervention or simulation systems.
- **Soft Tissue Modeling.** The development of sophisticated ex-vivo and in-vivo indentation devices should lead to a better understanding and new mathematical models of the mechanical behavior of human organs. In the context of surgery simulation, further optimization in soft tissue deformation is required to simulate a whole surgical intervention and not only a series of surgical tasks.
- **Real-time Coupling of Models with Observations.** This requires very fast inversion of realistic computational models. This will improve robot-assisted image-guided therapy in the presence of patient motion (brain shift, respiration, cardiac motion etc).

- **Miniaturized Robotics.** The advances in robotics research, in particular the design of new generations of highly accurate, easy-to-use miniature robotic guidance systems (e.g. the spine-assist system) might also contribute to the successful combination of computational models and medical imaging.
- **Microscopic Imaging.** New in vivo microendoscopy techiniques providing structural information on the tissues at the cellular level should also open combined with robotics and computational models, new venues for improving diagnosis and therapy.

9.4   Computational Disease Models

The collection and storage of biomolecular and clinical information is more accessible and cheaper than ever. A major challenge now is to make sense of the vast volumes of data being produced, which is where complex computational models can play a vital role.

Diseases such as HIV/AIDS, tuberculosis, hepatitis C, influenza and malaria affect large patient populations, making this a particularly important use of computer modeling. The models must be updated regularly to keep up with the rapid evolution of infectious agent's interactions between a pathogen and its host. A modeling approach based on molecular networks can reveal information about the relationship between a pathogen and its host. The development of dynamic models that show how infectious agents replicate within cells will be an important step forward, as will quantitative descriptions of pathogenic spread throughout tissue and organs. Computational models can predict the likely outcome of improved strategies for vaccine design, such as the best combination of an antigen with an agent to boost the immune response.

Most recent disease-modeling efforts focus on only a limited aspect of the disease process. In order to create more realistic and useful tools, it is important to integrate these approaches and develop more dynamic, large-scale models. This will be a challenge, not least because of the different timescales involved: models of disease progression and healing span days or even years, whereas chemical reactions can be completed in a matter of microseconds. Information based on computational disease models will benefit patients by improving diagnosis and prognosis, helping to develop new treatments and substantially reducing the risk of inadequate or even damaging therapy.

9.5   Computational Modeling of Tumor Response
     to Vascular-Targeting Therapies

Mathematical modeling techniques have been widely employed to understand how cancer grows, and, more recently, such approaches have been used to understand how cancer can be controlled. In the paper (Gevertz 2011), a previously validated hybrid cellular automaton model of tumor growth in a vascularized environment is used to study the antitumor activity of several vascular-targeting compounds of known efficacy. In particular, this model is used to test the antitumor activity of a clinically used angiogenesis inhibitor (both in isolation, and with a cytotoxic chemotherapeutic) and a vascular disrupting agent currently undergoing clinical trial testing. I demonstrate that the mathematical model can make predictions in agreement with preclinical/clinical data and can also be used to gain more insight into these treatment protocols. Vascular-targeting agents, as currently administered, cannot lead to cancer eradication, although a highly efficacious agent may lead to long-term cancer control.

The use of mathematical techniques in the drug development process is not a novel one. Pharmacokinetic (PK) and pharmacodynamic (PD) models have been utilized for decades to determine the relationship between drug dose and response. In particular, PK models study what the body does to a drug, including mechanisms of drug absorption and distribution (typically modeled through differential equations) and duration of drug effect. Mathematics has been employed in other ways to study tumor response to drug administration. While a comprehensive discussion of these approaches is beyond the scope of this paper, it is worthwhile to mention a number of interesting models that have been developed to understand tumor drug response. Chemotherapy, for example, has been extensively studied using mathematical models. Some of these models focus on the predicted efficacy of a chemotherapeutic treatment regime, its dependence on the immune system, the transport of chemotherapeutic agents, the development of drug resistance, and optimization of scheduling protocols.

Recently, PK/PD models have been coupled with models of tumor growth in order to explore drug dynamics and the resulting impact on tumor growth rates. The researcher has illustrated that the model can successfully predict, without any a priori knowledge, the antitumor activity of a number of vascular-targeting treatment protocols. The tumor microenvironment was shown to play an important role in drug activity. The predictions made by the model were verified by comparing to preclinical and clinical data wherever possible. The fact that the model could lead to predictions comparable to those made in preclinical and clinical trials is rather important. In order for clinical trials to reach these conclusions, millions of dollars were spent, many years of time were invested, and patients were put at risk of having an adverse response to the treatment. Mathematical models can be used to test the efficacy of cancer drugs and, importantly, rule out drugs that will not have significant antitumor activity. In the future will be used the mathematical model to test the efficacy of administering a drug cocktail of an AI and VDA, in an effort to learn if there are additive effects of combining these two vascular-targeting agents (Gevertz 2011).

9.6 Breast Tumor Simulation and Parameters Estimation Using Evolutionary Algorithms

An estimation methodology-based evolutionary algorithm using neural networks and genetic algorithms was developed (Mittal and Pidaparti 2008) to estimate the breast tumor parameters based on surface temperature profile that may be obtained by infrared thermography. The estimation methodology involves evolutionary algorithms using artificial neural network (ANN) and genetic algorithm (GA). The ANN is used to map the relationship of tumor parameters (depth, size, and heat generation) to the temperature profile over the idealized breast model. The relationship obtained from ANN is compared to that obtained by finite element software. Results from ANN training/testing were in good agreement with those obtained from finite element model. After ANN validation, GA is used to estimate tumor parameters by minimizing a fitness function involving comparing the temperature profiles from simulated or clinical data to those obtained by ANN. Results show that it is possible to determine the depth, diameter, and heat generation rate from the surface temperature data (with 5 % random noise) with good accuracy for the 2D model. With 10 % noise, the accuracy of estimation deteriorates for deep-seated tumors with low heat generation. In order to further develop this methodology for use in a clinical scenario, several aspects such as 3D breast geometry and the effects of no uniform cooling should be considered in future investigations.

References

Ackerman M (1998) The visible human project. Proc IEEE: Spec Issue Surg Simul 86(3):504–511
Alnaes M, Isaksen J, Mardal K-A, Romner B, Morgan M, Ingebrigtsen T (2007) Computation of hemodynamics in the circle of Willis. Stroke 38(9):2500–2505
Ayache N (2004a) Computational models for the human body: special volume (Handbook of Numerical Analysis), 1st edn. Elsevier Science Ltd., Amsterdam
Ayache N (2004b) Handbook of numerical analysis XII: computational models for the human body. Elsevier Science Ltd., Oxford
Bellamo N, Li N, Maini P (2008) On the foundations of cancer modelling: selected topics, speculations, and perspectives. Math Model Method Appl Sci 18(4):593–646
Bourquain H, Schenk A, Link F, Preim B, Peitgen H-O (2002) HepaVision 2: a software assistant for preoperative planning in living-related liver transplantation and oncologic liver surgery. Computer Assisted Radiology and Surgery (CARS): Proceedings of the 16th International Congress and Exhibition. Springer-Verlag NY Inc, Paris, pp 341–346
Buzug T, Lueth T (2004) Perspectives in image-guided surgery. Proceedings of the scientific workshop on medical robotics, navigation and visualization. World Scientific Publishing, Remagen
Clayton R, Panfilow A (2007) A guide to modelling cardiac electrical activity in anatomically detailed ventricles. Prog Biophys Mol Biol 96(1–3):19–43
Delingette H, Ayache N, Ciarlet P (2004) Soft tissue modeling for surgery simulation. In: Ayache N (ed) Computational models for the human body: special volume (Handbook of Numerical Analysis), 1st edn. Elsevier Science Ltd., Amsterdam, pp 453–550
Delingette H, Pennec X, Soler L, Marescaux J, Ayache N (2006) Computational models for image-guided Robot-assisted and simulated medical interventions. Proc IEEE 94(9):1678–1688

Gevertz J (2011) Computational modeling of tumor response to vascular-targeting therapies—part I: validation. Comput Math Method Med 2011:17

Giakoumaki A, Pavlopoulos S, Koutsouris D (2005) Multiple digital watermarking applied to medical imaging. In: Proceedings of the 27th annual international conference of the IEEE engineering in medicine and biology society—EMBS, article nr 2332, vol 4, pp 3444–3447, Shanghai, China, September 2005

Haug E, Choi H-Y, Robin S, Beaugonin M (2004) Human models for crash and impact simulation. In: Ayache N (ed) Computational models for the human body: special volume (Handbook of Numerical Analysis), 1st edn. Elsevier Science Ltd., Amsterdam, pp 231–452

Hunter P, Borg T (2003) Integration from proteins to organs: the physiome project. Nat Rev Mol Cell Biol 4:237–243

Istepanian R, Kyriacou E, Pavlopoulos S, Koutsouris D (2001) Effect of wavelet compression methodologies on data transmission in a multi-purpose wireless telemedicine system with mobile communication link support. J Telemed Telecare 7(1):14–16

Jannin P, Fitzpatrick J, Hawkes D, Shahidi R, Vannier M (2002) Validation of medical image processing in image-guided therapy. IEEE Trans Med Imaging 21(12):1445–1449

Mittal M, Pidaparti MR (2008) Breast tumor a simulation and parameters estimation using evolutionary algorithms. Model Simul Eng 2008:6

Noble D (2002a) Modeling the heart, from genes to cells to the whole organ. Science 295:1678–1682

Noble D (2002b) The rise of computational biology. Nat Rev Mol Biol 3(6):459–463

Pietka E (2008) Computation intelligence in medicine—data analysis and modelling. Model Simulat Eng 2008(215073):2. doi:10.1155/2008/215073. (Hindawi Publishing Corporation)

Reitinger B, Bornik A, Beichel R, Werkgartner G, Sorantin, E (2004) Tools for augmented reality based liver resection planning. SPIE Medical Imaging 2004: visualization, image-guided procedures, and display. San Diego, pp 88–99

Soler L, Nicolau S, Pennec X, Schmid J, Koehl C, Ayache N et al (2004) Virtual reality and augmented reality in digestive surgery. Proceedings of the IEEE International Symposium on Mixed and Augmented Reality (ISMAR'04). Washington, USA, pp 278–279

Starkie S, Davies B (2001) Advances in active constraints and their application to minimally invasive surgery. 4th International Conference on Medical Image Computing and Computer-Assisted Intervention (MICCAI'01). 2208. LNCS, Utrecht, pp 1316–1321

Stasis A, Loukis E, Pavlopoulos S, Koutsouris D (2003, April) Using decision tree algorithms as a basis for a heart sound diagnosis decision support system. In: Proceedings of the international 2003 IEEE-EMBS special topic conference on information technology applications in biomedicine-ITAB 2003, New solutions for new challenges, Birmingham, UK, pp 354–357

Taylor R, Stoianovici D (2003) Medical robotics in computer-integrated surgery. IEEE Trans Robotics and Autom 19(5):765–781

Chapter 10
Stent Deployment Computer Based Simulations for Health Care Treatment of Diseased Arteries

Georgia S. Karanasiou, Evanthia E. Tripoliti, Elazer R. Edelman, Lampros K. Michalis and Dimitrios I. Fotiadis

Abstract Endovascular stent deployment is one of the most commonly used techniques for the treatment of diseased arterial segments. Though these devices have eliminated the problem with recoil seen with balloon angioplasty alone there are idiosyncratic reactions that remain and mandate further definition and examination so as these can be eliminated. Chief amongst these problems are loss of lumen patency to clot, stent thrombosis (acute, subacute, late and very late), or to tissue overgrowth, instent restenosis (ISR). While these effects are to some extent class-related, each individual design and implantation procedures impacts outcome. The magnitude and diversity of the parameters that determine safety and efficacy defies empiric validation and limits how much experimentation can add to optimization. Differences in design, materials, arterial geometries, implantation procedures and local, regional and systemic forces and flows cannot be evaluated across the domains of interest and in reasonable time but they can be considered in computational models. High speed computer resources can solve complex coupled equations that cover an almost infinite range of perturbations and combinations of conditions and have become an invaluable tool in the armamentarium of

G. S. Karanasiou (✉) · E. E. Tripoliti · D. I. Fotiadis
Unit of Medical Technology and Intelligent Information Systems, Dept. of Materials
Science and Engineering, University of Ioannina, 45110 Ioannina, GR, Greece
e-mail: gkaranasiou@gmail.com

E. E. Tripoliti
e-mail: evi@cs.uoi.gr

D. I. Fotiadis
e-mail: dfotiadis@cs.uoi.gr

E. R. Edelman
Institute for Medical Engineering and Science and Cardiovascular Division Brigham and
Women's Hospital, Harvard Medical School, Boston, MA, USA
e-mail: ere@mit.edu

L. K. Michalis
Department of Cardiology, Medical School, University of Ioannina, 45110 Ioannina, Greece
e-mail: lamprosmichalis@gmail.com

D.-D. Koutsouris, A. A. Lazakidou (eds.), *Concepts and Trends in Healthcare Information Systems,* Annals of Information Systems 16,
DOI 10.1007/978-3-319-06844-2_10, © Springer International Publishing Switzerland 2014

the cardiovascular device designer and medical practitioner. We now present an extended review of computational modeling stent deployment and the emerging potential these resources provide.

Keywords Computational modeling · FEM · Stent · Atherosclerosis

10.1 Introduction

Computational modeling is a valuable tool for analyzing engineering and biomedical problems (Yang et al. 2013). In contrast to empiric studies its predictive value and time effectiveness will only rise with time as computer technology continues to expand exponentially. In the field of cardiovascular disease, computer based simulations is a well-recognized and widely adopted approach to understand the parameters that influence the success of the stent deployment procedure (Martin and Boyle 2011). One of the main advantages of computational modeling is that several "What if?" scenarios can be performed, using different stent designs or materials and this way evaluating devices before even be manufactured. The mechanical characteristics of the stents are tested, something which undoubtedly influences the cost in a very positive way. Furthermore, different stents are compared facilitating the evaluation of the most appropriate stent for patient specific diseased arterial segments. The scope of this chapter is to present the most recent studies of stent deployment simulations and take advantage of the current status of knowledge in this field. Finally, our approach of stent deployment in a reconstructed arterial segment is presented and compared to the abovementioned studies.

10.2 The Pathology of the Cardiovascular Disease

10.2.1 Cardiovascular Disease

Cardiovascular diseases (CVD) remain the main cause of human mortality and morbidity around the world (WHO 2010). Every year, millions of CVD patients experience death and disease due to arterial pathology. According to the World Health Organization in 2008, the percentage of mortality due to CVD was 30%, with 17.3 million people suffering coronary artery disease and 6.2 million stroke (WHO 2010). It is expected, that by 2030, almost 23.6 million people will die from CVD (Mathers and Loncar 2006).

The most preventable form of CVD is coronary artery disease (CAD). CAD is a disease that begins early in the childhood and progresses with age—becoming symptomatic over time for one in every 200 men and 300 women. While the precise mechanism behind this ubiquitous disease has not been fully delineated risk factors for CAD have long been identified (Boo and Froelicher 2012). To a great degree CAD, like all atherosclerotic processes and all diseases, is heavily moderated by genetic predisposition and age creating a non-modifiable risk. Yet, epigenetic factors are also dominant and these present a continuum of risk that can be manipulated and even treated. Blood cholesterol and blood pressure can be controlled with lifestyle modification, drugs and perhaps even emerging electromechanical approaches. Tobacco abuse, glucose control in diabetes mellitus, obesity and physical activity can similarly be modulated.

10.2.2 Atherosclerosis

The healthy arterial tissue is composed of three concentric layers to *tunics*: intima, media and adventitia. The intima is the innermost layer—comprised primarily of endothelial cells and some smooth muscle cells it senses luminal flows and forces and produces powerful vasoactive compounds. The media is the central coat and bears packets of smooth muscle cells aligned in lamellar units that respond to mediators of vasomotor tone to contract and relax alerting arterial diameter. The less dense outer coat, the adventitia, contains the microvasculature and nerves that perfuse and innervate the inner vascular tissue (Holzapfel et al. 2000). For those involved in computational modeling structure determines the boundary conditions and mechanical mesh geometry on which all models are based and driven.

Atherosclerosis, the main process of CAD, involves disruption of structure and function of the coronary arterial wall. Accumulation of fatty deposits, forming atherosclerotic plaques, in the inner surface of the arterial wall, underneath the endothelium change not only the geometry of the vessel but virtually all aspects of vascular biology (Libby 2013). The plaque is a combination of vascular smooth muscle cells, inflammatory cells, matrix and fatty deposits and it is covered by a fibrous cap (Bentzon and Falk 2013). The plaques are composed of cholesterol, calcium and other lipids that vary in morphology and in their pathophysiology. Based on Stary's classification, there are several stages in the progress of the atherosclerotic lesions, from Type I to Type VIII (Stary 2000). The disease begins as an accumulation of macrophage foam cells and may result to the fissuring, ulcerating and hemorrhaging of the arterial wall.

The arterial wall is normally smooth and flexible (Robertson and Watton 2013). As the plaque grows, the arterial wall thickens and stiffens. The blood flow circulation is disrupted and results in an insufficient oxygen-rich supply to the myocardium the artery perfuses (Silva et al. 2013). The obstruction of the blood flow can lead to angina (chest pain), myocardial infarction (heart attack) or even sudden cardiac death. In order to prevent such dysfunctions many treatment techniques are available, from medication prescriptions to interventional approaches and surgical procedures.

10.2.3   Treatment Options

Treating atherosclerotic arteries mainly aims at improving quality of life through symptomatic relief and restoration of vibrancy, and ideally at extending life expectancy. While preventive measures and life-style modification have greatest potential for early benefit years of poorly controlled blood pressure, dyslipidaemia and/or diabetes often requires pharmacologic control (Anderson et al. 2007). Often times however plaque decompensation is the first sign and more extensive intervention with surgery or devices is warranted.

Surgical Procedures (Arterial by Pass)

Arterial bypass is a procedure where a healthy arterial or venous segment, bypasses the occluded arterial region restoring blood flow (Cornwell et al. 2014). Such treatment for patients with CAD is called coronary artery bypass grafting (CABG) and can be performed either with the heart being stopped during the operation and the patient connected to a heart lung machine, or with the heart "off pump" performing normally. The in-hospital recovery period is on average 5 days (Peterson et al. 2002). In the last years, arterial by-pass surgery has been partially replaced by percutaneous coronary interventional procedures (PCI) due to its high rates of success, the quick recovery time and its cost-effectiveness (Sherman and Ryan 1995).

Percutaneous Coronary Intervention

Percutaneous coronary intervention (PCI) is a minimally invasive procedure used to unblock stenosed or occluded arterial segments (Khan 2006). Initially a long, thin tube with an inflatable balloon, called balloon-catheter is inserted into the diseased artery overlapping the region of stenosis. Then the balloon is inflated and pushes the arterial wall, opening the arterial lumen. Afterwards the balloon is deflated and removed from the treated artery. Despite the positive immediate effect of PCI, 30–40 % of the patients experience arterial re-narrowing after approximately 6 months, due to the elastic recoil of the arterial wall and the production of neointimal tissue (Giglioli et al. 2009). Moreover, the expansion of the balloon causes dissection, an arterial wall injury, which can lead to acute re-occlusion of the artery. The introduction of stents allows for a permanent implant to eliminate recoil but comes with a series of its own complications. Stenting is a combination of angioplasty and stent placement. The stent is a wire mesh tube that is most often inflated within the affected arterial segment and left in place to maintain arterial wall patency and prevent recoil and re-closure. The stent pushes back the plaque deposits, supports the arterial wall and results to blood flow restoration. Depending on the length of the arterial lesion, in some cases, it is necessary for more than one stent to be inserted (Silva et al. 2011). In the next section, the basic characteristics for optimal stent selection and deployment are described.

10.2.4   Coronary Artery Stenting

The evolution of the stenting procedure has significantly improved the clinical treatment of atherosclerosis. However, it is not a panacea in the treatment of the disease. First generation stents were typically comprised of rather inflexible, somewhat bulky metal struts and while they had a high acute success rate a chronic tissue overgrowth response limited efficacy. This overgrowth termed in-stent restenosis can be so severe as to induced myocardial infarction or necessitate intervention of its own. ISR was thought to arrive from the healing process following local injury induced with stent positioning Factors contributing to ISR are the induced arterial stresses after stent deployment, stent fracture and the positioning of a foreign body inside the artery (Surdell et al. 2007).

10.3   Stent

Stents must provide several performance characteristics such as an appropriate biomechanical behavior, flexibility, high radial strength, durability, radioopacity and corrosion resistance. These characteristics play a significant role not only in the phase of stent designing but also in the clinical choice of one device over another (Kwok 2013). A successful stent implantation requires controlled stent expansion and stent flexibility (Ormiston et al. 2011). Stent should possess radial strength sufficient to support the arterial wall, which with disease might have greater propensity for constriction. The stent should be biocompatible (Kathuria 2006), prevent the formation of thrombus (Balghith et al. 2013) and the development of late neointima. The choice of the appropriate material for stent manufacturing is critical. The stent material should be able to undergo 4 to 6-fold expansion and plastically deform to an inflated state. Stents should also have minimal elastic recoil combined with high radial strength. To achieve all the aforementioned mechanical characteristics the material should have high Elastic Modulus and low Yield stress. The commercially available stents are made of Stainless Steel, Nitinol shape-memory alloy, Cobalt-Chromium alloys, Platinum, Tantalum, or Gold (Lévesque et al. 2004).

Stents can be classified along many different lines—one involves the manner in which they are delivered and expanded in place. Two main types are used today: balloon expandable (BX) and self-expandable stents (SX). The balloon expandable stents are manufactured in the crimped state. The balloon is gradually inflated and the mounted stent expands. BX stents are mainly manufactured from Stainless Steel (SS), Cobalt—Chromium alloys and Platinum, as these materials provide good corrosion performance, high radial strength and great availability. The main advantage of balloon expandable SS stents is its biocompatibility—a property derived from the material itself and the minimum amount of the stent material that comes in contact with the arterial wall. Self-expandable stents are manufactured with a diameter higher than the arterial. Initially these stents are in a crimped condition.

When the self-expandable stent is delivered in the diseased arterial region, the constraint mechanism (usually a sheath) is taken away and the stent self-expands. The self-expansion of the stent derives from the mechanical properties of the stent material, usually a Nickel-Titanium alloy or a shape memory alloy material (Mortier and De Beule 2011).

Another crucial factor for stent classification is their size. The nominal diameter varies from 2–4 mm with lengths from 8 mm to more than 30 mm. The stent length should match the length of the stenosed area and the stent diameter should match the inner diameter of the artery. The stent should be placed in the appropriate arterial region to achieve the optimal stent deployment. The cardiologist decides which stent is to be placed. The inappropriate stent deployment can cause serious problems such as thrombosis or arterial rupture. Aiming to reach the optimal combination of strength and flexibility, different stent designs have been developed from helical spirals with few internal connectors to stents with sequential series of struts (Azaouzi et al. 2012). The struts can be connected in many different ways such as open cell connection, close cell connection, peak-to-peak connection or peak-to-valley connection. Many experimental studies, investigating the mechanical characteristics of stents, have been performed (Wang et al. 2005).

Since the experimental performance of stent deployment in a realistic artery is a difficult and complicated procedure, computational simulations have been proven a powerful tool in evaluating the response of stent and assess the effectiveness and accuracy of the stent implantation.

10.4 Computational Simulation Using the Finite Element Method (FEM)

An interesting and powerful computer based method for designing, modeling and simulating biomedical engineering problems is Finite Element Analysis (FEA) (Zienkiewicz et al. 2014). The Finite Element Method (FEM) is an effective numerical technique that transforms physical problems into equivalent structural and fluid mechanical forms that can be solved with a series of differential equations. FEA "approximates" solutions of a physical problems once they are well-defined and along as unique solutions can be found. The validity and value of the solution therefore depends on the quality of input data, the loads and the constraints (Babuska et al. 2001). These data require at least three distinct elements of computer aided engineering simulations: (a) Pre-processing, where a finite element model with its environmental factors is defined, based on the physical and mathematical problem, (b) Analysis solver, where a system of simultaneous algebraic equations is solved and (c) Post-processing, where the validity of the solution is examined and the desired and predefined results are observed. A detailed description of the three phases of FEA is provided next.

10.4.1   Pre-Processing

Before any analysis can commence the structure must be created in a mathematical form that can be appreciated by the computer. Solid modelers or 3D CAD software are often used, and increasingly geometric reconstructions are derived from medical image based sequences such as Intravascular Ultrasound (IVUS) (Balocco et al. 2014), (Zheng and Mengchan 2013), angiography or Computerized Tomography (CT). One major feature of FEA is that it allows for neglect of irrelevant mechanical forms. Structural features that do not have a significant mechanical impact can be omitted, simplifying the modeling and reducing the complexity.

The 3D geometry is imported to the FEM software and the appropriate boundary conditions are determined. The boundary conditions are essential for defining the mathematical model. The selection of the boundary conditions depends on the physics of the problem and is crucial for achieving correct results. Afterwards, the finite element "mesh" is generated. Mesh generation is a technique for dividing the domain into elements and solve the equations in a "simple" domain. The elements are joined in points called "nodes". The number of nodes presented in an element is crucial for the accuracy of the solution. The set of related continuous differential equations will be converted into linear algebraic equations and solved for the mesh element nodes. Since the linear algebraic equations will be solved in the nodes, a finer mesh with more nodes will lead to better and accurate results but it will need more computational time and memory requirements. The mesh should be as fine to lead to good results but as coarse to reduce computational time. A mesh that is not dense enough will create misleading results in the same way that an inadequate number of points will give the false impression of a curve fit for a single set of data. Mesh density must be high enough to remove false results and converge on singular solutions. Thus, the choice of a good mesh depends not only on a set of guidelines but also on the user's experience. The next step is to define the appropriate material properties for the involved components. A material model that describes the stress-strain relation for each material is selected. The commercial finite element software packages support the definition of many material models such as linear elastic, non-linear elastic, isotropic, orthotropic, hyperelastic, shape memory, etc.

10.4.2   Analysis Solver

Once the 3D geometry of the component is designed, then the material properties, the loads and constraints are determined and finally a system of algebraic equations of the finite element model is ready to be solved. The mathematical model must be chosen to match the equations—linear systems for linear equations, non-linear for non-linear cases. In the non-linearity case, a series of methodologies should be followed in order to "linearize" the problem. There are mainly three types of non-linearity; geometry, material and contact nonlinearity and in many physical problems more than one type is present. The finite element model is solved using special numerical methods and algorithms.

Fig. 10.1 Flowchart of the computational FEM

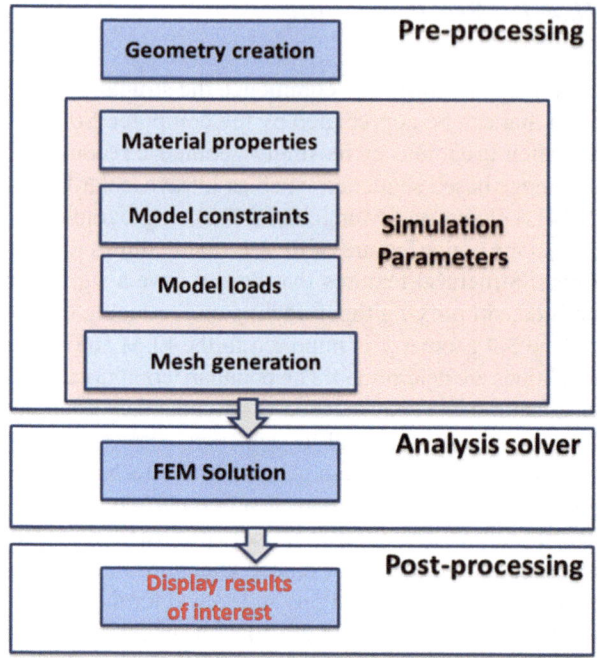

10.4.3 Post-Processing

After the finite element model has been solved, the results of the analysis are analyzed or "post-processed". Post-processing starts with the observation of potentially warnings or errors during the solution phase. Once the validity of the solution is checked, the quantities of interest are studied. Depending on the mathematical and physical form of the problem, different display options can be examined, such as the deformed shape, magnitude of principal stress, displacement magnitude, etc. Also the combination of large displacement motion with and fluid flow can be computed and displayed as well. The overall procedure is depicted in Fig. 10.1.

In short, computational simulation combined with the Finite Element Method is a mature, fully capable method of providing accurate results in a short time with a reduced possibility of failure.

10.5 Computational Modeling of Stent Deployment

Stent implantation in a diseased human artery is a complicated procedure that involves many simultaneous considerations from arterial geometry to lesion state, patient and disease specific characteristics and matching issues related to the availability of stents of specific materials and dimensions. Clinical success is predicated upon precise stent positioning and deployment accuracy.

Several computational studies have been carried out to investigate stent deployment performance and many different aspects of modeling have been presented—most require some form of simplification or assumptions of conditions in the face of limited actual data. The modeling of the diseased artery for example, can be reconstructed from patient specific data or images, but as these are not always available or may be unwieldy in the extreme are replaced by idealized structures like cylinders (straight, curved or even bifurcated). The atherosclerotic plaque, if modeled, can be stiff and calcified or soft. Other studies have investigated the type of stent delivery system using balloon expandable or self-expandable stents. Also the expansion of the balloon expandable stent can be simulated ignoring the presence of the balloon or assuming the balloon as a plane cylinder. For the modeling of balloon expansion two different approaches can be used; pressure and displacement driven processes. Further finite element analysis has been carried out to examine stent deployment using stents made of different materials, such as stainless steel (SS) and Cobalt-chromium (Co-Cr) stents. In the following section a number of the most recent research computational studies are summarized and presented.

10.5.1   Arterial Models

Patient Specific Arterial Models

Gijsen et al. (2008) examined stent deployment in a patient's specific coronary artery. For the 3D arterial lumen and wall reconstruction, biplane angiography and IVUS in the right coronary artery (RCA) were used as input data. The Bx velocity stent, made of 316 SS, was designed in its un-expanded state via a von Mises-Hill plasticity model with hardening. The artery was modeled using a hyperelastic isotropic model and a pressure of 1.0 MPa was applied to expand the stent. The arterial deformation and the arterial and stent stress distribution were presented. The lumen area for two proximal arterial regions were enlarged compared to the pre-stenting minimum arterial diameter. The stresses in the arterial wall were higher as the wall's thickness decreased and had a descending ratio from the lumen radially outwards. The stresses in the stent struts were higher near the connectors whereas the peak stresses were approximately 200 MPa. The effect of increasing the stent strut thickness from 0.1 mm to 0.14 mm was examined through a second stent deployment simulation. The results indicated that thinner struts require lower inflation pressure, thus they were preferable for limiting the possibility of arterial damage.

Mortier et al. (2010) studied the stent deployment simulation in curved bifurcations comparing three different stents; Cypher Select®, Endeavor® and Taxus Liberte® stent. The geometry of left coronary artery (LCA) was reconstructed based on rotational angiography using a 3D CAD software and was divided into three equal layers (intima, media and adventitia). These layers were assumed to behave

Fig. 10.2 The finite element model consisted of the artery, the plaque, the stent and the balloon. (Repro-duced from David Chua et al. 2004)

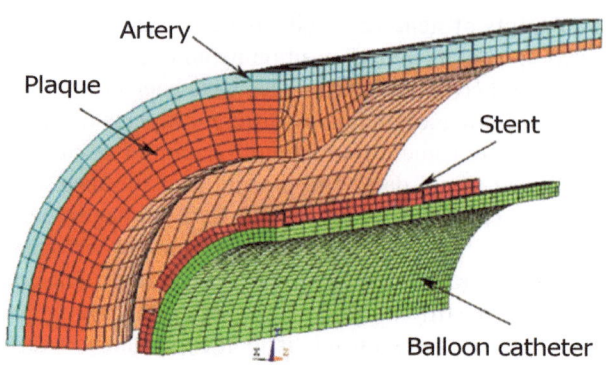

incompressible and non-linearly. The geometries of Cypher Select® (316 SS), Taxus Liberte® (316 SS) and Endeavor® stent (Co-Cr) were generated by Micro-CT imaging and they were modeled using elasto-plastic material models. For stent expansion, a semi compliant trifolded Raptor balloon, made of nylon-based material, was used. The balloon was modeled as a linear elastic material and its inflation was achieved by imposing pressure of 12 bars. The results revealed that the shape of the curved arterial tissues changed and more particularly all the stents resulted in the vascular straightening. This was possibly caused by the difference in radial stiffness between the stent and the artery. It has been proven that the alteration of the vascular curvature results to changes in the hemodynamic flow field (wall shear stress) and potentially to restenosis. This shows that stents should combine flexibility, in order to be easily positioned and minimize the vascular straightening, and stiffness, in order to sufficiently support the deformed arterial tissue. Regarding the induced arterial stresses, higher circumferential stresses were presented at the stent ends with 0.38 MPa, 0.15 MPa and 0.15 MPa for simulations using Cypher Select®, the Endeavor® and Taxus Liberte® stent correspondingly. Although the atherosclerotic plaque is not included in the FEM, this study represents one of the first attempts to examine the stent implantation in a curved arterial segment.

Idealized Arterial Models

Straight Cylinder

David Chua et al. (2004) presented results from a study carried out to examine the stent performance in an idealized arterial model. The diseased artery and the plaque were modeled as cylinders with the plaque being thinner in the proximal and distal ends (Fig. 10.2). The Palmaz-Schatz like stent, made of 316SS, was in initial contact with the polyurethane balloon component.

The material models used for the stent and the balloon were bi-linear elasto-plastic and hyperelastic materials respectively, while the artery and the plaque were assumed as linear isotropic. Regarding the modeling technique, a transient

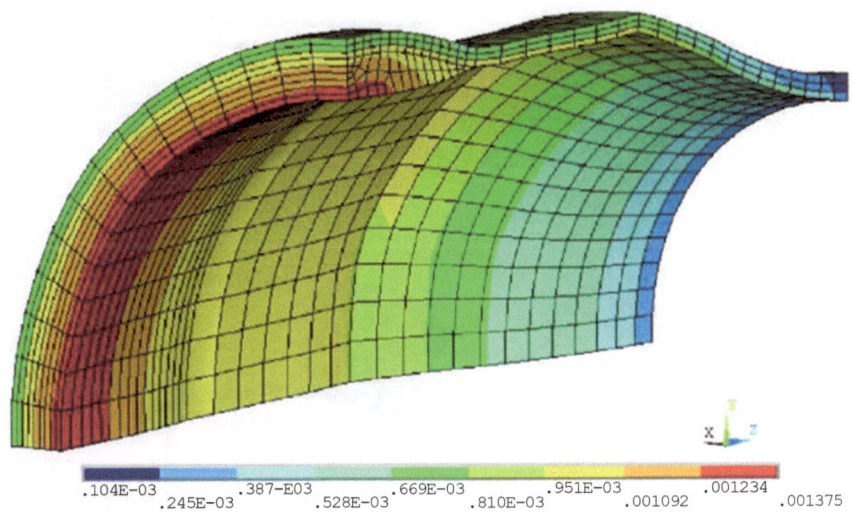

.104E-03   .387-E03   .669E-03   .951E-03   .001234
     .245E-03   .528E-03   .810E-03   .001092   .001375

Fig. 10.3 The resulted stress of the artery and the plaque component. (Reproduced from David Chua et al. 2004)

pressure was imposed to the inner balloon surface. The pressure increased from 0 to 2.65 MPa for 25 ms, then it sustained constant for 7 ms and finally the pressure decreased from 2.65 MPa to 0 MPa for 10 ms. It was observed that when the stent expanded inside the artery, the maximum stent diameter was not the same compared to the maximum free expansion diameter. The high von Mises stresses presented at the regions subject to the plaque component indicate the possibility of plaque rupture (Fig. 10.3).

Zhao et al. (2011) used the finite element method in stent deployment simulations, in order to understand and evaluate the alterations caused in the atherosclerotic arterial wall. The 3D geometry of the FEM was designed in a 3D CAD software. The FEM was similar to that reported by David Chua et al. (2004), but the balloon was ignored. The artery and the plaque were modeled as hyperelastic isotropic and incompressible materials correspondingly. The balloon's expansion was simulated through a uniform pressure of 2 MPa directly applied to the inner stent surface. The authors reported that a reduction in the stent's length by about 12.13 % of its original length was presented when the expanded stent reached its final diameter. The stent foreshortening resulted to the sliding between the stent and plaque and the increase of the contact pressure. This phenomenon might result to the injury of the vascular wall. Also a difference of 24 % was identified, between the final distal and central stent diameter (dogboning), caused by the lack of support at the distal end of the stent. The stent struts at distal end caused high stress on the arterial wall. Regarding the effect of stent deployment in the atherosclerotic plaque, in the contact area with the stent, high stresses of 2.651 MPa appeared. Aiming at minimizing the dogboning effect, a second stent (S2) was designed, where the thickness

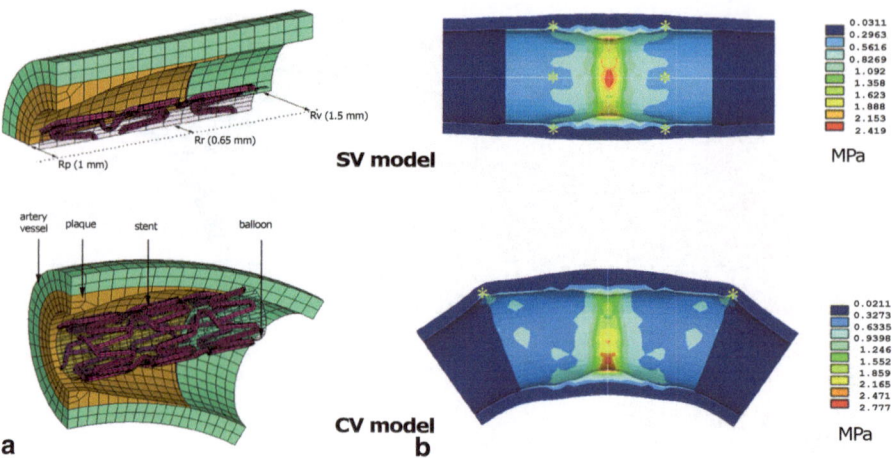

Fig. 10.4 a SV and CV finite element models, **b** Arterial and plaque stress distribution for the SV and CV models. The star symbol presents the area of highest arterial stress for the SV model (0.174 MPa) and the CV model (0.517 MPa). (Reproduced from Wu et al. 2007)

of the distal struts was increased from 0.09 mm to 0.15 mm. The dogboning effect was approximately decreased from 24–10 %, while the maximum plaque stress was reduced from 2.651 MPa to 1.355 MPa. The results of this study provided crucial information for the stent performance and highlighted the necessity of optimizing the stent design.

Curved Idealized Artery

Wu et al. (2007) studied the biomechanical performance of a stent implanted both in idealized, straight (SV model) and curved (CV model), arteries. The SV model included an idealized straight cylinder and a parabolic plaque whereas the curved artery was modeled based on the SV model with a curvature of 0.1 mm^{-1} in a local toroidal coordinate system (Fig. 10.4). The material properties were the same for both models. The artery and the plaque were considered as hyperelastic materials, the stent (316SS) was modeled as a bilinear elastoplastic material and the balloon was modeled as a rigid body. The expansion of the balloon in the SV model was achieved by increasing its diameter to 3.3 mm. In the CV model, the contact was initially deactivated using a specific technique of "element birth and death". The stent expanded due to the displacement—driven boundary condition on the inner balloon's surface. According to the authors, the SV model conformed to the arterial segment in contrast to the CV model. In the CV model, the stent expansion resulted to the straightening of the artery. Also, high stresses were observed in the plaque at the inner curvature and in the artery at the outer curvature. Comparing the SV and CV arterial stresses, the maximum CV stresses were three times larger than the maximum SV stresses. Concluding, these FEM models are a valuable tool for examining the stent deployment in straight and curved diseased arteries and assist in testing the conformability of the existing stents (Fig. 10.4).

10.5.2   Loading Scenarios

Gervaso et al. (2008) modeled stent deployment using three different stent expansion techniques. The artery was modeled as a hollow cylinder and divided into three equal layers (intima, media and adventitia). All the layers were modeled as hyperelastic materials. The Cordis BX-velocity stent (316SS) was modeled as an elasto-plastic material while the semi-compliant balloon was modeled with an isotropic, linear-elastic material. The first simulation (confined-LOAD model) was achieved through imposing directly a pressure to the stent surface. In the second simulation (confined—CYLINDER model), the stent expansion was modeled through a displacement-driven procedure applied to the balloon surface. In the last simulation (confined—BALLOON model), stent deployment was achieved by imposing pressure to the inner surface of a polymeric deformable balloon. The confined-LOAD model presents concentration on radial stresses near to the central section, whereas the maximum circumferential stresses appear in the contact area of the stent struts. In the confined-CYLINDER model stent expansion generated a uniform imprint on the arterial wall (Fig. 10.5). In the confined-BALLOON model the "dogboning" effect appeared while further increase of the pressure had no significant effect on the arterial wall stresses. These different methods of expansion showed that the expansion methodology altered the results and that the deformed shapes and the occurred arterial stresses had significant differences. It is thus concluded that the loading scenario is crucial for the accuracy and correctness of the results.

10.5.3   Stent Design

Gu et al. (2012) compared the effect of stent deployment on the arterial stresses by conducting three simulations with different stent designs and materials (Palmaz–Schatz® stent, Express® stent, and Multilink® stent). The artery was modeled as a straight cylinder and the plaque had a paradolic shape; both components were defined by a hyperelastic isotropic constitutive material model. The Palmaz–Schatz® stent (316SS), Express® stent (316SS) and Multilink® stent (Co-Cr) were modeled as elasto-plastic materials. The balloon component was not included in the modeling technique. For all the models, the stent expansion was simulated by imposing a uniform displacement to the inner surface of the stent. The results showed that the percentage of the stented arterial wall area with von Mises stress over 0.08 MPa was approximately 2.7, 3.6 and 1.6 % for the Palmaz–Schatz® stent, Express® stent and Multilink® stent, respectively. Since the Multilink stent had thinner struts compared to the other two stents, it was speculated that thinner struts provoke a lower

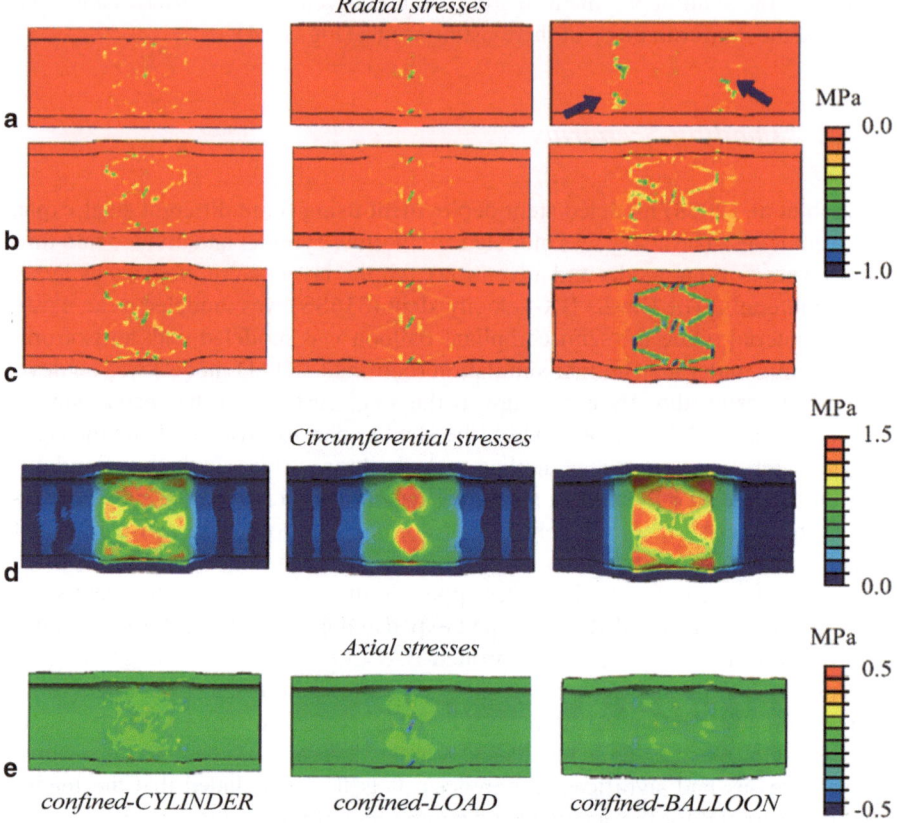

Fig. 10.5 Radial, circumferen-tial and axial stress for the three models. **a** Radial stress at the beginning of the stent-arterial contact and **b** Radial stress at the middle expansion, **c** Radial stress at the end phase of stent deployment, **d** Circumferential stress at the end phase of stent deployment and **e** Axial stress at the end phase of stent deployment. (Repro-duced from Gervaso et al. 2008)

possibility in causing an arterial injury. The impact of the operator's skills and the effect of stent malpositioning were examined by a second simulation. In this simu-lation, the Palmaz–Schatz® stent was deployed closer to the thinner plaque edge and the results revealed that the stresses in the arterial wall increased by 12.7%.

10.5.4   Plaque Composition

Pericevic et al. (2009) evaluated the influence of three different plaque types on the arterial wall followed by stent deployment. The FEM was similar to that re-ported by Gu et al. (2012) and the expansion was simulated using the Cobalt alloy Driver® stent (Medtronic). Depending on the stiffness of the plaque component,

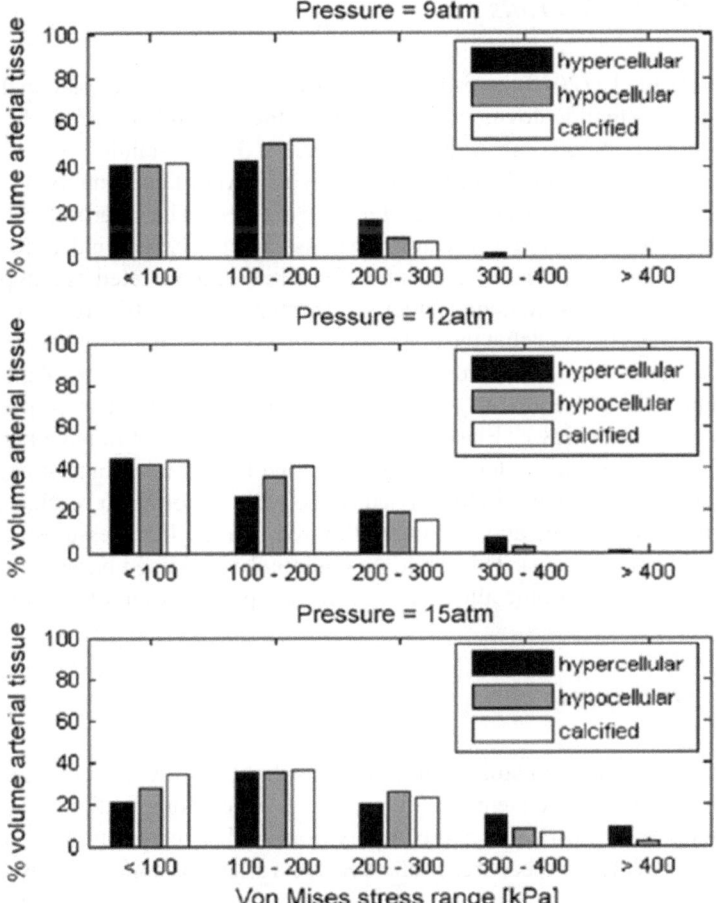

Fig. 10.6 Distribution of the ar-terial volume in specific stress ranges for three different inflation pressures. (Reproduced from Pericevic et al. 2009)

cellular, hypocellular and calcified plaques were selected. All these plaque types were modeled as hyperelastic materials, while the stent was modeled as a bi-linear elasto-plastic material. For all cases, a linear pressure of 15 atm was directly applied to the inner surface of the stent. The results showed that as the inflation pressure increased, the percentage of arterial volume in high stress altered accordingly to the plaque type. More specifically, the stiff plaque protected the arterial tissue by absorbing the high stresses (Fig. 10.6). Thus, it was concluded that the presence of a calcified plaque in a stenotic diseased artery does not increase the risk of potential arterial injury. However, this is not happening with the soft plaques; the risk of arterial damage or plaque rupture is greater in this case.

10.5.5   Stent Materials

Tammareddi and Li (2010) investigated the effect of the stent material on the arterial tissue during stent deployment. The design of the stent was based on the Palmaz-Schatz® stent and four materials were selected: 316 L stainless steel (316SS), cobalt-chrome alloy (CoCrMo), titanium alloy (Ti6Al4V) and unalloyed annealed tantalum. The FEMs consisted of the artery and the stent. The atherosclerotic plaque and the balloon were ignored. The artery was assumed to be a cylinder, divided into three equal sublayers (intima, media and adventitia) and modeled as a hyperelastic material. The stent was expanded under a uniform pressure until it reached a diameter 3 mm. It was observed that the dogboning altered accordingly to the elastic modulus of the stent material. More specifically, Tantalum, Steel and Cobalt Chrome stents (similar Elastic modulus) had a similar dogboning effect in contrast to the Titanium alloy stent (lower Elastic modulus) which presented to have higher dogboning. The pressure-diameter graph revealed that the Tantalum and stainless steel stent required low pressure (approximately 0.6 MPa) in order to reach a diameter 3 mm, while the Chrome and Titanium alloy required higher pressures (1.32 MPa and 1.2 MPa respectively). This could be potentially explained based on the lower elongation of cobalt chrome alloy that governs the plastic strain of the stents.

10.5.6   Our Approach

From the aforementioned studies, it is obvious that the FEM provides great capabilities in optimizing the stent deployment procedure. Computational simulations have resulted to sophisticated and complex models that represent more accurately the stent deployment procedure. Moreover, the variety of commercially available stents and the different material models used have assisted in improving the modeling of stent implantation. The idealized arterial models resulted enormously to the understanding of the structural performance of stents. However, there is an increasing need for examining the behavior of these stents within realistic arterial models. Gijsen et al. (2008) and Mortier et al. (2010) utilized patient specific arterial segments in the modeling of stent deployment and these studies presented a deep insight into the stent performance.

To the best of our knowledge, there has not been any study investigating stent deployment in a reconstructed artery including the characterized plaque in the region of stenosis. Stent simulations in patient specific arteries including characterized plaques could improve and optimize the selection of appropriate stent materials and designs and generally the stent deployment technique. We performed a study of modeling stent deployment in 3D reconstructed arterial geometry with a characterized plaque component (Karanasiou et al. 2013, 2014).

A 62-year old male patient (BMI 27.8) with coronary syndrome was examined. The blood data revealed high levels of cholesterol and hypertension problems.

Fig. 10.7 Geometry of the
fi-nite element model

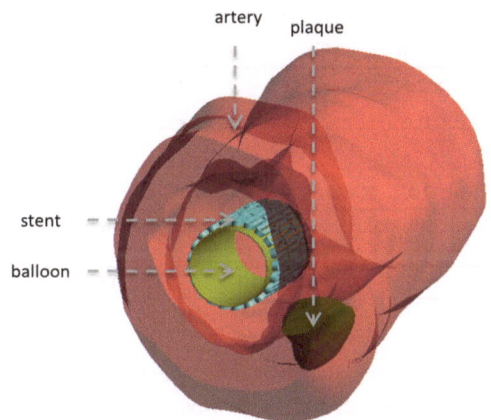

For the 3D reconstruction of the arterial segment, a methodology introduced by
Bourantas et al. (2005) was adopted, where IVUS and angiography data were employed. The IVUS catheter (Atlantis SR 40 MHz, Boston Scientific Corporation,
Natick, MA, USA) was placed into the coronary artery and after injecting contrast
agent, the angiographic images were viewed from two orthogonal sides. The catheter was pulled back at an approximately constant speed of 0.5 mm/sec and the
extracted data were acquired for detecting the lumen and media-adventitia borders.
A specific algorithm was used to represent the luminal and media adventitia point
clouds by placing the 2D detected lumen and media-adventitia borders on the 3D
catheter path. As far as the 3D reconstructed characterized plaque is concerned,
the methodology introduced by Athanasiou et al. (2012) was employed. This semi-
automated methodology mainly consists of three phases. In the first phase the region where plaque exists (ROI) was semi-automatically detected. In the second
phase, a set of features, intensity and geometrical features were extracted for each
pixel of the ROI. In the last phase, these pixels were classified using a Random
Forest classifier. In order to define the finite element model, the geometry of the
artery, the plaque, the balloon and the stent were defined. The stent geometry, based
on the Open stent design (Open Stent Design), was specifically designed for this
arterial segment. To minimize the computational time only a fraction of the stent's
total length was used. The balloon component was modeled as a plane cylinder and
was in initial contact with the outer surface of the balloon. The stent-balloon component was appropriately positioned inside the 3D reconstructed arterial segment
in the region of stenosis. The arterial and plaque length were 17.54 and 3.27 mm,
respectively, while the plaque's thickness varied from 1.05 to 1.40 mm. The finite
element model comprised of the artery, the plaque and the balloon stent device in its
unexpanded state is presented in Fig. 10.7.

The deformation analysis was conducted using the ANSYS 12.1 software (AN-
SYS, Canonsburg, PA). The artery, the plaque and the stent were discretized by

Table 10.1 Hyperelastic coefficients for the arterial wall and the balloon

Coefficients	C_{10}	C_{01}	C_{20}	C_{11}	C_{30}
Artery	0.0189	0.00275	0.08572	0.5904	0
Balloon	1.0318	3.6927	–	–	–

Table 10.2 Material properties of the SS304 stent

Young modulus (GPa)	Shear modulus (GPa)	Tangent modulus (GPa)	Yield stress (MPa)	Poisson ratio
193	75×103	0.692	207	0.27

tetrahedrons elements and the balloon was discretized by hexahedron elements. The density of the mesh was selected on the basis of minimizing the contact areas occurring penetration. In order to certify the quality of the chosen mesh, a mesh sensitivity check was employed, which revealed that the number of the elements was sufficient for numerically accurate results.

The mechanical behavior of the involved components can be described using several material models. In this study, the artery and the balloon were modeled as hyperelastic materials using a third order five parameter Mooney-Rivlin hyperelastic material model, defined by a polynomial form (Eq. 10.1).

$$W = C_{10}(I_1 - 3) + C_{01}(I_2 - 3) + C_{20}(I_1 - 3)^2 + C_{11}(I_1 - 3)(I_2 - 3) + C_{30}(I_1 - 3)^3 \quad (10.1)$$

where W is the strain energy density function of the hyperelastic material and I_1, I_2, I_3 are the strain invariants. The coefficients of Eq. 10.1 derived from the study of Eshghi et al. (2011) are presented in Table 10.1.

The hyperelastic material models are not suitable for describing the non-recoverable deformation of the arterial and plaque interlining. Considering the fact that if both the artery and the plaque were modeled by hyperelastic material models, the resulted recoil ratio would be 100 %, the calcified plaque was modeled as a linear isotropic material model. The Young Modulus was 2.7 MPa and the Poisson's ratio was 0.4913. The stent was assumed to be made of Stainless Steel (SS304) and was modeled using a bi-linear elasto-plastic material (Table 10.2).

The stent was initially in contact with the balloon and the stent expansion was modeled imposing a radial displacement to the inner surface of the balloon. In order to avoid rigid body motion, specific boundary conditions were applied to the finite element model. More particularly, the arterial ends were tethered in all directions and the stent was allowed to expand only radially. Regarding the contact pairs, the balloon-stent contact pair had a frictionless contact while the artery-plaque contact pair was considered to be bonded. The von Mises stresses of the arterial and plaque component for three different cross sections along the arterial longitudinal axis; before (position 1), in (position 2), and after (position 3) the stenotic area are presented in Fig. 10.8.

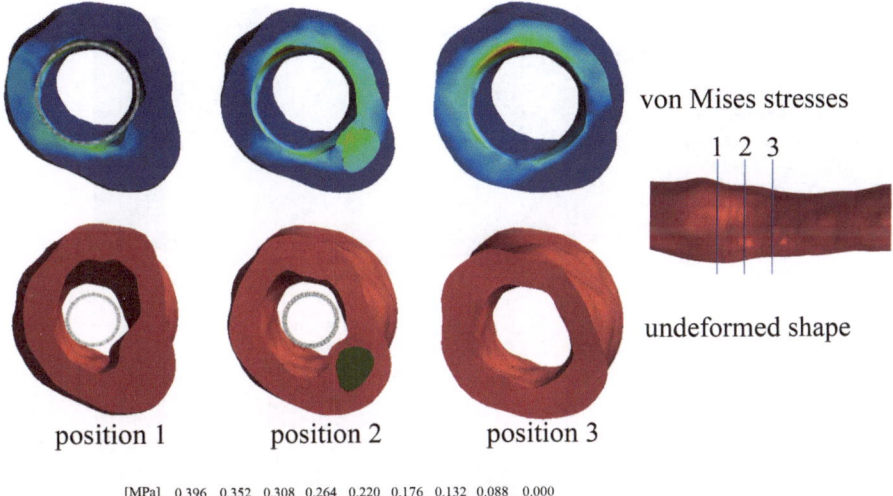

von Mises stresses

1 2 3

undeformed shape

position 1   position 2   position 3

[MPa] 0.396 0.352 0.308 0.264 0.220 0.176 0.132 0.088 0.000

Fig. 10.8 Arterial wall and plaque von Mises stresses for three cross sections

In the first and second row, the von Mises stresses and undeformed shape are presented. The arterial wall is deformed more than the plaque, possibly due to the plaque stiffness. The stresses presented in these two components appear to have differences. The arterial stresses have a descending ratio when going from the arterial lumen outwards, whereas the maximum stresses are depicted at the area across the stenosis.

A longitudinal cross section in the arterial wall shows the increase in the arterial stresses behind the stent struts (Fig. 10.9). It is believed that the fracture of the atherosclerotic plaque is highly associated with the increase of stress (David Chua et al. 2004), thus the examination of the stress in the plaque component is important. The maximum stresses occurred in the plaque component appear in the stent-arterial contact, in the area where the plaque is pushed by the stent (Fig. 10.9).

In some recent studies (Mortier et al. 2010), the modeling of the stent expansion was simulated while the atherosclerotic plaque was ignored. Thus, we decided to pay attention towards the importance of including or not the 3D characterized plaque in the FEM (Karanasiou et al. 2013). The stent deployment was simulated for two cases. Both models consisted of the artery and the stent—balloon device. The second model included additionally the plaque component in the area of stenosis. The material properties, the boundary conditions and the loading technique were the similar to that reported by (Kavanasiou et al. 2014). The arterial stresses for three different cross sections; before (position 1), in (position 2), and after (position 3) the stenotic area along the arterial longitudinal axis were shown for

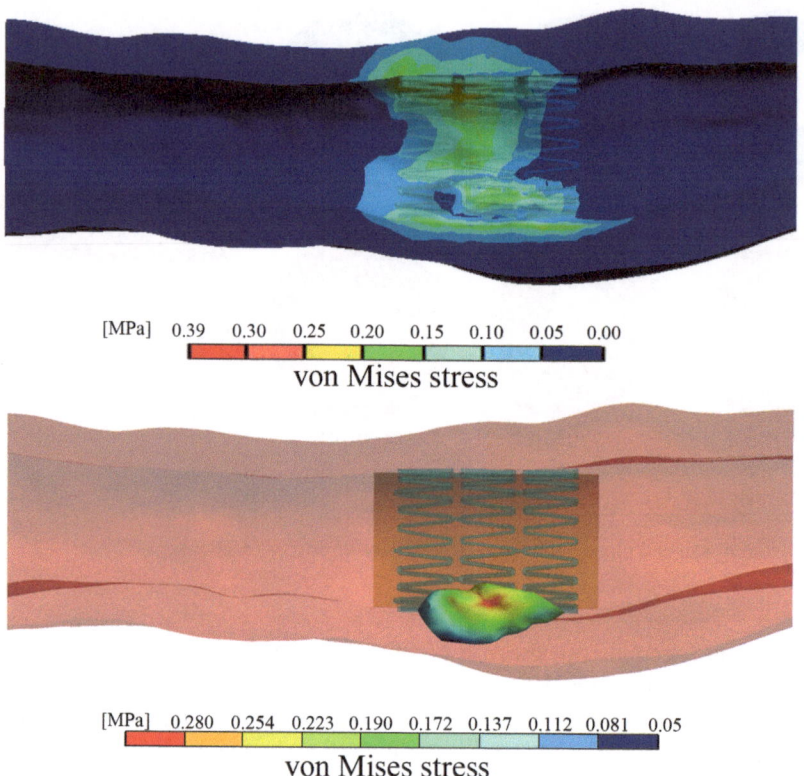

Fig. 10.9 Arterial wall and plaque von Mises stress results

both cases (Fig. 10.10). The difference in the arterial stress is mainly depicted in region of stenosis, where the plaque exists. Also, the second model presents to have higher stresses in this region compared to the first one. It is revealed that the existence of the calcified plaque resulted to the increase of the induced stresses in the area of stenosis. It is also interesting to highlight that in the contact area of the stent struts-arterial wall, for both models, an increase in the arterial stresses appears, but high stresses appear in different areas (Fig. 10.11).

In the first model, the maximum arterial stresses were presented in two different areas. In the second model, the maximum arterial stresses were concentrated in one arterial location. It must be noted that despite the fact that the difference in the maximum arterial stresses was not significant, in the plaque region the difference in the induced stresses ranged from 58–87%. This study demonstrated the criticality of including the plaque geometry and composition in the stent deployment simulations. Moreover, more precise data of the plaque composition could be crucial for predicting the development of plaque rupture.

This study introduces the idea of personalized medicine and is different from existing approaches that examine either idealized geometries or ignore the plaque component.

Fig. 10.10 von Mises stresses for three cross sections. The FEM model **a** with the plaque component and **b** without the plaque compo-nent

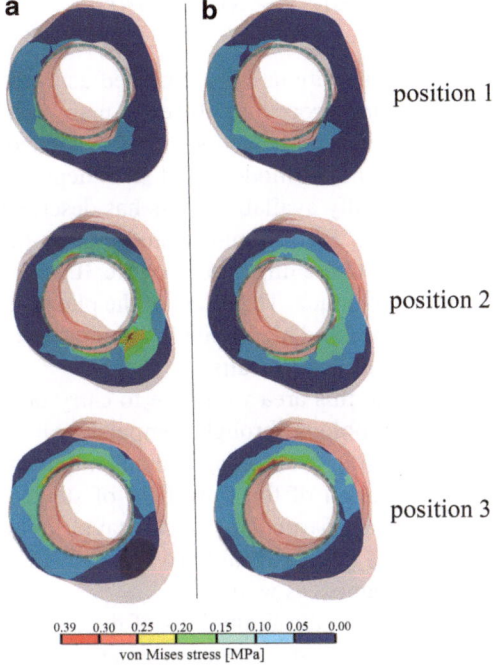

Fig. 10.11 von Mises stresses for the models **a** with and **b** without the plaque compo-nent, respectively

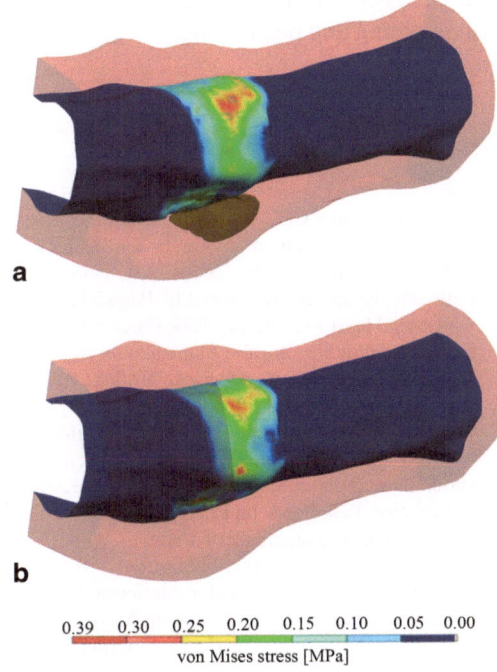

10.6 Conclusions—Future Work

Computational simulations have emerged as a useful tool for assessing and optimizing the stenting procedure. To date, many studies are based on the FEM and examine the mechanical behavior of the stents and the impact of stent deployment in the arterial wall. The modeling of stent deployment in 3D arterial segments using 3D commercially available stents has described the biological behavior of the diseased segments. Some sophisticated models have examined the importance of the stent design and the importance of the 3D reconstructed arterial morphology in the simulation technique. The effect of the plaque composition and morphology has been also examined and highlighted the importance of including the atherosclerotic plaque for more accurate results.

Future work in this area would be to carry out a deep investigation of the atherosclerotic morphology through computational modeling aiming at widening the knowledge in this field and give recommendations for improving treatment. Moreover the examination of the flow field of stented arterial segments would be of much interest. More particularly, the behavior of hemodynamic parameters such as Wall Shear Stress (WSS) would provide valuable information to the cardiologists and the stent designers as well.

Generally, despite the limitations of the aforementioned studies, it must be acknowledged that these studies are of great significance for evaluating different aspects of stent performance. Concluding, the combination of computational modeling and FEA yielded the generation of innovative numerical studies that may assist stent designers, in developing new stent designs, and the cardiologist in optimal stent choosing and positioning.

References

Anderson JL, Adams CD, Antman EM, Bridges CR, Califf RM, Casey DE Jr, Chavey, WE, 2nd, Fesmire, FM, Hochman JS, Levin TN, Lincoff AM, Peterson ED, Theroux P, Wenger NK, Wright RS, Smith SC Jr, Jacobs, AK, Halperin JL, Hunt SA, Krumholz HM, Kushner FG, Lytle BW, Nishimura R, Ornato JP, Page RL, Riegel B (2007) American College of Cardiology, American Heart Association Task Force on Practice Guidelines (Writing Committee to Revise the 2002 Guidelines for the Management of Patients With Unstable Angina/Non ST-Elevation Myocardial Infarction), American College of Emergency Physicians, Society for Cardiovascular Angiography and Interventions, Society of Thoracic Surgeons, American Association of Cardiovascular and Pulmonary Rehabilitation, Society for Academic Emergency Medicine: ACC/AHA 2007 guidelines for the management of patients with unstable angina/non ST-elevation myocardial infarction: a report of the American College of Cardiology/American Heart Association Task Force on Practice Guidelines (Writing Committee to Revise the 2002 Guidelines for the Management of Patients With Unstable Angina/Non ST-Elevation Myocardial Infarction): developed in collaboration with the American College of Emergency Physicians, the Society for Cardiovascular Angiography and Interventions, and the Society of Thoracic Surgeons: endorsed by the American Association of Cardiovascular and Pulmonary Rehabilitation and the Society for Academic Emergency Medicine. Circulation 116:e148–e304

Athanasiou LS, Karvelis PS, Tsakanikas VD, Naka KK, Michalis LK, Bourantas CV, Fotiadis DI (2012) A novel semiautomated atherosclerotic plaque characterization method using grayscale intravascular ultrasound images: comparison with virtual histology. IEEE Trans Inf Technol Biomed. (Publ IEEE Eng Med Biol Soc) 16:391–400

Azaouzi M, Makradi A, Belouettar S (2012) Deployment of a self-expanding stent inside an artery: a finite element analysis. Mater Des 41:410–420

Babuška I, Strouboulis T (2001) The finite element method and its reliability. Oxford University Press, Oxford

Balghith MA, Alghamdi AM, Ayoub KM, Saleh AA, Aziz MS, Algahtany M, Almasood F, Albargy GM (2013) Stent thrombosis is a major concern in clinical practice: a single Saudi center experience. J Saudi Heart Assoc 25:233–238

Balocco S, Gatta C, Ciompi F, Wahle A, Radeva P, Carlier S, Unal G, Sanidas E, Mauri J, Carillo X, Kovarnik T, Wang C-W, Chen H-C, Exarchos TP, Fotiadis DI, Destrempes F, Cloutier G, Pujol O, Alberti M, Mendizabal-Ruiz EG, Rivera M, Aksoy T, Downe RW, Kakadiaris IA (2014) Standardized evaluation methodology and reference database for evaluating IVUS image segmentation. Comput Med Imaging Graph. 38(2):70–90. doi:10.1016/j.compmedimag.2013.07.001. Epub 2013 September 6.

Bentzon JF, Falk E (2013) Chapter 47—atherosclerosis, vulnerable plaques, and acute coronary syndromes. In: Ginsburg GS, Willard HF (eds) Genomic and personalized medicine, 2nd edn. Academic Press, London, pp 530–539

Boo S, Froelicher ES (2012) Cardiovascular risk factors and 10-year risk for coronary heart disease in Korean women. Asian Nurs Res 6:1–8

Bourantas CV, Kourtis IC, Plissiti ME, Fotiadis DI, Katsouras CS, Papafaklis MI, Michalis LK (2005) A method for 3D reconstruction of coronary arteries using biplane angiography and intravascular ultrasound images. Comput Med Imaging Graph. (Off J Comput Med Imaging Soc) 29:597–606

Cornwell LD, Preventza O, Bakaeen F (2014) Chapter 21—coronary artery bypass surgery. In: Levine GN (ed) Cardiology secrets, 4th edn. W.B. Saunders, Philadelphia

David Chua SN, MacDonald BJ, Hashmi MSJ (2004) Finite element simulation of slotted tube (stent) with the presence of plaque and artery by balloon expansion. J Mater Process Technol 155–156:1772–1779

Eshghi N, Hojjati MH, Imani M, Goudarzi AM (2011) Finite element analysis of mechanical behaviors of coronary stent. Procedia Eng 10:3056–3061

Gervaso F, Capelli C, Petrini L, Lattanzio S, Di Virgilio L, Migliavacca F (2008) On the effects of different strategies in modelling balloon-expandable stenting by means of finite element method. J Biomech 41:1206–1212

Giglioli C, Valente S, Margheri M, Comeglio M, Chiostri M, Romano SM, Saletti E, Falai M, Chechi T, Gensini GF (2009) An angiographic evaluation of restenosis rate at a six-month follow-up of patients with ST-elevation myocardial infarction submitted to primary percutaneous coronary intervention. Int J Cardiol 131:362–369

Gijsen FJ, Migliavacca F, Schievano S, Socci L, Petrini L, Thury A, Wentzel JJ, Steen AF, van der Serruys PW, Dubini G (2008) Simulation of stent deployment in a realistic human coronary artery. Biomed Eng OnLine 7:23

Gu L, Zhao S, Froemming SR (2012) Arterial wall mechanics and clinical implications after coronary stenting: comparisons of three stent designs. Int J Appl Mech 04:1250013

Holzapfel GA, Gasser TC, Ogden RW (2000) A new constitutive framework for arterial wall mechanics and a comparative study of material models. J Elast Phys Sci Solids 61:1–48

Karanasiou GS, Sakellarios AI, Tripoliti EE, Petrakis EG, Zervakis ME, Migliavacca F, Dubini G, Dordoni E (2013) Modeling stent deployment in realistic arterial segment geometries: the effect of the plaque composition. 13th IEEE International Conference on BioInformatics and BioEngineering (IEEE BIBE 2013). Chania.

Karanasiou GS, Sakellarios AI, Tripoliti EE, Petrakis EGM, Zervakis ME, Migliavacca F, Dubini G, Dordoni E, Michalis LK, Fotiadis DI (2014) Modeling of stent implantation in a human stenotic artery. In: Romero LMR (ed) XIII mediterranean conference on medical and biological engineering and computing 2013. Springer International Publishing, pp 1045–1048

Kathuria YP (2006) The potential of biocompatible metallic stents and preventing restenosis. Mater Sci Eng A 417:40–48

Khan MG (2006) Chapter 9—angioplasty/coronary balloon. In: Khan MG (ed) Encyclopedia of heart diseases. Academic, Burlington, pp 57–60

Kwok O-H (2013) Stent "concertina:" stent design does matter. J Invasive Cardiol 25:E114–E119

Lévesque J, Dubé D, Fiset M, Mantovani D (2004) Materials and properties for coronary stents. Adv Mater Process 162:45–48

Libby P (2013) Chapter 8—atherosclerosis. In: Creager MA, Beckman JA, Loscalzo J (eds) Vascular medicine: a companion to braunwald's heart disease, 2nd edn. W.B. Saunders, Philadelphia, pp 111–125

Martin D, Boyle FJ (2011) Computational structural modelling of coronary stent deployment: a review. Comput Method Biomech Biomed Engin 14:331–348

Mathers CD, Loncar D (2006) Projections of global mortality and burden of disease from 2002 to 2030. PLoS Med 3:e442

Mortier P, De Beule M (2011) Stent design back in the picture: an engineering perspective on longitudinal stent compression. EuroIntervention J Eur Collab Work. (Group Interv Cardiol Eur Soc Cardiol) 7:773, 775

Mortier P, Holzapfel GA, De Beule M, Van Loo D, Taeymans Y, Segers P, Verdonck P, Verhegghe B (2010) A novel simulation strategy for stent insertion and deployment in curved coronary bifurcations: comparison of three drug-eluting stents. Ann Biomed Eng 38:88–99

Open SD, http://www.nitinol.com.

Ormiston JA, Webber B, Webster MWI (2011) Stent longitudinal integrity bench insights into a clinical problem. JACC Cardiovasc Inter 4:1310–1317

Pericevic I, Lally C, Toner D, Kelly DJ (2009) The influence of plaque composition on underlying arterial wall stress during stent expansion: the case for lesion-specific stents. Med Eng Phys 31:428–433

Peterson ED, Coombs LP, Ferguson TB, Shroyer AL, DeLong ER, Grover FL, Edwards FH (2002) Hospital variability in length of stay after coronary artery bypass surgery: results from the society of thoracic surgeon's national cardiac database. Ann Thorac Surg 74:464–473

Robertson AM, Watton PN (2013) Chapter 8—mechanobiology of the arterial wall. In: Becker SM, Kuznetsov AV (eds) Transport in biological media. Elsevier, Boston, pp 275–347

Sherman DL, Ryan TJ (1995) Coronary angioplasty versus bypass grafting. Cost-benefit considerations. Med Clin North Am 79(5):1085–1095

Silva J, Carrillo X, Salvatella N (2011) Simultaneous two-vessel very late stent thrombosis and coronary aneurysm formation after sirolimus-eluting stent implantation: an intravascular ultrasound evaluation. J Invasive Cardiol 23:E128–E131

Silva T, Sequeira A, Santos RF, Tiago J (2013) Mathematical modeling of atherosclerotic plaque formation coupled with a non-newtonian model of blood flow. Conf Pap Math 2013:1–14

Stary HC (2000) Natural history and histological classification of atherosclerotic lesions: an update. Arterioscler Thromb Vasc Biol 20:1177–1178

Surdell D, Shaibani A, Bendok B, Eskandari MK (2007) Fracture of a nitinol carotid artery stent that caused restenosis. J Vasc Interv Radiol JVIR 18:1297–1299

Tammareddi S, Li Q (2010) Effects of material on the deployment of coronary stents. Adv Mater Res 123–125:315–318

Wang Y, Yi H, Ni Z (2005) Computational biomechanics and experimental verification of vascular stent. In: Hao Y, Liu J, Wang Y, Cheung Y, Yin H, Jiao L, Ma J, Jiao Y-C (eds) Computational intelligence and security. Lecture Notes in Computer Science Volume 3801. Springer, pp 870–877

WHO | Global status report on non communicable diseases 2010. WHO. http://www.who.int/nmh/publications/ncd_report2010/en/. Accessed April 2011

Wu W, Wang W-Q, Yang D-Z, Qi M (2007) Stent expansion in curved vessel and their interactions: a finite element analysis. J Biomech 40:2580–2585

Yang X-S, Koziel S, Leifsson L (2013) Computational optimization, modelling and simulation: recent trends and challenges. Procedia Comput Sci 18:855–860

Zhao S, Gu L, Froemming SR, Hammel JM, Lang H (2011) Finite element analysis of stent deployment in a stenotic artery and their interactions. (iCBBE) 2011 5th International Conference on Bioinformatics and Biomedical Engineering. pp 1–4

Zheng S, Mengchan L (2013) Reconstruction of coronary vessels from intravascular ultrasound image sequences based on compensation of the in-plane motion. Comput Med Imaging Graph 37:618–627

Zienkiewicz OC, Taylor RL, Fox D (2014) Chapter 15—computer procedures for finite element analysis. In: Zienkiewicz OC, Taylor RL, Fox D (eds) The finite element method for solid and structural mechanics, 7th edn. Butterworth-Heinemann, Oxford, pp 589–595

Chapter 11
Development of Collaborative Modular Assembly Micro-Robot Colonies for Use in Natural Orifice Transluminal Endoscopic Surgery: The LABYRINTH Approach

Dimitra Iliopoulou, Georgios Papantonakis, Alexandros Perrakis, Athina A. Lazakidou, Maria Petridou, Kostas Giokas, Nikos Katevas and Dionysios-Dimitrios Koutsouris

Abstract From the mid-1980s up to date, the progress in the field of surgery is rapid. In late 90s, laparoscopic surgery had already been established from both practical and theoretical point of view. This, along with the evolution of technology, paved the way towards the broad application of minimally invasive surgery. During the very first interventions robots were tools with minor roles besides the operation table (e.g. Probot). The introduction of the daVinci system, made the breakthrough towards the wide application of robotic assisted surgery, and still today maintains the lead position in the field. Recently, NOTES (Natural Orifice Transluminal Endoscopic Surgery), gave another dimension to minimally invasive surgery. The main innovation in NOTES is that the endoscope and other surgical tools are inserted to human body through natural holes such as mouth anus etc. Endoscopic surgery is a well-developed method and therefore a wide variety of tools are already existing. Based on this and in order to support this technique, various types of micro-robots have been developed, that are building upon the NOTES concept and are supporting

D. Iliopoulou (✉) · G. Papantonakis · A. Perrakis · K. Giokas · D.-D. Koutsouris
Biomedical Engineering Laboratory, School of Electrical and Computer Engineering, National Technical University of Athens, Heroon Polytechneiou Str. 9, 15780 Zografou, Athens, Greece
e-mail: dilio@biomed.ntua.gr

D.-D. Koutsouris
e-mail: dkoutsou@biomed.ntua.gr

N. Katevas
Department of Automation Engineering, Technological Educational Institute of Sterea Ellada, 3440 Psahna, Evia, Greece

A. A. Lazakidou
Department of Nursing Faculty of Human Movement and Quality of Life Sciences, University of Peloponnese, Orthias Artemidos & Plateon, 23100 Sparta, Greece
e-mail: lazakid@uop.gr

M. Petridou
School of Computer Science & IT Jubilee Campus, The University of Nottingham, Wollaton Road, NG8 1BB Nottingham, UK
e-mail: psxmp4@exmail.nottingham.ac.uk

D.-D. Koutsouris, A. A. Lazakidou (eds.), *Concepts and Trends in Healthcare Information Systems,* Annals of Information Systems 16,
DOI 10.1007/978-3-319-06844-2_11, © Springer International Publishing Switzerland 2014

like their conventional counterparts endoscopic operations biopsies. Concurrently, in the medical field there has been the development of nanosurgery techniques which consequently led to development of nanorobots in order to support this trend. The last some of those equipped with biosensors and actuators. This paper proposes the so-called L.A.BY.R.IN.TH (Life Aided By Robotic Intrabdominal Therapists) as a holistic approach towards an integrated system based on NOTES.

Keywords Laparoscopic surgery · Minimally invasive surgery · DaVinci · NOTES · Endoscopes · Micro-robots · Nanosurgery · Biosensors · L.A.BY.R.IN.TH

11.1 Introduction

Almost two decades ago, laparoscopic surgery began as innovative experiments aiming at surgery without scars. The experiments were successful and paved the way to minimally invasive surgery. In general, minimally invasive surgery is the method which when applied concludes to relatively small incision to the skin, (half to two centimeters long) instead of the relatively larger (about 15 cm) which are caused by conventional surgery. In the recent years new techniques like SILS (Single Incision Lap-band Surgery) and robotic surgery have been established (Westebring-van der Putten et al. 2008; Walid and Heaton 2010). Laparoscopic surgery is performed trough two to four incisions depending on the actual operation (appr. half a centimeter each), which are used as insertion points for the laparoscopic tools. Laparoscopic surgery is supported by telescopic camera which is inserted through a small incision in the abdominal wall (appr. 1 cm). In order to enable adequate field of view, the abdominal cavity is inflated with carbon dioxide. During the endoscopic surgery the surgeon is able to see the operation field trough the video collected by the endoscopic camera and also adjust the field of view according to the operation demands. Nowadays laparoscopic surgery is well established and applied in several cases like cholecystectomy, hernia treatment, appendectomy, treatment of gastroesophageal reflux, treatment of esophageal achalasia (also called thoracoscopic treatment), kardiomyotomis etc. One of the main advantages of laparoscopy surgery is that there is a minimal tissue damage in order to reach the point of interest, which subsequently concludes to a minimal recovery time for the patient. This is because the surgeon is able to reach the region of interest without the large surgical incisions that occur with the conventional operations. This usually results in less pain after surgery, faster recovery, shorter admission times and costs. In the common case the patient can be discharged from the hospital the day after (Laparoscopic Surgery. http://el.wikipedia.org/wiki).

Robotic surgery emerged from robotics and telemedicine technology. Until recently it was not possible to perform remote surgeries without having the patient and the surgeon at the same place. Remote surgeries require strict medical approvals. Modern information technologies have advanced several fields involved in robotic surgery and medical procedures. During the last years robotic surgery evolved and was able to offer flexible tools with larger workspace, more DoF and higher precision giving the surgeons the ability to better use their skills and be supported by advanced techniques e.g 3D visual content of the surgical field (Ahmed et al. 2009). Thus, by the help robotic surgery technologies operations that were considered in the past as exceptional cases are now considered routine surgeries. Surgery with the help of robots is the most recent advancement in the field of laparoscopy and minimally invasive surgery. Robotic surgery is currently the most promising method since it overcomes the limitations of laparoscopy (2D vision, ergonomic issues, limited of degrees of freedom, etc). Benefits include: movement freedom during the operation, advanced tools e.g. enhanced information in 3D through augmented reality images, higher precision, robustnest etc. (Lanfranco et al. 2004; Robotic Surgery http://library.thinkquest.org/03oct/00760; Kostantinidis 2008).

Although robotic surgical technology is constantly enhancing in recent years, it has not yet been possible to overcome some important limitations that characterize it. One of the main disadvantages of robotic surgery is its cost. Two relatively recent studies have shown that the increased cost of robotic surgery compared to that of conventional methods is mainly due to the initial purchase cost of robotic systems and annual maintenance costs. Another disadvantage of robotic surgery is the large mass of the systems used today. Both the robot body (equipped with robotic arms) and the central surgeon's console, occupy considerable space in the operating room. In terms of perception and control, robots are controlled by computers, thus share many of the weaknesses that the last present, especially on issues related sensor fusion. Due to principal design decisions, surgical robotic systems have limited ability to integrate and utilize information from ad hoc sensors, despite the fact that they embed the computational power required to handle complex three-dimensional images. In the common case there is no autonomous robot movements. The lack of compatible equipment and relevant standards are also contributing to the limitations. Tactile feedback is an important element that surgeon needs to have. "Replication" of the actual feel of human tissue being manipulated by surgical tools through tactile feedback, is under experimental stage although some approaches have been presented (Lanfranco et al. 2004; Robotic Surgery http://library.thinkquest.org/03oct/00760; Morris 2005).

11.2 The da Vinci Surgical System

The robotic da Vinci system has been developed by Intuitive Surgical Inc. in 1995. The main aim was to offer robotic surgery solutions that can be widely applied. Using technology developed by IBM and MIT, the company developed robotic arms and tools that can support surgery through small incisions.

The da Vinci system consists of the surgeon's console, which includes the main computer, special drivers, footswitches and the control console itself. The surgical tower is situated besides the patient, consists of a central brace that can support up to four robotic arms (depending on the version of the system) (Camarillo et al. 2004). Detachable surgical instruments may be attached to the second or the third robotic arm, while the main arm manipulates the endoscopic imaging system. This system provides a high resolution three-dimensional image of the surgical field (Gary et al.). The three-dimensional imaging system used, called InSite provides the surgeon with real three-dimensional images of the surgical field, matching eye-hand-instrument and the required natural depth perception for precise tissue manipulation (Gary et al.) http://biomed.brown.edu/Courses/BI108/BI108_2005_Groups/04/davinci.html. The overall system includes a comprehensive range of innovative, removable (EndoWrist) surgical instruments, which provide surgeons the physical ability and the range of motion required for delicate operations through small incisions. Incorporated tools have been designed with seven degrees of freedom and joints imitating the manipulation features of human hands EndoWrist Instruments, Intuitive Surgical. Inc.

The da Vinci SHD system is an improved version of the initial da Vinci system. It provides enhanced features, like HD displays, with enhanced resolution and clarity (as required for detailed depiction of the levels of tissue anatomy), panoramic viewing, larger viewing area, digital zoom capability (helping the to reduction of interference between the endoscope and the surgical instruments), stereo imaging endoscopes etc. Also there is improved dexterity and precision, (Intuitive Movement technology) that enable enhanced precision of the EndoWrist tools, better ergonomics (surgeon's body posture and optimal alignment hands and eyes), provisions for fast and safe preparation of the system before the surgery, faster and controlled access to the patient etc. There is a fourth robotic arm and an new advanced user interface that includes integrated monitor with touch screen, TilePro technology with multiple inputs for the presentation of critical patient information, LED and status icons and telestration tools for improved surveillance and communication of the surgical team The TilePro display enables the presentation of three dimensional video of the surgical field, along with two additional video sources, such as ultrasound and electrocardiograph (EKG) The daVinci Surgical System, Intuitive Surgical. Inc.

11.3   Natural Orifice Transluminal Endoscopic Surgery (NOTES)

Laparoscopic Surgery has practically replaced the conventional open surgery in many surgeries. Aiming at lesser invasive techniques, research community investigated the option of performing e.g. intra-abdominal surgery through natural holes, by the use of flexible endoscopes or approaching the peritoneal cavity through an incision in the stomach wall, vagina or bowel. Endoscopic surgery through natural holes or Natural Orifice Transluminal Endoscopic Surgery (NOTES), is the most modern technique of minimally invasive surgery widely applied to operations in abdominal cavity. This technique removes the need of skin incisions as insertion of surgical tools is made through natural holes of the human body (e.g. mouth, anus, vagina). Most of interventions reported are at an experimental stage on animals. Although reported as successful, there are limitation as regards the actual clinical practice (http://www.intuitivessurgical.com/products). Only a few NOTES have been performed in humans. The potential benefits to the patient from this innovative technique are numerous. There is a significant reduction of postoperative pain because there are no incisions in the abdominal wall. Also, the amount of general anesthesia administered is significantly reduced even in comparison to laparoscopy. Also the suppression of the immune system that has been occurred after surgery, is expected to be much smaller. There is a reduced use of postoperative painkillers, and faster recovery from surgery (Camarillo et al. 2004).

Flexible endoscopes are the main tools used in minimally invasive methods. The dimensions of a typical endoscope are, 10 mm (diameter) by 70–180 mm (length). Endoscopes are inserted into an organ/cavity mainly for samples picking or for the actual treatment. There are various types of endoscopes lately a new generation of advanced endoscopes have been presented. The endoscope "HARP" consisting of an inner and outer "snake" made of rigid cylindrical connectors, which are connected together (Degani et al. 2006). By pulling or relaxing the wires, the endoscope can be rigid or flexible, which is similar to ShapeLock technology. Also the endoscopic system "ViaCath" consists of a toolholder, a flexible shaft and a joint with an actuated end, mechanical properties of which are assessed, but still need validations in models and animal models (Abbott et al. 2007). The USGI Medicine developed a prototype named "Cobra", which has three independent "hands" controlled by a robotic interface (The Incisionless Operating Platform, USGI Medical. Inc). Olympus has developed a standard dual channel therapeutic endoscope, called the "R" endoscope for NOTES, allowing it to be placed close to the target area and then to be secured (Yonezawa et al. 2006). The improved flexible endoscopes are useful for some direct motion intra-abdominal procedures. However, there are still deficiencies due to their inherent characteristics. An important point is that the flexibility makes them difficult to handle tissue. Due to the small size of the endoscope channels, end-operators of most organs are small and weak. Larger with more channels allow some degrees of freedom but they are still insufficient. Some instruments require the removal of the device for changing tools each time a new tool is required. Moreover, the complexity of the devices does not allow a physical controlled movement of the tip and thus the end of the instrument doesn't perform precise maneuvers.

The NOTES is based on flexible gastroscopes that enter the peritoneal cavity through the stomach, the bladder, the vagina, and the gut. Research aims in advancement at topics, like, the ideal passage in the peritoneal cavity, the exact point to conduct the hole on the instrument which can differ depending on the type of surgery and intraabdominal locating of the surgical field, and finally the most appropriate technique to perform the hole. Also medical research is looking for the most suitable method of closing the incision after the surgery, which will ensure nearly 100 % safety and reliability of the process and will prevent the dispersion of bacteria from the organ through which the hole is made to access the peritoneal cavity, which can lead to the development of intra-abdominal inflammatory complications (Knight et al. 2005). Several methods have been developed of the creation of the insertion points. According to the technique of transurethral/transvesical access based on the Seldinger technique an ureteroscope is positioned through the urethra into the bladder, which expands using CO_2. Incision performed in the dome of the bladder, and a diameter guide with flexible tip is inserted into the peritoneal cavity. After completing the surgery the CO_2 is being removed from the peritoneal cavity, followed by the exit of ureteroscopes and entering a urethral Foley catheter (Lima et al. 2006, 2007). According to another technique the access is performed through the intestinal system. The incision at the front edge of the colon can be made either by palpation of the abdominal wall, either, unlike the collection of fluid, intraluminally. Most surgeons use the endoscopic scalpel for conducting a small incision (2–3 mm) in the wall of the colon (Fong et al. 2007; Wilhelm et al. 2007; Raju et al. 2005, 2008). Once the scalpel passes through the wall of the colon, the endoscope can been easily inserted because the insertion itself causes a subsequent expansion of the initial hole. In contrast to the transabdominal access and because of the lesser thickness of the colon wall, the method does not require the use of an expander. There is relevant bibliography on transabdominal access, presenting the advantages of the universal application of the method on both sexes (Romanelli et al. 2008). By means of palpation of the upper abdomen and under endoscopic guidance, the part of the stomach wall which is in direct contact with the peritoneum corresponding to the anterior abdominal wall, is recognized. By means of an intradermal injection with a large needle and under endoscopic guidance, a guide enters through it into the lumen of the stomach. By the use of specially designed endoscopic scalpel which is able to carve and cauterize tissues, the part of stomach wall positioned adjusting the driver is been transected, throughout its thickness and for a length of 3 mm. An expansion of the hole, from 3 to 12 mm, is caused by the use of a 18 to 20 mm diameter expander which is guided by the driver (Blessing et al. 2005). There is also a widely used technique which involves the use of the guide (inserted endoscopically into the peritoneal cavity), which presents sufficiently safe results also on humans (Merrifield et al. 2006). Also, the experience gained by gynaecologists through transvaginal surgery led to the knowledge of access points in vagina.

In addition to the access methods there are methods used for closing the access hole. The injuries of adjacent organs must be avoided and more importantly it should provide the option of full closure of the edges of the hole, in a similar way with traditional surgical closure in two layers, mucosa and serosa liner. For closing the transurethral access, there is a three steps technique (a) pass a needle through the edge of the hole; open a T-tag system and release suture from the needle retained in the outer surface of the bladder, (b) the needle captures the opposite end of the incision, followed by a Tag system release and (c) knotting and cutting of suture is achieved by a special mechanical system. The incision is closed by pulling the sutures from both ends up to be included in the capture system, so the seams are cut and removed. Most recently a team conducted a successful closure of an access road using endoloop, which was introduced through trocar 15 mm in the peritoneal cavity, while using a endoscopic clamp 2 mm for the bladder (Metzelder et al. 2009).

Methods for closing the incisions on the abdominal cavity are divided into four categories: systems of simple suture, automatic stapling devices, clips use and mechanical obstruction. In simple seaming systems there are the T-Fastener systems which comprise a seam of nonabsorbable material (monofilament) mounted on a metal T-shaped restraint system (T-tag), which bears on the edge a long empty needle in which is fitted the automatic release closing system (Sumiyama et al. 2007; Matthews et al. 2002). Still, there is the Eagle Claw system whose mechanism uses two antiparallel jaws (at 23 mm), which move rapidly and simultaneously, one to hold the tissue and the other consisting of a nylon non-absorbable suture $3-0$ with a detachable needle attached to a curved slot, is being inserted to the tissue with the union of two jaws. Then, the needle trapped in the plastic connector to the second jaw and the knot is completed by tying the suture, bringing the plastic jack on the mucosa (Pham et al. 2006; Chiu et al. 2008). There is also the USGI G-Prox needle whose technique involves capturing the two ends of the hole with a 19 pin gauge (helped by a toothed capture tool)in the ends of which two grids are adapted (by the use of non-absorbable sutures). Once they both release, pulling one edge of the suture causes an approaching to the grids followed by the approaching of the edges of the incision (Arezzo and Morino 2010; Swanstrom 2006). Regarding automatic stapling systems, the devices have the PMI SurgASSIST system suitable for use from flexible endoscopes, based on the same principles as those of classic and laparoscopic surgery. The startup of the device is relatively easy, however, the required manipulation of the tissue, for the correct positioning between the legs of the device, is extremely difficult and potentially time consuming (Sherwinter and Eckstein 2009; Kaehler et al. 2006). Clips are applied by the use of the so-called jumbo clips, placement of which starts from both ends of the incision stomach and progressively directed towards it's center (thereof the use of 4–6 clips per section are required) (Von Delius et al. 2008). Furthermore, Over-the-scope clips are used which are made of Nitinol, a material with significant flexibility, which can approaches the edges of significant voids. Immediately after their release from the device, and applying them on the deficit, they return to their original size and shape, exercising considerable pulling power and approaching automatically the edges of the hole (Kirschniak et al. 2007; Rolanda et al. 2009; Schurr et al. 2008). Finally a system of mechanical obstruction is the Nitinol cardiac septal occluder. It consists of a device capable of self-tapping, umbrella-shaped, with two layers, one on the inside and one on the outside surface for blocking communication made of nitinol, lattice-like grid, interposed between them a smaller diameter structure, as a connecting link. To prevent possible detachment, the umbrella-shaped structure has special support from non-permeable material. After extensive tests of these methods he IRCAD medical team of Strasbourg, it concluded that this device is currently the perfect selection for closing the gastric hole after the access (Arrezzo and Morino 2010).

11.4   Notes Micro-Robots

The development of micro electromechanical systems (or MEMS) in the late twentieth century enabled the development of robots in very small size (less than a centimeter) which were called Micro-Robots. Due to the small size of micro-robots, the mass production costs have dropped to low levels. When built and deployed in large numbers small-robots presenting similar behavior (robotic swarms) they could collaborate and develop as a team different functionality features compared to the individual robot and therefore all together perform a specific function (Zygomalas et al. 2014). However, design of micro-robot have to take care of critical issues like low energy consumption at least for the most energy consuming functions (e.g. motion). Energy consumption is also critical for other functions like data acquisition and transmission. Developments in this area include advanced robotic system for in vivo exploration of the abdominal cavity, equipped with wireless cameras in a form of a pill, which can swallowed and move in the body (Zygomalas et al. 2012). Commercially available devices in this are include the PillCam SB, a capsule shaped device equipped with a video acquisition device and a light source, which transmits images at a rate of two images per second. This produces more than 50,000 images during a period of 8 h (Given Imaging's PillCam SB 2009). The micro-robots that have been built or studied so far can be divided into six categories: (i) In vivo fixed base camera micro robots, (ii) In vivo mobile camera micro-robots (iii) in vivo mobile biopsy micro-robots, (iv) In vivo endoluminal mobile micro-robots (v) In vivo cooperation micro-robots (vi) In vivo dexterous micro-robots.

11.4.1   In Vivo Fixed Base Camera Micro Robots

Representative examples in this category include two systems. The first is a three axis device encapsulated in an aluminum case of 15 mm diameter and 60 mm height The motion is produced by a DC permanent magnet motor which is used to impart motion to the tilt mechanism. The device is controlled by the surgeon by the use of external switches. The device can rotate in two axes and change angles. This allows the surgeon, to observe the peritoneal cavity in depth according to the needs of the specific intervention. On board LEDs provide the required illumination. The second is an in-vivo stereoscopic imaging platform with 5-DOF. The device, is encapsulated in a 11/16" tube and it is equipped with two miniature cameras and five motors. The motors provide the differential motion required to the onboard cameras in order to produce the stereoscopic view of the surgical field. At the initial stage at which the device is inserted in the body, the cameras are retracted and protected by an outer shell. At the stage at which the device is located at appropriate position inside the peritoneal cavity, a motor rotates an inner shell to expose the cameras. Once this happens, the cameras can be tilted together or move independently along their axis and at a range of angles in order to produce stereoscopic vision of the points of interest. Although not currently materialized, this device is mature enough and is to be committed to physical prototype, aiming in-vivo tests on surgery models, animals etc. (Forgione 2009; Rentschler et al. 2008).

11.4.2   In Vivo Mobile Camera Micro-Robots

In this category the most representative device is that of a micro-robot with 2-DOF for motion, in a configuration of two independent motors. The wheels have been designed with the precaution that the robot has to travel and cross the abdominal organs without causing tissue damage. The device is 75 mm in length and 15 mm in diameter. This robot is controlled by the operator by a joystick. There is an additional DOF for the onboard camera. Special provisions facilitate a set of tools that enable the change of their position relative to the imaging lens. (Forgione 2009; Rentschler et al. 2008).

11.4.3   *In Vivo Mobile Biopsy Micro-Robots*

When designing biopsy robots, there are some specific requirements that differentiate this robot category to those as above. The three main requirements are: The robot should have sufficient clamping force in order to cut and remove tissue. The robot should have sufficient grip not only to pass through the abdominal cavity, but also enough to pull out the sample (in the case the cut was not clear). The robot should provide effective visual feedback, to serve the purposes of both the exploration and the biopsy procedures. Examples of devices in this category that are fulfilling all the three main requirements as above have been already developed. Such an example is composed by a mobile platform for visual feedback and effective tissue sampling. The device is equipped with two independently controlled wheels enabling forward, backward and rotational motion, along with features for biopsy forceps activation and vision system control (Mark et al.).

11.4.4   *In Vivo Endoluminal Mobile Micro-Robots*

In this category a set of subunits (micro-robots) that collaboratively present the overall system functionality. The subunits are inserted through natural holes (e.g. by swallowing). After the insertion the subunits are in-vivo assembled in the region of interest (e.g. esophagus, stomach, colon etc.) and form a larger structure that presents overall articulation, manipulation and exploration features, that are different to the features of the individual subunits. A representative example in this category is the Assembling Reconfigurable Endo-luminal Surgical System. There are variations in the approach that a modular robotic system can follow. According to one of those approaches all modules (subunits) follow a homogeneous shape and all subunits are identical except for one or two surgical or diagnostic units. In this approach, the interconnection is not critical because the subunits can be connected without taking into account the special e.g. sequential combination or a specific orientation. Since the configurations depend of the degrees of freedom implied by homogeneous in series connected subunits, the path planning and the overall control is not complicated. According to another approach, the overall modular robotic system is using heterogeneous subunits which in the general case consist of one or more branching units, structural units and additional functional units. Such a robot configuration enables surgical interventions that require peculiar and non-conventional reach and in general operations that cannot be served by the serial configuration model of the previous approach. However, the advanced features bring associated high demands e.g. for the advanced kinematics to control the overall robot, the difficulties during the initial in-vivo assembly etc. Advantages of the approach include the variety of topologies that can be implemented through a redeployment or through the repeated connection and disconnection of the subunits. From the surgical point of view the procedures and the steps that have to be follow are almost identical for both of the above approaches. Before the operation the stomach needs to be expanded (e.g. consumption of a liquid) to enable vision. The stomach fluid also serves the needs to have a reference plane for the subunits. The reference place makes the initial assembly easier and faster. Shortly after, the initial configuration is achieved (according to the preoperative plan) the main aim of the intervention may start (Harada et al. 2010.

11.4.5   In Vivo Cooperation Micro-Robots

In this category the overall robot is composed by three purpose dedicated micro-robots that each present a specific functionality: an imaging robot, a lighting robot and a retraction robot. This category is different to previous one because the micro-robots are not linked together in an overall robot assembly. However, in a kind of similarity to the previous category each of them acts complementary to each other, although there is not central control. Each micro-robot is designed for specific surgical tasks. Typical design examples include: imaging robots of appr. 12 mm long, consisting of an outer tube containing an inner tube with a lens, camera and three DC motors. Lighting robots with an outer tube on which LEDs are mounted. In the common case the lighting robot is attached to the abdominal wall by the help of an external magnetic handle. Retraction robots that consist of (in the common case two) magnets and a sampling device. Magnetic DC micromotors within the body of the robot provide the required rotational motion and activate the sampler. All three modules need to have the appropriate sizes so that can be inserted through a standard laparoscopic trocar or through a natural orifice during NOTES (Tiwari et al. 2010; Farritor et al. 2013).

11.4.6   In Vivo Dexterous Micro-Robots

Dexterous in vivo micro-robots are designed and target use in a similar way to the standard laparoscopic tools. The design principle of this robot category is to replace laparoscopic tools by robotic devices that can present similar linear and angular motion and ability to apply forces and torques on tissues like the conventional laparoscopic tools. The overall aim is to have and operational replacement of conventional laparoscopic tools for those cases that remote interventions are required. Typical designs in this category consists of micro-robots that are inserted in peritoneal cavity and an external control console. In the common case dexterous micro-robots are equipped with two prismatic arms, each of them connected to a central body with a rotational joint. Each arm has either a clip or a cautery tool that enables it to handle the tissues. Onboard there is a pair of cameras for stereo vision feedback, and appropriate lighting sources. Control is achieved by joysticks for the rotation of the joints and extension of the arms.

The device in mounted by magnets that hold it on the inner wall of the abdominal wall (Tiwari et al. 2010; Farritor et al. 2013).

The technological challenges resulting from this approach through natural holes cannot be overcome using standard devices. In this sense, in vivo micro-robots will become useful tools. Because of their nature these small tools will be expertly, friendly, easy to use and cheap. The enormous advances in microtechnology and the culture change that occurs in the technological community have already created an open source basis for developing systems. This potentially offers great opportunities in many research groups to work on the development of systems focusing particularly in adapted micro-tools. This overcomes another important limitation of previous robotic era which is the limited patenting because of the companies currently dominate the medical robotics market. The result should be a powerful and cost-efficient way for mass production of robots for many different specific applications. Moreover, while the DaVinci robotic system was used to overcome specific difficulties met during some highly complex processes, it must be considered that the desired goal of NOTES procedures should be the effective treatment of some high risk disease.

11.5   Nanorobotics

The present era of nanotechnology has reached to a stage where scientist are able to develop and programme complex machines that are built at molecular level which can work inside the patient body. The research and development of nanorobots with embedded nanobiosensors and activators offers new tools to medical doctors (Goicoechea et al. 2007). Integrated machine control systems in tiny environments differ from conventional control techniques. Approaches based on control technique "feed forward control", are sought to effectively promote new medical technologies. The use of small appliances in surgical and medical treatments is a fact, which has brought many improvements in clinical procedures in recent years. A first series of nanotechnology prototypes for molecular machines investigated in different ways (Cavalcanti et al. 2007). More complex molecular machines or nanorobots having integrated nanosystems represent new tools for medical procedures. The use of nanorobots may advance biomedical intervention (Leary et al. 2006) with minimally invasive surgeries, help patients who need constant body function monitoring, and improve treatment efficiency through early diagnosis of possibly serious diseases. Implantable devices in medicine have been used for continuous patient data acquisition. Patient monitoring can help in preparing for neurosurgery (Sauer et al. 2005), early stage diagnostic reports to fight cancer, and blood pressure control for cardiology problems. The same approach is quite useful in monitoring patients with diabetes.

11.5.1 DNA Based Nanorobots

Nature chooses DNA mainly as an information carrier. There is no mechanical features assigned to it. There are certain features like energy conversion, sensing which make the DNA an attractive choice for the construction of artificial nanomachines. In recent years, DNA has found use in not only mechanochemical, but also in nanoelectronic systems as well (Seeman 2003). Single stranded DNA (ss-DNA) is very flexible and cannot be used where rigidity is required; however, this flexibility allows its application in machine components like hinges or nanoactuators. The DNA based nanomachines and nanorobotics were used to identify the cancerous region of the body parts. These DNA based nanorobotics are the markers in the detection of many type of cancers.

11.5.2 Applications of Nanorobots in Disease Diagnosis

Nanorobots are expected to enable new treatments for patients suffering from different diseases, and will result in a remarkable advance in the history of medicine. Studies targeted at building biosensors and nanokinetic devices, required to enable medical nanorobotics operation and locomotion, have also been progressing (Pohl and Jovin 1972). The use of nanorobots may advance biomedical intervention with minimal invasive surgeries, and help patients who need constant body functions monitoring, or ever improve treatments efficiency through early diagnosis of possible serious diseases (Stracke et al. 2000). One possible utilization of the nanorobots would be the attachment on white blood cells or other closely floating inflammatory cells so that tissues can be reached faster and the healing process to start earlier. One obvious application is the administration of accurate dosage in chemotherapy related cases (Onion 2006). A similar approach could work with HIV drug delivery. Nanorobots can also take part in or even process chemical reactions required when organs are injured. Another possible application is the monitoring and control of glucose level in diabetes patients (Cavalcanti et al. 2006).

11.5.3 Treatment of Artery Occlusion

An important possible feature of medical nanorobots will be the capability to locate atherosclerotic lesions in stenosed blood vessels, particularly in the coronary circulation, and treat them mechanically, chemically or pharmacologically

(Wright et al. 2005). Heart problem is the world biggest killer. The nanorobots must be equipped with the necessary devices for monitoring the most important aspects of disease pathogenesis. Teams of nanorobots may cooperate to enable exploration, or diagnosis or even treatment. The present state of the art in technology can support such attempts (Chandran 1992).

11.5.4   Nanorobots in Cancer Detection and Treatment

Nanorobots could be a very helpful and hopeful in the therapy of cancer patients, since current treatments like radiation therapy and chemotherapy often end up destroying more healthy cells than cancerous ones. The nanorobots will be able to distinguish between different cell types that is the malignant and the normal cells by checking their surface antigens. This may be achieved by the use of chemotactic sensors keyed to a specific antigen on the target cells. By the use of chemical sensors the nanorobots can be indicate and detect different levels of E- Catherin and beta–catenin in primary and metastatic phases. Once identified the cancer cells, appropriate treatment methods can be locally applied (e.g. radiation locally at the cell, injection of antigen etc.)

11.5.5   Nanorobotics Control in Brain Aneurysms

Endovascular treatment of brain aneurysms, arteriovenous malformations, and arteriovenous fistulas are biomedical problems expected to benefit from current research and developments in the field of medical nanorobotics. The advent of bio-molecular science and new manufacturing techniques is advancing the miniaturization of devices from micro to nanobioelectronics. A first series of nanotechnology prototypes for molecular machines are being investigated in different ways in the diagnosis of brain aneurysm. More complex molecular machines, or nanorobots, having embedded nanoscopic features represent new tools for medical procedures (Vadali and Musunuri 2007). For analysis, a real time simulation based on clinical data is implemented, demonstrating sensor and nanorobot behavior capabilities for detection of abnormal vessel dilatation in cases of cerebral aneurysm. The use of real time 3D prototyping and simulation are important tools for medical nanorobots research and development. (Freitas 2005).

11.6   Research Experiments

11.6.1   Direct Nano-Injection into Cell

Nano-bio science and technology are strongly investigated through the micro/nano scale techniques based on the local environmental measurements and controls (Leary et al. 2006). It has developed the novel single cell nanosurgey system based on micro/nanomanipualtors under various microscopes under wet/semi-wet/ dry conditions. The local stiffness evaluation, local cutting, and local extraction of biological organism are presented by micro-nanoprobes based on an Environmental-Scanning Electron Microscope (E-SEM) nanorobotic manipulation system for future cell diagnosis and surgery system (Ahmed et al. 2008, 2010). In the system, the unique nanomanipulation system is developed inside the E-SEM. Using conventional electron microscope, a vacuums chamber is needed for nano-scale high resolution imaging. On the other hand, the E-SEM can be used for a direct observation of water-containing samples with nanometer high resolution by specially built secondly electron detector in the nanometer scale observation resolution. The evaporation of water is controlled by the low sample temperature and high sample chamber pressure. In this work, the OM and E-SEM is combined to realize biological specimen analysis by optical microscope image including fluorescent imaging, and nano-scale manipulation by E-SEM imaging. This system will be applied as future nano-surgery system based on nanomanipulation system for biological specimen. The nanoprobe has a neck to break itself after inserting into biological specimen. At the tip of nanoprobe, the indicator or injection material can be attached and covered by sealing materials. The nano-scale small size probe is important to make the damage to biological specimen as minimum. The hybrid microscope can observe and determine the injection point and viability condition of biological sample from OM imaging. The width of nanoprobe is ~600 nm, and the width of neck is ~200 nm. The height of nanoprobe is ~400 nm. The nanoprobe has a sharp tip to insert the probe into biological sample smoothly. The tip angle is ~45 degrees. The probe is fabricated by focused ion beam (FIB) process. The nanoinjection technique is needed to transport fluorescent materials or specific biological organism into specific cell as in-vivo experiment. The system will be applied as future nano-surgery system based on nanomanipulation system for biological specimen to realize gene-deliver or electrophysiologic applications and novel cell diagnosis.

11.6.2 Nano Knife for Single Cell Cutting

Research on individual cells could benefit the understanding of biological processes. Single cell cutting is an important links in single cell analysis (Huang et al. 2008). For instance, it has been widely used for the specimen preparation of single cell slices (Hess 2007; Leis et al. 2009; Mobius 2009). It also benefited the single cell surgery and operation fields. Generally, the diamond and glass knives are used for the cell sample cutting. However, these knives always have an edge angle larger than 20°. It bends the sections sharply away from the block face, inducing compressive stresses on the upper surface of the section relative to the bottom (Richter et al. 1991). The compression force caused by the knife edge angle influences the inner structure of the sample, or even leads to cracking of the sample surface. A nano knife fabricated from a carbon nanotube (CNT) was developed to replace the conventional diamond knife for the cell cutting task. The result shows the compression to sample can be reduced greatly when using the oscillating diamond knife (Singh et al. 2009). An environmental scanning electron microscope (ESEM) allows real-time observation of biological samples under high humidity environment at nanoscale. We have developed the nanorobotic manipulation system inside an ESEM. The result showed that the strength of nano knife was capable for single cell cutting task. This nano knife had an edge angle only 5°, which was much smaller than the diamond knife (larger than 20°). The small knife edge angle combining with the oscillation cutting could reduce the compression to the cell. As we can see from the results, the single cell with a diameter 4 μm was cutting to two parts without bursting. The slice angle between the two slices was around 16° and the deformation of the cell during and after cutting was very small. It meant the physical damage to the single cell caused by oscillating nano knife was small. The traditional method for compression evaluation is based on the observation of the slice sample after cutting, in which a long time period is required. In our method, the deformation of the nano knife beam and cell can be seen directly and the oscilating cutting force can be measured as well. Therefore, the study of compression to cell is easier and the evaluation and optimizationof operating parameters can be realized faster. In conclusion, the oscillating nano knife can be used for single cell cutting task. In the future work, it will studied and optimized the cutting parameters to reduce the cell comprehension further (Shen et al. 2009; Green and Olson 1990; Botstein et al. 1997).

11.7 Labyrinth

11.7.1 Aim

According to the current trends in treatment and diagnosis and based on the recent development of robotics technology, it is evident that a new area starts which deserves to be further explored and developed. The concept, "LABYRINTH", stands for "Life Aided BY Robotic Intrabdominal Therapists" and it is an attempt to holistically present robotic solutions based on the NOTES approach. The overall aim is to present a set of robotic modules,hereinafter called "MINOS-MR" (Minimal Invasive and Natural Orifice Surgical Micro -Robots) that are fully compliant with NOTES procedures. In NOTES there are still several open topics that need to be addressed and resolved in an integrated and fully functional manner. Several researchers in the past have achieved great and important results as regards some of the subtopics, and the work in the latest developments in the field are giving promising results.

LABYRINTH, aims at the advancement of the state-of the-art building up on these results and offering a holistic and integrated analysis of the overall problem of NOTES. The concept aims at delivering to the scientific community an integrated solution addressing in all the details all the relevant aspects and offering the complete example on which future work and implementation can be based on. The proposed concept aims at the integrated analysis and process of all relevant aspects, ranging from the high level man-machine-interface and system deployment in surgeons' daily practice, down to low level technical issues like interferences between wireless communication, wireless power systems and actuators. The proposed concept aims at delivering, innovative advanced methods, in-silico prototypes of MINOS-MR and experimental set-ups of key technological issues related to NOTES and MINOS-MRs.

Overall, LABYRINTH concept aims at increasing the surgical abilities of the surgeons and furthermore improve the quality of life of surgical patients. It could have a major impact on the healthcare systems, in terms of hospitalization time and costs, and general health management. The minimal invasive surgery approaches and methods currently applied could be further evolved with the use of micro-robot colonies proposed by the concept. Tele-surgery would be also evolved and thus distant or isolated populations could benefited by the proposed approach.

11.7.2 Methods

In order to achieve its aim, LABYRINTH will be deployed around 3 main objectives:

a. Requirement studies and analysis aiming detailed acquisition, analysis and process all the required aspects that will provide a stable base ground on which the design of MINOS-MR will be based on.
b. The in-silico design and development of collaborative modular reconfigurable MINOS-MR that are in compliance with NOTES and applicable to real life minimal invasive surgery applications.
c. Studies, designs, developments, experimentation and evaluation with key technological issues that are consisting barriers at the current state-of-the-art technologies in NOTES.

These objectives are governed by an overall objective: to deliver the LABYRINTH approach in a way that can easily be industrialized without the need of revising any of the design of MINOS-MR modules or any other design principles.

11.7.3 Overview and Initial Specifications of the MINOS-MR Modules and the MINOS-MR

The prototype of the modular micro-robot will consist of the MINOS-MR modules that can enter in the abdominal cavity through the natural orifices of the human body. In addition to the MINOS-MR modules and respective MINOS-MR configurations and MINOS-CS (MINOS Control Station) will be designed, implemented and evaluated in-silico.

The MINOS-MR modules will be designed to be lightweight, waterproof and biocompatible. The components will be designed using as much as possible basic 3D objects in order to create simple forms and enable a targeted low cost manufacturing prospective. The modules will be studied and designed in all the details in order to enhance their potential of use in real operational environments e.g. modules will have different colors coding depending on their use to ease the surgeon during the operation. The dimensions of each module will be designed not to exceeding an overall volume of $25 \times 10 \times 10$ mm allowing for potential introduction of the modules into the human body via swallowing. A limited classes of modules will be developed so as to facilitate the production of large number and low cost units.

At a minimum configuration of the MIMOS micro robot, the following basic types of MINOS-MR modules will be designed, developed and evaluated in-silico:

a. a camera module
b. an operational-surgical instrument toolbox module, and
c. a connection module.

The MINOS-MR modules will be equipped with specifically selected motors (rotational and/or linear) consisted of preferably of-the-self components in order to keep the overall cost low and make the future fabrication of the prototypes easier (of-the-self miniaturized motors with high gear ratios). Alternatives to motors will be also investigated e.g. motion by inertia produced by a spinning mass or by the use of memory wires. Special studies will be devoted to the formation of the shape of the modules in order to achieve both the maximum functionality for the targeted application field and at least 3 DoFs (depending on the overall micro-robot configuration). Permanent magnet configurations along with micro activation rotation mechanics will be explored for the coupling/decoupling procedures of the modules.

The camera module will be designed in order to be equipped with at least one true color camera with the appropriate lighting device. Research efforts will be devoted to the design of a camera module that would enable 3D image capturing. Given that 3D is an essential requirement, especially in cases where the MINOS-MRs are used for tele-operation, there are two important issues that need to be investigated: (a) the potential need for the design of a localization subsystem (absolute or relative) in order to provide a reference coordinate frame for the cameras to provide the 3D view. In this case two identical camera modules could serve the objective of 3D image capturing. (b) Acquisition of the camera(s) signal in real time. Image capturing can be accomplished even in low-bandwidth links. However, the application environment implies transmission of the image data in real time over wireless links. Furthermore, there are other limitations beyond the bandwidth that influence the requirement of real-time 3D image data, like the interference between the transmission link with other equipment operating in the same environment e.g. wireless power transmission devices, and the limitations imposed by the regulations in operating rooms. These along other important issues e.g. field of view, data representation and augmented reality issues, will be the core of the research as regards the camera module.

The **operational-surgical toolbox module** will be designed in order to be equipped with appropriate laparoscopy like surgical instruments, like grasping and dissection tools, forceps etc. Several of the tooltips used in the surgeon daily practice will be integrated in this module. Operation scenarios and requirements studies will provide information of the common/conflicting issues related to the tools e.g. actuation method, applied force/torque etc. that will be required. At least two tooltips (cutting, fetching) will be designed and integrated on the operational-surgical module. Special efforts will be devoted in order to design the module in order to carry more than one tooltip. Force feedback and/or tool position and state sensors will be studied and incorporated in the design in order to provide the operator, through the appropriate instrumentation, haptic sense and feedback.

The **connection module**. It is the module that provides the mechanical interconnection between the MINOS-MR modules. The debate has been built around the arguments for an integrated connection mechanism on-board the individual modules and a standalone connection module. It has been decided that the experimentation of a standalone connection module may provide a method that also be could be applied on individual modules. Therefore the studies will be first focused on the connection module as an integrated component in the individual modules and if this fails then the design of a standalone connection module will be implemented.

The most important issue as regards the connection module is the (self-) assembly functionality that is required for MINOS-MRs. The functionality of the modular micro-robot is based on the assembly of the modules. In order to study the optimum functionality a dipper analysis will be made. This will consist of the investigation of the final form, assembly type and configuration of the micro-robots. The modules have to be assembled in series with a specific order (depending on the operation scenario) as to form a worm-like modular micro-robot with a particular function. The robot could be pre-assembled or self-assembled. The type of the micro-robot that is assembled depends on the primary module, which will be the camera module or the operational module. If magnets are placed on the matching faces, the magnetic force will attract the different modules toward each other and the magnetic torque will orient them. In addition, electro-magnets provide a reversible connection allowing for disconnection. However, electro-magnets consume high amounts of power. Each module should be able to connect to any other module in order to increase the number of possible configurations of the micro-robot. The mating faces should be connected in a unique orientation to enable kinematic configurations without the need for additional orientation sensors. There are three cases: the assembly of modules to form and operational micro-robot can be performed: a) before the introduction of the MINOS-MR into the human body, b) afterwards, directly in the stomach or in the abdominal cavity. In the second case, the modules should be swallowed or entered into the abdominal cavity in a specific order. However, this type of assembling will require more time because of the modules' passive motion. The gastric motility and the liquid content of the cavity e.g. stomach, may accelerate or prevent the assembly of the modules. The modules during the assembly process should move in such a way that the energy consumption of the overall system is minimized. A large number of forces like gravity, magnetic force/torque, friction etc., between the modules, and the intrabdominal organs, in addition to the some unpredictable initial conditions may possibly interact from misaligned assembly to no interaction at all. Externally applied magnets may allow the guided assembly of the micro-robot, making it more predictable (Giakoumaki et al. 2004).

Several methods will be investigated as regards the essential (self-) assembly issue. Solutions incorporating permanent magnets are the most promising mainly because of the zero energy consumption. However, the control of the self-assembly functionality is heavily depended on the probabilities of the relevant position of the modules in the operation environment and in addition, permanent magnets, may interfere with other functional elements like actuators or wireless transmitters. Electromechanical or electromagnetic coupling of the modules presents advantages, like ease of control, while there are disadvantages, like the high energy consumption. Decoupling procedures to allow MINOR-MR modules to exit the operation environment are straight forward in electromechanical methods, while quite difficult in methods based on permanent magnets. The research team strongly considers a hybrid method according to which the final coupling power is provided by permanent magnets, while the control of the coupling/decoupling is provided by low consumption electromechanical mechanism.

All the MINOS-MR modules will be designed to be equipped with a wireless data transmitter. The role of the wireless transmitter is twofold: in one hand to enable inter-module communication and communication of the modules to the micro-robot control station in order to enable the wireless control of the MINOS-MR, and on the other hand to enable medical/operational data (e.g. visual information, force feedback to be transferred to the MINOS-CS) (Istepanian R. et al. 2001).

Although the notion of MINOS-CS sounds quite technical, the research team does not neglect important aspects like the man-machine interface and other operation related aspects. These aspects will be fully incorporated into the design and ported to the implementation of the MINOS-CS and the respective functionality of the MINOS-MRs.

Energy consumption is of great concern and without power supply the micro-robot will become immobilized and useless if not problematic for the rest of the operation. In the common case, the human intervention is required to ensure continued functionality; however the surgeon and the operation team would and should not have the time to deal with this issue. Long-term autonomous functionality would be required by micro-robots without recharge and without human intervention. The overall system should be easily adapted to different surgical operations, as well as multiple cooperating micro-robots. MINOS-MR modules will require power. The operation environment implies a lot of limitations and rises several issues like, time required before any of the MINOS-MR are connected to the mains to be recharged, batteries vs. wired vs. wireless power transmission, etc (Lamprinos et al. 2005). Nowadays there are available thin film batteries that can provide power of up to 20 mAh. However, autonomous operation of modules might require much more of that power, and therefore an alternative should be found. The design principle as regards the power issue is: incorporation of an on-board battery to provide a minimum autonomy between recharges and a method to provide power during the operation. Wired power would be a direct solution to the problem; however the research team aims at the development of methods that would meet the most of the demanding requirements. Therefore, the wireless power transmission power will be investigated. The proposed approach foresees implementation and testing of experimental set-ups of wireless power transmission (though inductance). The frequency and the volume required as well as the limitations imposed by the regulations in the operation room are some of the problems that need to be addressed.

11.7.4 In-Silico, Design, Development, Experimentation and Evaluation

For the design, development and functional experimentation and evaluation of the MINOS-MR there are several options. Complex robotic configurations and set-pus, with several micro-robots, in a shared environment will be designed. Specific properties of each robotic configuration, such as DoFs, shape, texture, mass, etc., will be evaluated under various operative scenarios. Simulation, experimentation and evaluation will include also the incorporation of simulated sensors and actuators in each of the evaluation scenarios. Also the physics of the application environment imply further limitations and difficulties. The micro-robots will not be operating in homogeneous environments; therefore it is required to take into incorporation the physics parameters. The fundamental physics governing the micro-robots remains the same, but the relative importance of physical effects changes (Morris 2005). Fluid viscosity and surface effects such as electrostatics dominate over volumetric effects such as weight and inertia, and the generation and storage of power becomes difficult. The above characteristics will be taken in account. The world of a surgical micro-robot consists of fluid-filled lumens and cavities, as well as soft tissues. Surgical micro-robots must be designed specifically to work in these environments (the intrabdominal environment will be simulated using simple 3D structures with physical characteristics of the human tissues and organs).

MINOS-CS will be also included in the simulation, experimentation and evaluation either within the built-in integrated development environment or with third party development environments. The overall objective is to experiment and evaluate the MINOS-MRs in realistic simulation environments simulating all the physical environment of operation. The MINOS-CS man-machine-interface is of great importance, especially as regards the user friendliness and ease of use. In the light of the a potential future industrial exploitation of the design and the research results, it is essential that the MINOS-CS adapts the methods and procedures that the surgeons are currently using, and in the case the research proposes new methods then these methods should be at least evaluated by the relevant professionals.

11.7.5 Operation Modes

For the purposes of experimentation and evaluation, the following operation modes are foreseen: (a) real time full control of the individual MINOS-MR modules and there components (e.g. tooltips). This mode will be mainly used for the testing of the system and will allow experimentation with the functionality of components and sub-components, (b) semi-automatic control of the MINOS-MRs: in this mode the operator will be provided with a limited set of high level operation commands that will enable him/her to operate the MINOS-MR without requiring full control of the individual DoFs of the micro-robot. It is expected that this mode will be the most preferable operation mode, (c) automatic control of the MINOS-MRs: in this mode the operator will be enabled to perform a full set of high level commands e.g. approach more, cut etc. without requiring considering how the MINOS-MR will actually implement those. This mode is not expected to be in favor of the professionals but it is included in the work in order to investigate the limits between semi-automatic and automatic control mode and help the research team define the set of high level commands that might enhance the exploitation potential of the overall system.

11.7.6   Potential Impact

It is well known that in-body robotic medical interventions will benefit tremendously by decreasing considerably the physical dimensions of the hardware and payloads. Micro robots and individual devices can very easily prove to be the solution to this problem. The LABYRINTH approach aims to provide designs for solutions that integrate a micro-robotic system (comprised by modules) that is lightweight, appropriately sized and present the required functionality for operations following the NOTES concept. The MINOS-MR colonies will be designed to be reconfigured; a property that will help to establish operation sites on remote and inaccessible environments and in turn, initiate a whole micro-scale industry. The surgical micro-robots will begin to colonize and build a new intrabdominal surgical world. They will carry out operations on patients in hostile and remote environments, like war fields, space missions and otherwise isolated populations. These module and reconfigurable micro-robots will assemble habitats that can be completely constructed by remote control. Tele-surgery may be a realistic low cost surgical solution carried out even with the aid of non-specialized paramedical personnel, "just put these micro-robots in the natural orifices".

11.8   Conclusion

The concept of surgical micro-robotic colonies is innovative and can potentially put new perspectives in the field of surgery, increasing the possibilities for true scarless tele-surgery. Cooperative modular micro-robots could operate in such a way to accomplish complex surgical interventions. The development of the innovative wireless controlling solution with bi-directional feedback designed as stated above will provide the surgeon with simple but efficient remote controlling capabilities. Also the 3D visual feedback of remote environment and the use of other sensors will help in tele-operation.

Some of these micro-robotic assemblies will execute specific tasks, while others perform a number of different operations. These micro-robot colonies will interact, collaborating to build, repair, and manipulate an intrabdominal micro-world. Micro-robots have the potential to perform tasks that are currently difficult or impossible, and they will undoubtedly lead to the development of surgical therapies not yet conceived offering minimal pain and trauma to the surgical patient. It should however be understood that applications that benefit from intrabdominal surgical micro-robots are in a relatively early stage (conceptual), albeit the field is advancing extremely fast. In a few years specialized micro-robots (we can call them intrabdominal therapists) will be vitally important during surgery.

References

Abbott DJ, Becke C, Rothstein RI, Peine WJ (Oct 2007) Design of an endoluminal NOTES robotic system. IEEE/RSJ International Conference on Intelligent Robots and Systems (IROS '07). San Diego, Calif, USA, e-ISBN: 978-1-4244-0912-9, pp 410–416

Ahmad MR, Nakajima M, Kojima S, Homma M, Fukuda T (2008) In-situ single cell mechanics characterization of yeast cells using nanoneedles inside environmental-SEM. IEEE Trans Nanotechnol 7(5):607–616

Ahmad MR, Nakajima M, Kojima S, Homma M, Fukuda T (2010) Nanoindentation methods to measure viscoelastic properties of single cells using sharp, flat and buckling tips inside ESEM. IEEE Trans Nanobioscience 9(1):12–23

Ahmed K, Khan MS, Vats A, Nagpal K, Priest O, Patel V, Vecht JA, Ashrafian H et al (Oct, 2009) Current status of robotic assisted pelvic surgery and future developments. Int J Surg 7(5):431–440

Arezzo A, Morino M (Feb, 2010) Endoscopic closure of gastric access in perspective NOTES: an update on techniques and technologies. Surg Endosc 24(2):298–303. (Epub 2009 Jun 30. Review)

Blessing WD Jr, Ross JM, Kennedy CI, Richardson WS (Dec, 2005) Laparoscopicassisted peritoneal dialysis catheter placement, an improvement on the single trocar technique. Am Surg 71(12):1042–1046

Botstein D, Chervitz SA, Cherry JM (1997) Genetics—yeast as a model organism. Science 277(5330):1259–1260

Camarillo DB, Krummel TM, Salisbury JK Jr (2004) Robotic technology in surgery: past, present, and future. Am J Surg 188(Suppl to Oct, 2004):2S–15S

Cavalcanti A, Hogg T, Shirinzadeh B, Liaw HC (2006) Nanorobot communication techniques: a comprehensive tutorial.,9th International Conference on Control Automation, Robotics and Vision, 2006 ICARCV, Grand Hyatt, Singapore, e-ISBN:1-4214-042-1, pp 1–6

Cavalcanti A, Shirinzadeh B, Fukuda T, Ikeda S (2007) Hardware architecture for nanorobot application in cerebral aneurysm. 7th IEEE conference on Nanotechnology 2007, IEEE-NANO 2007, Hong-Kong, e-ISBN:978-1-4244-0607-4, pp 237–242

Chandran KB (1992) Cardiovascular biomechanics (New York University Biomedical Engineering Series). New York University Press, pp 32–41

Chiu PW, Lau JY, Ng EK, Lam CC, Hui M, To KF, Sung JJ, Chung SS (Sept, 2008) Closure of a gastrotomy after transgastric tubal ligation by using the Eagle Claw VII: a survival experiment in a porcine model (with video). Gastrointest Endosc 68(3):554–559. (Epub 2008 Jul 16)

Degani A, Choset H, Wolf A, Zenati MA (May, 2006) Highly articulated robotic probe for minimally invasive surgery. In Proceedings of the IEEE International Conference on Robotics and Automation (ICRA '06). Orlando, Fla, USA, pp 4167–4172

EndoWrist Instruments (n.d.) Intuitive Surgical Inc. http://www.intuitivesurgical.com/

Farritor SM, Lehman AC, Oleynkov D (2011) Miniature in vivo robots for notes. Surgical Robots. Springer, pp 123–138, ISBN: 978-1-4419-1126-1

Fong DG, Ryou M, Pai RD, Tavakkolizadeh A, Rattner DW, Thompson CC (Oct, 2007) Transcolonic ventral wall hernia mesh fixation in a porcine model. Endoscopy 39(10):865–869

Forgione A (2009) In vivo microrobots for natural orifice transluminal surgery. Current status and future perspectives. Surgical Oncology xx:1–9

Freitas RA Jr (2005) Nanotechnology, nanomedicine and nanosurgery. Int J Surg 3(12):1–4

Gerhardus D (July/Aug, 2003) Robot-assisted surgery. The future is here. J Healthcare Manage 48(4):242–251. http://www.entrepreneur.com/tradejournals/article/106226723_3.html

Giakoumaki A, Pavlopoulos S, Koutsouris D (2004) A multiple watermarking scheme applied to medical image management. In: Proceedings of the 26th Annual International Conference of the IEEE Engineering in Medicine and Biology Society-EMBS, 5:3241–3244. San Francisco, CA, USA, September 2004

Goicoechea J, Zamarreño CR, Matias IR, Arregui FJ (2007) Minimizing the photobleaching of self-assembled multilayers for sensor applications. Sens Actuator B-Chem 126(1):41–47. http://dx.doi.org/10.1016/j.snb.2006.10.037

Green ED, Olson MV (1990) Chromosomal region of the cystic-fibrosis gene in yeast artificial chromosomes—a model for human genome mapping. Science 250(4977):94–98

Guthart GS, Salisbury J, Jr. (2000) The IntuitiveTM telesurgery system: overview and application. IEEE International Conference on Robotics and Automation. Proceedings ICRA 2000, San Fransisco CA, ISBN: 0-7803-5886-4, pp 618 -621 v.1

Harada Kanako, Oetomo Denny, Susilo Ekawahyu, Menciassi Arianna, Daney David, Merlet Jean-Pierre (2010) A reconfigurable modular robotic endoluminal surgical system: vision and preliminary results. Robotica 28:171–183. (© Cambridge University Press 2009)

Hess MW (2007) Cryopreparation methodology for plant cell biology. Cell Electron Microsc 79:57–100

http://biomed.brown.edu/Courses/BI108/BI108_2005_Groups/04/davinci.html

Huang W-H, Ai F, Wang Z-L, Cheng J-K (April, 2008) Recent advances in single cell analysis using capillary electrophoresis and microfluidic devices. J Chromatogr B Analyt Technol Biomed Life Sci 866(1–2):104–122

Istepanian R, Kyriacou E, Pavlopoulos S, Koutsouris D (2001) Effect of wavelet compression methodologies on data transmission in a multi-purpose wireless telemedicine system with mobile communication link support. J Telemed Telecare 7(1):14–16

Kaehler G, Grobholz R, Langner C, Suchan K, Post S (Jan, 2006) A new technique of endoscopic full-thickness resection using a flexible stapler. Endoscopy 38(1):86–89

Kirschniak A, Traub F, Kueper MA, Stuker D, Konigsrainer A, Kratt T (Dec, 2007) Endoscopic treatment of gastric perforation caused by acute necrotizing pancreatitis using over-the-scope clips: a case report. Endoscopy 39(12):1100–1102

Knight CG, Lorincz A, Cao A, Gidell K, Klein MD, Langenburg SE (April, 2005) Computer-assisted, robot-enhanced open microsurgery in an animal model. J Laparoendosc Adv Surg Tech 15(2):182–185

Kostantinidis K (2008) Advanced of robotic surgery. http://robotic.kkonstantinidis.com/index.php/2008-10-23-16-20-35

Lanfranco A, Castellanos A, Desai J, Meyers W (Jan, 2004) Robotic surgery: a current perspective. Annal Surg 239(1):14–21. http://www.pubmedcentral.nih.gov/articlerender.fcgi?artid=1356187

Lamprinos IE, Prentza A, Sakka E, Koutsouris D (2005) Energy-efficient MAC protocol for patient personal area networks. In: Proceedings of the 27th Annual International Conference of the IEEE Engineering in Medicine and Biology Society-EMBS, article Nr 1011, 4:3799–3802. Shanghai China, September, 2005

Laparoscopic Surgery http://en.wikipedia.org/wiki/Laparoscopic_surgery

Leary SP, Liu CY, Apuzzo MLI (2006a) Toward the emergence of nanoneurosurgery: Part III—nanomedicine: targeted nanotherapy, nanosurgery, and progress toward the realization of nanoneuro- surgery. Neurosurgery 58(6):1009–1025. http://dx.doi.org/10.1227/01.NEU.0000217016.79256.16

Leary SP, Liu CY, Apuzzo MLJ (2006b) Toward the emergence of nanoneurosurgery. Neurosurgery 58:1009–1026

Leis A, Rockel B, Andrees L, Baumeister W (Feb, 2009) Visualizing cellsat the nanoscale. Trends Biochem Sci 34(2):60–70

Lima E, Henriques-Coelho T, Rolanda C, Pego JM, Silva D, Carvalho JL, Correia-Pinto J (June, 2007) Transvesical thoracoscopy: a natural orifice translumenal endoscopic approach for thoracic surgery. Surg Endosc 21(6):854–858

Lima E, Rolanda C, Pego JM et al (2006) Transvesical endoscopic peritoneoscopy: a novel 5 mm port for intra-abdominal scarless surgery. J Urol 176:802–805

Matthews BD, Walsh RM, Kercher KW, Sing RF, Pratt BL, Answini GA, Heniford BT (May, 2002) Laparoscopic vs open resection of gastric stromal tumors. Surg Endosc 16(5):803–807. (Epub 2002 Feb 8)

Merrifield BF, Wagh MS, Thompson CC (April, 2006) Peroral transgastric organ resection: a feasibility study in pigs. Gastrointest Endosc 63(4):693–697

Metzelder M, Vieten G, Gosemann JH, Ure B, Kuebler JF (Dec, 2009) Endoloop closure of the urinary bladder is safe and efficient in female piglets undergoing transurethral NOTES nephrectomy. Eur J Pediatr Surg 19(6):362–365

Mobius W (2009) Cryopreparation of biological specimens for immunoelectron microscopy. Annal Anat 191(3):231–247

Morris B (Sept, 2005) Robotic surgery: applications, limitations, and impact on surgical education. Med Gen Med 7(3):72. http://www.pubmedcentral.nih.gov/articlerender.fcgi?artid=1681689

Onion Am (2006) RoboSnail tackles any terrain—slime not included. ABC News. http://abcnews.go.com/Technology/story?id=1525599

Onion Am. RoboSnail tackles any terrain- slime not included, abcNEWS 2006, http://abcnews.go.com/Technology/story?id=1525599

Pham BV, Raju GS, Ahmed I, Brining D, Chung S, Cotton P, Gostout CJ, Hawes RH, Kalloo AN, Kantsevoy SV, Pasricha PJ (July, 2006) Immediate endoscopic closure of colon perforation by using a prototype endoscopic suturing device: feasibility and outcome in a porcine model (with video). Gastrointest Endosc 64(1):113–119

PillCam SB, Given Imaging Ltd. (2009) Innovative Solutions-Capsule Endoscopy. http://www.givenimaging.com

Pohl FM, Jovin TM (1972) Salt-induced co-operative conformational change of a synthetic DNA: equilibrium and kinetic studies with poly (dG-dC). J Mol Biol 67:375–396. http://dx.doi.org/10.1016/0022-2836(72)90457–3

Raju GS, Fritscher-Ravens A, Rothstein RI, Swain P, Gelrud A, Ahmed I, Gomez G, Winny M, Sonnanstine T, Bergstrom M, Park PO (Aug, 2008) Endoscopic closure of colon perforation compared to surgery in a porcine model: a randomized controlled trial (with videos). Gastrointest Endosc 68(2):324–332. (Epub 2008 Jun 17. Erratum in: Gastrointest Endosc. 2008 Sep;68(3):616)

Raju GS, Pham B, Xiao SY, Brining D, Ahmed I (Nov, 2005) A pilot study of endoscopic closure of colonic perforations with endoclips in a swine model. Gastrointest Endosc 62(5):791–795

Rentschler ME, Dumpert Jason, Platt SR, Oleynikov D, Farritor SM, Iagnemma K (2006) Mobile in vivo biopsy robot. Proceedings 2006 IEEE International Conference on Robotics and Automation 2006, ICRA 2006,Orlando FL, ISBN: 0-7803-9505-0, pp 4155–4160

Rentschler ME, Platt SR, Berg K, Dumpert J, Oleynikov D, Farritor SM (Jan 2008) Miniature in vivo robots for remote and harsh environments. IEEE Trans Inf Technol Biomed 12(1):66–75

Richter K, Gngi H, Dubochet J (July, 1991) A model for cryosectioning based on the morphology of vitrified ultrathin sections. J Microsc 163(1):19–28

Robotic Surgery http://library.thinkquest.org/03oct/00760

Rolanda C, Lima E, Silva D, Moreira I, Pego JM, Macedo G, Correia-Pinto J (Dec, 2009) In vivo assessment of gastrotomy closure with over-the-scope clips in an experimental model for varicocelectomy (with video). Gastrointest Endosc 70(6):1137–1145. (Epub 2009 Jul 31)

Romanelli JR, Mark L, Omotosho PA (2008) Single-port laparoscopic cholecystectomy with the TriPort system: a case report. Surg Innov 15:223–228

Sauer C, Stanacevic M, Cauwenberghs G, Thakor N (2005) Power harvesting and telemetry in CMOS for implanted devices. IEEE Trans Circ Sys 52:2605–2613. http://dx.doi.org/10.1109/TCSI.2005.858183

Schurr MO, Arezzo A, Ho CN, Anhoeck G, Buess G, Di Lorenzo N (2008) The OTSC clip for endoscopic organ closure in NOTES: device and technique. Minim Invasive Ther Allied Technol 17(4):262–266

Seeman NC (2003) DNA in a material world. Nature 421:427–431. http://dx.doi.org/10.1038/nature01406

Shen Y, Nakajima M, Ahmad MR, Fukuda T, Kojima S, Homma M (2009) Single cell injection using nano pipette via nanorobotic manipulation system inside E-SEM. 9th IEEE Conference on Nanotechnology, IEEE-NANO 2009, Genoa, e-ISBN: 978-981-08-3694-8, pp 518–521

Sherwinter DA, Eckstein JG (July, 2009) Feasibility study of natural orifice transluminal endoscopic surgery inguinal hernia repair. Gastrointest Endosc 70(1):126–130. (Epub 2009 Feb 27)

Singh G, Rice P, Mahajan RL, McIntosh JR (March, 2009) Fabrication and characterization of a carbon nanotube-based nanoknife. Nanotechnology 20(9):095701

Stracke R, Böhm KJ, Burgold J, Schacht H, Unger E (2000) Physical and technical parameters determining the functioning of a kinesin- based cell-free motor system. Nanotechnology 11(2):52–56. http://dx.doi.org/10.1088/0957-4484/11/2/302

Sumiyama K, Gostout CJ, Rajan E, Bakken TA, Deters JL, Knipschield MA (Jan, 2007) Endoscopic full-thickness closure of large gastric perforations by use of tissue anchors. Gastrointest Endosc 65(1):134–139

Swanstrom LL (Nov, (2006) Current technology development for natural orifice transluminal endoscopic surgery, (Article in Spanish). Cir Esp 80(5):283–288

The Incisionless Operating Platform, USGI Medical Inc. http://www.usgimedical.com/eos/index.htm

The daVinci Surgical System, Intuitive Surgical Inc. http://www.intuitivesurgical.com/

Tiwari MM, Reynoso JF, Lehman AC, Tsang AW, Farritor SM, Oleynikov Dmitry (27 June, 2010) In vivo miniature robots for natural orifice surgery: state of the art and future perspectives. World J Gastrointest Surg 2(6):217–223

Vadali Shanthi MS (2007) Prospects for medical robots. AZojono: J Nanotechno 3:1–9

von Delius S, Gillen S, Doundoulakis E, Schneider A, Wilhelm D, Fiolka A, Wagenpfeil S, Schmid RM, Feussner H, Meining A (Nov, 2008) Comparison of transgastric access techniques for natural orifice transluminal endoscopic surgery. Gastrointest Endosc 68(5):940–947. (Epub 2008 Jun 17)

Walid MS, Heaton RL (2010) Laparoscopy-to-laparotomy quotient in obstetrics and gynecology residency programs. Arch Gyn Ob 283(5):1027–1031

Westebring-van der Putten EP, Goossens RHM, Jakimowicz JJ, Dankelman J (2008) Haptics in minimally invasive surgery—a review. Minim Invasive Ther 17(1):3–16

Wilhelm D, Meining A, von Delius S, Fiolka A, Can S, Hann vonWC, Schneider A, Feussner H (May, 2007) An innovative, safe and sterile sigmoid access (ISSA) for NOTES. Endoscopy 39(5):401–406

Wright EM, Sampedro AD, Hirayama BA, Koepsell H, Gorboulev V, Osswald C (2005) Novel glucose sensor. United States patent US 0267154

www.intuitivesurgical.com/products/davinci_surgical_system

Yonezawa J, Kaise M, Sumiyama K, Goda K, Arakawa H, Tajiri H (2006) A novel double-channel therapeutic endoscope ("R-scope") facilitates endoscopic submucosal dissection of superficial gastric neoplasms. Endoscopy 38(10):1011–1015

Zygomalas A, Giokas K, Koutsouris, D (2012) "Modular assembly micro-robots for Natural Orifice Transluminal Endoscopic Surgery, the future of minimal invasive surgery", International Journal of Reliable and Quality e-Healthcare, vol. 1 (4), pp 43–55

Zygomalas A, Kehagiaç I, Giokas K, Koutsouris D (2014) Miniature surgical robots in the era of NOTES and LESS: dream or reality? Surg Innov. doi:10.1177/1553350614532549, published online 14 May 2014

Chapter 12
Impacts of Robotic Assisted Surgery on Hospital's Strategic Plan: A Social Cost Approach

Charalampos Platis, Emmanuel Zoulias and Stelios Zimeras

Abstract In this paper presented a methodological approach of the possible effects, considering various aspects, of incorporating robotic systems in complex environments like hospitals. In particular we examine the implementation of robot-assisted surgery systems which are of key importance within hospital's environment. Although robotic systems are quite new and not widespread, due to various reasons, it has been identified that those systems affect seriously the whole operation of the hospital. The analysis take into account the different aspects like Surgical, Economic, Organizational, Structural as well as Legal issues, Ethical issues and Patient issues that are related to the implementation of robotic surgery in a hospital. Harmless of the surgical robotics in hospitals might affect the economical and social structure of the public system leading to direct and effective decisions to overcome the problematic. For that reason, calculation of social cost of harm could be introduced over time (t) as a proposed social measure to define the variability of social indicator on society.

Moreover we present the various stakeholders that are involved in the application of robotic systems within a hospital and their different key role, how they influence the use of such systems. The hectic aspect of economic sustainability is discussed taken into account terms of running costs, investment costs, and costs for patients and caregivers. Implementation of robotic systems is a part of a serious strategic plan of the hospital and could start composing a SWOT analysis in order to reveal Strengths, Weaknesses, Opportunities and Threats regarding Medical, Technical, Social and Ethical aspects. Specific problems such as lack of resources and coordination necessities such as restructuring and finally weaknesses in the production of services can be managed with innovative solutions such as of Robotic Surgery.

Keywords Robotic Assisted Surgery · Social cost · Hospital strategic plan · SWOT

S. Zimeras (✉)
Department of Mathematics, Direction Statistics and Actuarial-Financial Mathematics,
University of the Aegean, 83200 Karlovassi, Greece
e-mail: zimste@agean.gr

C. Platis
National Centre for Public Administration and Local Government, Institute of Training,
Pireos 211, 17778 Tavros, Greece

E. Zoulias
National Centre for Public Administration and Local Government, Information Systems and
Technical Support, Pireos 211, 17778 Tavros, Greece

D.-D. Koutsouris, A. A. Lazakidou (eds.), *Concepts and Trends in Healthcare Information Systems,* Annals of Information Systems 16,
DOI 10.1007/978-3-319-06844-2_12, © Springer International Publishing Switzerland 2014

12.1 Introduction

Modern hospital environment is highly connected to technology and engineering. A vast number of technological equipment is wide spread in a hospital, from laboratories to intensive care and from short term care to operating theater. Therefore technological innovations are close related in hospital environment and the level of offered health care. Consequently technological equipment is of key importance regarding the strategic plan of the hospital on various aspects as well as the economic view. Within this paper we try to present the effect of robotic systems use in hospital environment and the effects on the strategic plan and economic aspects. Robotic surgery transforms the surgery procedure to an operation that the surgeon remotely-controlled robotic arms, which may affect the performance of procedures.

At the same time the use of robotics surgical operators (surgical assistance) may effect the economic budget either the hospital or the patients leading us to the investigation of the social cost modelling. Social cost is a term that is sometimes used in economic discussions to refer to the costs that are experienced by others when specific types of goods and services are purchased. This is different from the concept of private cost, which focuses on the costs that an individual experiences when choosing to purchase a specific good or service. The idea behind understanding social cost is to help determine if the production and sale of certain goods creates enough benefits to the general populace that the costs to those same people is offset. In order to model the social cost and defined as an important variability factor for the society, the definition of social cost must be introduced, as well as the types of social cost must be defined. Based on these types, important factors that effect in calculation could be introduced and statistical measures could be proposed.

From the early 80s robotic surgery systems are used in medical procedures. Passing almost three decades tremendous growth has been experienced in the market of robotic surgery mainly in terms of medical equipment innovation and development. The major advantages of these systems include improved surgical outcomes, accurate procedure execution and rapid post-surgical recovery of the patient. Robotic technology has been adopted in hospitals use rapidly over the last decade both in the United States and Europe. The da Vinci Surgical System introduced in 1999 for minimally invasive surgery. Up to 31 December 2012, 2.585 da Vinci Systems have been installed in approximately 2025 hospitals worldwide. Approximately 450,000 da Vinci procedures were performed in 2012, up approximately 25 % compared to 2011 (http://www.intuitivesurgical.com). Nowadays many procedures are performed robotically than laparoscopically as in the previous years. In Greece there were established six robotic systems and a number of more than 1000 operations have been performed (http://www.roboticsurgery.gr).

12.2 Experimental

Although robotic systems are quite new and not widespread, due to various reasons, it has been identified that those systems affect seriously the whole operation of the hospital. The analysis take into account the different aspects like Surgical, Economic, Organizational, Structural as well as Legal issues, Ethical issues and Patient issues that are related to the implementation of robotic surgery in a hospital. Moreover there were various stakeholders that are involved in the use of robotic systems within a hospital and their different key role.

High reliability in healthcare is founded to be the most important key aspect based on which care is delivered, called organizational culture, and that has important influences on patient satisfaction and care give (Pronovost et al. 2006). A set of strategies and factors have to be considered while introducing new robotic technologies into clinical scenario. As far as the surgical issues the important aspects are the effectiveness, patient safety. The benefits of robot-assisted surgery derive from the enhanced precision, better visualization, and easier articulation of instruments and the elimination of tremor. These parameters should allow for more precise interventions on various high difficulty and importance situations like anatomical structures such as blood vessels, nerves and other tissues can be spared. Studies directly comparing robot-assisted surgery to either laparoscopic or open surgery, however, are scarce (Ballini et al. 2008; Adams 2006; Ontario Ministry of Health and Long-Term Care 2004; Tooher and Pham 2004).

From the economic point of view the robot-assisted surgery should be examined in terms of cost and if it is or not more expensive than the other alternatives. Aspects like equipment costs, specialized labor costs should be taken into account with their irregularities. In general there is a fundamental need of cost-effectiveness analyses based on RCTs performed by experienced surgeons and including the long term impact of surgery on clinical outcomes and on health related quality of life (Camberlin et al. 2009). Costs of robot-assisted surgery are partly dependent upon technical repairing and maintenance costs, as well as disposables costs as some specific instruments are preprogrammed to be used for only a limited number of times. The cost-effectiveness analysis is very important to see if robotic-assisted surgery is effective. Robotic surgical systems have high fixed costs, with prices ranging from $ 1 to $ 2.5 million for each unit. Surgeons must perform 150 to 250 procedures to become adept in their use (Barbash and Glied 2010). In addition to that it is stated that costs of robots are high and do not justify the use of this technology considering the lack of benefits for patients (Breitenstein et al. 2008).

Robotic-assisted procedures like all other informational technology systems introduce new aspects in terms of Legal, Ethical and Patient issues. The terms of consent and professional confidentiality are key principles in all medical activities from a legal point of view and technology changes the traditional way. In any case patient should be provided with clear and complete information concerning the whole proposed operation. In terms of medical liability there is no change from the traditional legal rules. From an ethical point all new and needed information should be provided to the patient in order to be able to compare with alternative procedures, to feel confident with surgical team training experience, technology efficiency and extra costs.

New technology seriously affects organizational and structural formation of any organization as well as a hospital's environment. To adopt a robotic system in the surgery life of any hospital might need making decisions about formatting the surgical robotic team, the robotics program, reviewing clinical cases, approving proctors, training staff member and surgeon (Zender and Thell 2010) rearranging the hospital's work flow and safety procedures. Surgical robots are different from other equipment such as operating blood analysis, imaging or microscopes and more over they are not traditional operating room instruments. In addition to that all operating staff should be equally and highly trained from surgeons and surgical assistant as well as all personnel. In addition to that new staff appeared in the operating room, since such high technology equipment need the presence of appropriate technical staff. In this way, emerging problems may be quickly identified and addressed (Herron and Marohn 2007).

Implementation of robotic systems is a part of a serious strategic plan of the hospital. The strategic plan of a hospital consolidates all the above issues and is of a key importance in order to run efficiently a hospital. A very important and effective tool is SWOT analysis. This analysis reveals Strengths, Weaknesses, Opportunities and Threats regarding Economical, Medical, Technical, Social and Ethical aspects (Pickton and Wright 1998).

12.3 Social Cost Definition

As social cost is defined the cost imposed to the society from an event, action or policy (Deardorff 2006). From the general point of view social cost could be defined as the cost that includes the private cost, the public expenditure and the external cost affecting the society from an event, action or policy change (Kopp and Fenoglio 2002; Diomidous et al. 2009). Private costs include the costs borne directly from drug users and the private external costs borne by private agents who are not substance users. Public costs include public expenditure government budget, resources by local government public costs, resources by health public costs (Kopp and Fenoglio 2002).

From the point of type the social cost is divided in direct and indirect. Direct cost includes the value of services used to overcome the negative effects of surgical operation. Indirect cost describes the value of services based on surgical operation. If we concentrate on health and economical earnings health cost describes the costs of treating patients before the surgical operation and productivity costs represent the earnings by using surgical assistance operators and earnings by people who are relatives to the patients.

Investigating the impact of social costs in the society, leads us to study these information that related to private, public and external costs as well as analyzes the

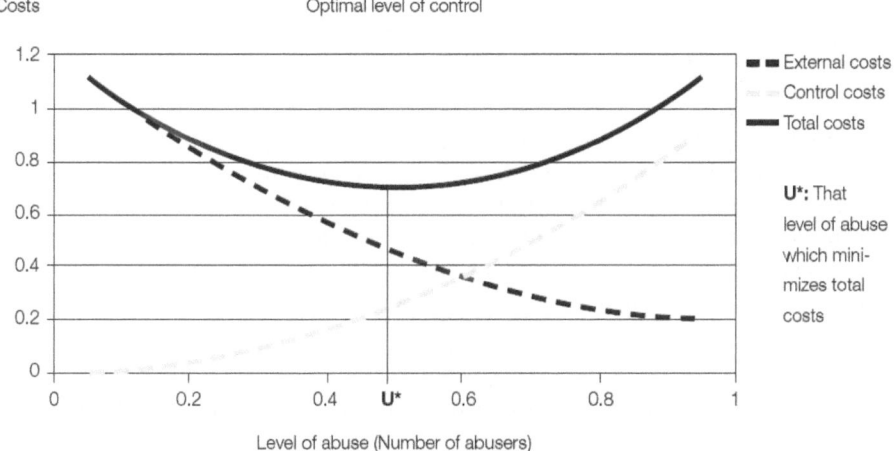

Fig. 12.1 Control costs, external costs and the optimal level of control (Melberg 2010)

affects of government policies such as prevalence of use considering the cost-of illness approach. Cost of illness (COI) studies measure the value of net resources that are unavailable for other purposes considering the effects of a health condition (Choi et al. 1997). From economic point of view, the process involved in a policy analysis based on the social costs must be presented using economic evaluation techniques.

The cost-of-illness approach is based on the idea that a disease or a social problem imposes costs when resources are used as a result of the disease or the social problem, whereas they could have been used differently.

Figure 12.1 illustrates the economical explanation between control costs, external costs and the optimal level of control considering the cost-of-illness approach. The horizontal axis measures the number of users of a substance. The government can try to reduce the number of patients and this will reduce the external cost as a result of abuse (health costs), but it requires higher control costs (treatment) (Melberg 2010).

Costs that related to social costs are the hospital costs where involves the costs with surgery and the costs without surgery. The cost of hospitalisation with surgery (Ch^{with}) for n pathologies is:

$$C_h^{with} = \sum_{i=1}^{n} \left(RA_i^{men} * NS_i^{men} \right) * c_i + \sum_{i=1}^{n} \left(RA_i^{women} * NS_i^{women} \right) * c_i$$

where i is the pathology studied ($i=1, \ldots, n$), RA corresponds to the risk characteristic to the risk factor considered, NS is the number of hospitalisations with surgery, c_i is the mean cost of a hospitalisation with surgery for the pathology i. The cost of hospitalisation without surgery ($Ch^{without}$) for n pathologies is thus:

$$C_h^{without} = \sum_{i=1}^{n}\left(RA_i^{men}*NS_i^{'men}\right)*c_i'+\sum_{i=1}^{n}\left(RA_i^{women}*NS_i^{'women}\right)*c_i'$$

where i is the pathology studied ($i=1, \ldots, n$), RA corresponds to the risk characteristic to the risk factor considered, NS' is the number of hospitalisations without surgery, c_i' is the mean cost of a hospitalisation without surgery for the pathology i. For the calculation of the overall risk characteristic to the risk factor concerned, in order to determine the share of non-hospital health care costs characteristic to that risk factor, the total annual number of visits or consultations (NV_i, $i=1, \ldots, n$) for each pathology is considered, and the total annual number of visits (NV) is given

by $NV = \sum_{i=1}^{N} NV_i$. Combination between Attributable Risk (AR) with NV gives us $RA_i = 1 \Rightarrow NV_i = NV_i$ and $RA_i = 0 \Rightarrow NV_i = NV_i^*$, where $NV_i = RA_i - NV$ and $NV_i^* = (1 - RA_i)NV_i$. The overall risk (RA_g) based on the risk factor under consideration when calculating the non-hospital health care costs of that risk factor

is $RA_g = \dfrac{\sum_{i=1}^{N} NV_i}{NV}$. The total annual spending on non-hospital health care (D) for

a given risk factor is: $D = \dfrac{\sum_{i=1}^{N} NV_i}{NV} \times CV + \sum_{I=1}^{n} CA_i + \sum_{i=1}^{n} CP_i$, where CP_i is the cost of

medicine for pathology i attributable to a particular risk factor, CV is the total annual cost of visits to doctors and CAi is the total annual cost of treatment.

12.4   Theory

The suggested tool of SWOT analysis is presented within this part of this paper. The suggested strengths, weaknesses, opportunities and threads are the outcome of literature review (http://www.intuitivesurgical.com, Camberlin et al. 2009) and knowledge. A SWOT analysis of adopting robotic system in hospital is presented in the following part (Table 12.1).

The financial effects of robotic surgery application are examined within this paper comparing data from a medium size urban hospital in Athens for 2012 and already published data from United States of America (Center for Evidence-based Policy Oregon Health & Science University 2012). In the Table 12.2 below the discharges for three operations groups are presented with the corresponding hospitalization days of the medium size hospital. The reimbursement in Greek health system is based on fix costs of operations (Greek DRGs). In Table 12.2 we present the fix cost price that the hospital receives as well as the days that are officially paid.

Table 12.1 SWOT analysis

Strengths	Weaknesses
Lowers the risk of infection	Limited sterility
Lower operating procedure execution time	Limited dexterity and hand-eye coordination
Shorter hospital stay	Long set-up time of robot and the operating room
Removal of the tremor and high accuracy during surgery	Social
Magnification of the working field	High purchase costs that make the acquisition of a group of devices really onerous
Less scarring and improved cosmetics	Open surgery has a better costs/effectiveness ratio
Reduced trauma to the body	High maintenance/repair costs
Reduced blood loss and need for transfusions	Slow amortization
Less post-operative pain and discomfort	Minimally invasive procedures are expensive because of surgeon specialization and training
Robotic system needs low space in the operating room	
Simulates traditionally surgery for surgeons but provides telescopic precision social	
Speeds patient's recovery and return to normal activities	
Opportunities	Threats
Expand the application fields of robotic	Without a competitive plan of development of researches it could remain a niche sector too high costs too less application fields open surgery or laparoscopic techniques would be predominant
Improve the cooperation of many research centers	Finite number of hospitals potential users aimed towards larger hospitals
Positively improve research though the data that collects and can be provided	Requires doctors to be trained extensively
	Liability from accidents/malfunctions of robots

Table 12.2 Operations, number of discharges and hospitalization days vs price reimbursement and days

Fix reimbursement greek DRGs				
Operations groups	Discharges	Days	Days paid	Price
Operations perianal and dermoid disease (bladder fistula, abscess, etc.)	29	109	2	626 €
Operations hernia (inguinal, umbili-cal hernia, etc.) without coexisting disease—complications	26	105	2	868 €
Nasal operations	25	71	2	600 €

Table 12.3 Operations, total costs, number of discharges and hospitalization days vs price reimbursement and days

Operations groups	Hospital's reimbursement for all cases per operation group	Extra days of hospitalization	27% days of hospitalization	Cost save for days (hospitalizations cost 80 €)
Operations perianal and dermoid disease (bladder fistula, abscess, etc.)	18.154 €	51 (188%)	−14	1.120 €
Operations hernia (inguinal, umbilical hernia, etc.) without coexisting disease—complications	22.568 €	53 (198%)	−14	1.120 €
Nasal operations	15.000 €	21 (142%)	−6	480 €
	55.722 €			2.720 €

We selected three operation groups among 75 groups in order to prove the reduction in hospitalization only costs that might have a medium size urban hospital by implementing robotic surgery.

Table 12.3 presents the total amount of money reimbursement for a medium size hospital for the cases described in Table 12.2 as well as the extra days of hospitalization revealing inefficiency due to traditional surgery methods that the hospital engage. After the elaboration of data provided by Center for Evidence-based Policy Oregon Health & Science University, year 2012 in Table 12.3 we estimate based on a mean of 27% of reduction in hospitalization days using robotic surgery. Implementing robotic surgery a hospital can save about 5% only from the hospitalization costs. In last column is presented the reduction of total costs that a hospital can save in case of robotic surgery use. This cost reduction only results from less of hospitalization days.

12.5   Results and Discussion

The aspects of the SWOT analysis that affect the cost of robotic surgery implementation are numerous. Some them are lower operating procedure execution time, shorter hospital stay, less post-operative pain and discomfort, robotic system needs low space in the operating room, speeds patient's recovery and return to normal daily activities, high purchase costs that make the acquisition of a group of devices really onerous, high maintenance/repair costs, requires doctors to be trained extensively. All those aspects, except the initial installation fix cost ranging from $ 1 to $ 2.5 million for each unit (Barbash and Glied 2010) and the high cost of service and consumables, can reduce the cost and discomfort in contrast to open operation procedures.

As far as the costs that presented in Table 12.2 we can conclude that in case of robotic operation implementation in such a medium size urban hospital for only three common operations we have a reduction in hospitalization days of approximately 5 % or in economic word a cost reduction of 2.720 €. The calculation is based on the reduced fix fee of 80 €. This save is only gained from the hospitalization costs. In order to have a precise number of money save, based on the results of SWOT analysis, we have to take into account some indirect costs that can be saved, like drugs, extra cost for doctors and other paramedical personnel, the availability of beds and operation theatres for more operations, labour costs due to immediate return in work of the patient.

12.6   Conclusions

The main conclusions of the study are that although for some cases robotic surgery proved not to be cost effective, in total and taking into account all aspects that are involved in a hospital, robotic surgery is worth implementing. A further study should be done with data of big hospitals and more operations. The data used for the example of the study was in raw format and not enough qualitative. This paper aims to provide a foundation for further and more detailed studies that will include also other hospital functional parameters such consumables, medicines, indirect costs etc. Those parameters will have a direct relationship with both the economic view of the hospital as well as with patient's satisfaction and quality of life. The compensation of hospitals and health service providers highly affects Greek health care. In addition to that indirectly affects in exaggerated degree social security system of the country. As a result those studies will be of great interest on the part of the Social Funding.

References

Adams E (2006) Bibliography: robotic surgery—update 2006. Boston: Technology Assessment Unit, Office of Patient Care Services, US Department of Veterans Affairs (VATAP) PUB: KCE Reports 104 Robot-assisted surgery 125 Technology Assessment Unit, Office of Patient Care Services, US Department of Veterans Affairs (VATAP). 2006:11 XPT Report

Ballini L, Minozzi S, Pirini G (2008) La chirurgia robotica; il robot da Vinci. Bologna: Osservatorio regionale per l'innovazione; 2008, September (167–2008). http://asr.regione.emilia-romagna.it/wcm/asr/collana_dossier/doss166.htm

Barbash GI, Glied SA (2010) New technology and health care costs—the case of robot-assisted surgery. New Engl J Med 363:8. nejm.org. Accessed 19 Aug 2010

Breitenstein S, Nocito A, Puhan M, Held U, Weber M, Clavien PA (June, 2008) Robotic-assisted versus laparoscopic cholecystectomy: outcome and cost analyses of a case-matched control study. Ann Surg 2008 Jun 247(6):987–993. doi:10.1097/SLA.0b013e318172501f

Camberlin C, Senn A, Leys M, De Laet C (2009) Robot-assisted surgery: health technology assessment KCE reports 104C, The Belgian Health Care Knowledge Centre

Center for Evidence-based Policy Oregon Health Science University (2012) Robotic Assisted Surgery, Health Technology Assessment Program, UPDATED FINAL EVIDENCE REPORT, Health Technology Assessment Program (HTA), Washington State Health Care Authority, May 3, 2012

Choi BC, Robson L et al (1997) Estimating the economic costs of the abuse of Tobacco, Alcohol and Illicit Drugs: a review of methodologies and Canadian data sources. Chronic Dis Can 18(4):1–67

Herron DM, Marohn M (Nov, 2007) The SAGES-MIRA robotic surgery consensus, a consensus document on robotic surgery prepared by the SAGES-MIRA Robotic Surgery Consensus Group . A consensus document on robotic surgery. Surg Endosc 2008 Feb 22(2):313-325

Deardorff A (2006) Terms of trade glossary of international economics. World Scientific Publishing, USA

Diomidous M, Zimeras S, Jonh Mantas J (2009) Aspects of social cost concerning Illicit Drug use: analysis based on index numbers. Rev Clin Pharmacol Pharmacokinet 23(3)

http://www.intuitivesurgical.com

http://www.roboticsurgery.gr

Kopp P, Fenoglio P (2002) Calculating the social cost of illicit drugs. Methods and tools for estimating the social cost of the use of psychotropic substances. Council of Europe Publishing. http://www.emcdda.europa.eu/attachements.cfm/att_1362_EN_public_expenditure.pdf

Melberg HO (2010) Conceptual problems with studies of the social cost of alcohol and drug use. Nordic Stud Alcohol Drugs 27(2010):287–303

Ontario Ministry of Health and Long-Term Care (2004) Computer-assisted surgery using telemanipulators. Toronto: Medical Advisory Secretariat, Ontario Ministry of Health and Long-Term Care (MAS) PUB: Medical Advisory Secretariat, Ontario Ministry of Health and Long-Term Care (MAS). 2004:36 ISB 0779463773 XPT Systematic review

Pronovost PJ, Berenholtz SM, Goeschel CA, Needham DM, Sexton JB, Thompson DA, Lubomski LH, Marsteller JA, Makary MA, Hunt E (Aug, 2006) Creating high reliability in health care organizations. Health Serv Res 41(4 Pt 2):1599–1617

Pickton DW, Wright S (1998) What's swot in strategic analysis? Strat Chang 7:101–109. doi:10.1002/(SICI)1099-1697(199803/04)7:2<101::AID-JSC332>3.0.CO;2-6

Tooher R, Pham C (2004) Da Vinci surgical robotic system: technology overview. Stepney, SA: Australian Safety and Efficacy Register of New Interventional Procedures—Surgical (ASERNIP-S) XSE: ASERNIP-S Report No. 45 PUB: Australian Safety and Efficacy Register of New Interventional Procedures—Surgical (ASERNIP-S). 2004:117 ISB 0909844658 XPT Systematic review

Zender J, Thell C (July, 2010) Developing a successful robotic surgery program in a Rural Hospital. AORN J 92:72–83. doi:10.1016/j.aorn.2009.10.024 (© AORN, Inc., 2010)

Chapter 13
Feature Analysis of Blind Watermarked Electromyogram Signal in Wireless Telemonitoring

Nilanjan Dey, Goutami Dey, Sayan Chakraborty and Sheli Sinha Chaudhuri

Abstract Presently ample amount of work has been done in the field of tele-monitoring that involves sharing of biomedical signals and medical images through wireless media. Transmission of biomedical and medical signals over unsecured open network may cause various alteration and corruption of these signals and images which can lead to loss of decisive data. High level of security and confidentiality is required for exchanging information between various hospitals and diagnostic centers. Authenticity, verification of signal integrity, and achieved control over the copy process can be proved by adding watermark as the "ownership" information in multimedia content. The EMG signal is a perceptive diagnostic tool which is used for detection of various muscle related diseases by measuring and recording the muscle electrical signal. In the first part of this present work two novel blind-watermarking mechanisms are proposed namely Session Key Based Blind-Watermarking Mechanism and Self Recovery Based Blind-Watermarking Mechanism, into the Electromyogram (EMG) signal. Both these mechanisms are based on Stationary Wavelet Transformation (SWT) and Spread-Spectrum. In these approaches, the generated watermarked signal having a fair level of imperceptibility and distortion is examined with the original EMG signal. The Peak Signal to Noise Ratio (PSNR) of the original EMG signal vs. watermarked signal and the correlation value between the original and extracted watermark image are calculated for both of the mechanisms. Finally, the second part of this paper presents a comparative study of EMG features between the original and watermarked EMG signal.

Keywords EMG · Stationary wavelet transformation (SWT) · Spread-spectrum · Blind watermarking

N. Dey (✉) · G. Dey · S. Chakraborty
JIS College of Engineering, Kalyani, West Bengal, India
e-mail: neelanjan.dey@gmail.com

G. Dey
e-mail: goutamidey783@gmail.com

S. Chakraborty
e-mail: sayan.44@rediffmail.com

S. S. Chaudhuri
Jadavpur University, Kolkata, West Bengal, India
e-mail: shelism@rediffmail.com

D.-D. Koutsouris, A. A. Lazakidou (eds.), *Concepts and Trends in Healthcare Information Systems,* Annals of Information Systems 16,
DOI 10.1007/978-3-319-06844-2_13, © Springer International Publishing Switzerland 2014

13.1   Introduction

The electronic mobilization of clinical information is done across medical organizations or hospital systems to facilitate access to and retrieval of clinical data for mutual study of diagnostic and therapeutic case studies in order to get more precise and improved diagnosis. Such communication for exchanging medical data through signals requires high security and authenticity. Watermark embedding (Rey and Dugelay 2002; Voyatzis et al. 1998; Potdar et al. 2005; http://www.webmd.com/brain/electromyogram-emg-and-nerve-conduction-studies) in signals may cause degradation of the resultant signal. As the signals convey vital information which is used for detection of diseases, hence any kind of degradation of these signals can lead to erroneous diagnosis. Embedding of watermark in EMG signal compromises the diagnosis value of medical signal. To achieve watermarking technique in medical information is a challenging task.

EMG test is suggested by the doctors when the patient has symptoms of weakness as it shows impaired muscle strength. Problems in a muscle, the nerves supplying in a muscle, the spinal cord, or the area of the brain that controls a muscle can cause these symptoms. EMG is able to detect the difference between muscle weakness caused by injury of a nerve attached to muscle and due to neurologic disorders. EMG is done to find out the diseases that damages muscle tissue, nerves, or the junctions between nerves and muscles. These problems may include a herniated disc, amyotrophic lateral sclerosis (ALS), or myasthenia gravis (MG) (Raez et al. 2006; http://www.medicinenet.com/electromyogram/article.htm; http://www.nlm.nih.gov/medlineplus/ency/article/003929.htm; http://www.guluindependenthospital.com/neurophysiology.html).

EMG stands for Electromyography, able to study the muscle electrical signal (Semmlow 2011). Muscle tissues conduct electrical potentials that are known as Muscle Action Potential. EMG is sometimes referred to as myoelectric activity. The information present in this muscle action potential can be recorded by the EMG. There are two main issues to be concerned while detecting the EMG signal. First is the signal to noise ratio, which represents the ratio of energy of the EMG signal to the energy in the noise signal. Distortion means any kind of change in the signal due to noise. The second issue, which must be taken care of during the detection of the EMG signal, is to avoid any kind of distortion in the signal that means relative contribution of the frequency components in the signal must not be altered. Invasive electrodes and non-invasive electrodes are two different kinds of electrodes that are used to acquire muscle signal. EMG is directly mounted on the skin when it acquires from the electrodes. The EMG signal is a composite signal of all the muscle action potentials that occurs in muscles under the skin. At any moment, EMG signal can be positive or negative voltage as the muscle action potential occurs at a random interval of time. Individual muscle action potentials also may be caught by inserting wire or needle electrodes directly in the muscle.

Following equation shows a simple model of the EMG signal:

$$X(m) = \sum_{r=1}^{N-1} h(r)e(m-r) + W(m) \qquad (13.1)$$

where, $x(m)$ is modeled EMG signal, $e(n)=$ point processed, represents the firing impulse, h(r) represents the MUAP, $W(m)=$ zero mean addictive white Gaussian noise and N is the number of motor unit firings (Ramirez and Hu 2011).

According to Zecca et al. there are three types of feature in EMG signal control systems (Brachtl et al. 2004):

(1) Time Domain, (2) Frequency Domain, (3) Time—frequency domain.

The time domain features are computed based on signal amplitude. The frequency domain is based on signal's estimated power spectrum density and is computed by parametric methods. Englehart has explained in his thesis that time—frequency domain includes the energy of both time and frequency domain by representing more accurate description of the physical phenomenon.

Watermarking is the technique of embedding information into a 1-D or 2-D signal for safety and security purpose. Watermarking of digital media content is very popular as a method to protect intellectual property rights of the content owners (IV054).

A watermarking scheme is said to be blind if it does not require the original signal or any other data (Chan and Cheng 2003) for extraction of the watermark from the watermarked signal. Watermark is embedded with the help of an embedding algorithm and a pseudo-random key. Blind watermarking provides a scope for the authentication of the original signal or to provide patient information (Electronic Patient Report). Every watermarking scheme, being able to recover the original data, should provide a way of authenticating the signal. In addition, if it is possible to analyze that a copy has been made leading to some form of data degradation and/or corruption that can be conveyed through a relevant analysis, then a scheme should be developed that imposes a check on: (i) the authenticity of the data n, (ii) its fidelity.

In 2-D signal processing, watermarking technique can be catalogued either as spatial domain or as transformed domain. Inserting least significant bit (LSB) (Hernández et al. 2000) is quite basic as well as simple and it is a common approach to embed information in an image in special domain. Vulnerability to every slight image alteration and manipulation is the limitation of this scheme. Conversion of image from one format to another could destroy information concealed in LSB. Watermarked image can be easily detected by statistical analysis, such as histogram analysis. This scheme involves replacement of N number of least significant bit of each pixel of the container image with the data of the watermark. Watermark is degraded as the value of N increases. In frequency domain analysis, data can be kept hidden by the help of discrete cosine transformation (DCT) (Tao and Dickinson 1997; Anumol and Karthigaikumar 2011). The major limitation of this technique is the blocking artifact. DCT pixels are arranged into 8×8 blocks that are each transformed into 64 DCT coefficients. The alteration of a single DCT co-efficient alters all 64-image pixels in that block. Discrete wavelet transformation (DWT) approach (Jiansheng et al. 2009; http://en.wikipedia.org/wiki/Stationary_wavelet_transform) is one of the modern schemes of watermarking. In this scheme, the imperceptibility and degradation of the watermarked 2-D signal is acceptable. Proposed technique of watermarking deals with a stationary wavelet transformation based blind watermark

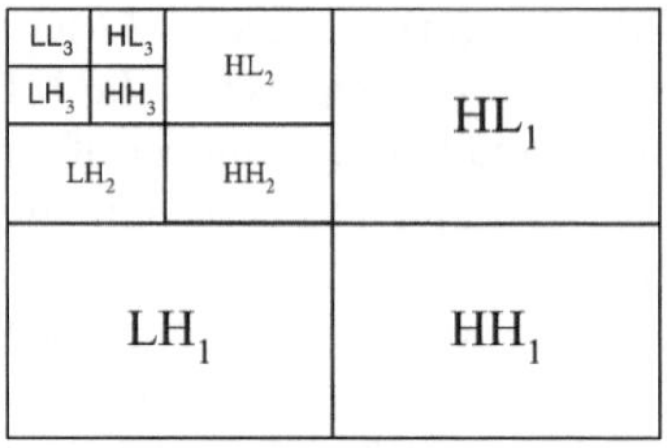

Fig. 13.1 Three phase
decomposition using DWT

| LL₃ | HL₃ | | |
| LH₃ | HH₃ | HL₂ | |

Fig. 13.1 table:

LL₃ HL₃	HL₂	HL₁
LH₃ HH₃		
LH₂ HH₂		
LH₁	HH₁	

technique where the pseudo-random key for the embedding process is generated by
a session key or from the signal itself. The second type of extraction mechanism of
the watermark is self-recoverable. A comparative study is done for the features of
Original and Watermarked EMG signal to measure the diagnostic value changes as
an effect of watermarking.

13.2 Methodology

13.2.1 Stationary Wavelet Transformation

The wavelet transform illustrates a process of a multi-resolution decomposition in
terms of an image expansion onto a set of wavelet basis functions. Discrete wavelet
transformation (DWT) has a property of the space frequency localization. DWT application in 2D signals corresponds to the processing of 2D filter image in each of
the dimensions. The input image is divided into 4 non-overlapping multi-resolution
sub-bands by the filters, that is, approximation coefficients (LL_1), vertical details
(LH_1), horizontal details (HL_1) and diagonal details (HH_1). The sub-band (LL_1) is
further processed to attain the next coarser scale of wavelet coefficients, until the
final scale "N" is obtained. When "N" is obtained, $3N + 1$ sub-band are attained consisting of the multi-resolution sub-bands, LL_X and LH_X, HL_X and HH_X, where "X"
ranges from 1 to "N". LL_X sub-bands stores most of the image energy (Fig. 13.1).

Stationary Wavelet Transform (SWT) (Hoštálková and Procházka 2006) is the
modification of the Discrete Wavelet Transform to make it translation-invariant in
nature that does not decimate coefficients at every transformation level. Transla-
tion-invariance is obtained by discarding the down samplers and up samplers in
DWT and up sampling the filter coefficients by the factor of $2^{(j-1)}$ in the jth level
of the algorithm. It is an innately redundant technique, as the output of each level
consists of the same number of samples as the input. So for the decomposition of N
levels, there are redundancies of N in the wavelet coefficients. The given algorithm
proposed by Holdschneider is also known as "algorithm à trous" which refers to
introducing zeros in the filters (Fig. 13.2).

Haar wavelet is not differentiable and therefore is not continuous. This property
can act as an advantage for the analyzing the signals with abrupt transitions.

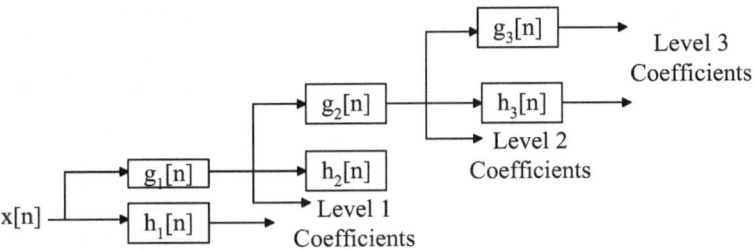

Fig. 13.2 Three phase decomposition using DWT

13.2.2   Signal De-noising

Artificially added random noise (Jiansheng et al. 2009; Dey et al. 2012d; http://ncalculators.com/statistics/signal-noise-ratio-calculation.htm) in the signal is discarded by thresholding of the SWT coefficients up to level 2 using sym 4 wavelet function. The thresholding method, a soft global threshold δ of an estimated value that is given by the following equation is used.

$$\delta = \sigma \sqrt{2 \log L} \qquad (13.2)$$

Where the noise is Gaussian with standard deviation σ of the SWT coefficients and L is the number of samples of the processed signal.

Thresholding is either soft or hard. In soft and hard thresholding, the entire signal values zeroes out if the signal values are smaller than δ. In case of soft thresholding the subtraction of δ from the signal values is larger than δ.

13.3   Proposed Method

a. Preprocessing of Electromyography signal
   Step 1. EMG signal is loaded.
   Step 2. Any DC offset present in the signal is removed.
   Step 3. Resultant signal is rectified.
   Step 4. Linear Envelope is obtained from the rectified signal (Fig. 13.3).

Watermark Embedding and Extraction

1. Watermark embedding and extraction using session based key

Watermark Embedding
   Step 1. Conversion of the rectified EMG signal into the largest possible square 2-D signal takes place, which is followed by decomposition into four sub bands (Ca1, Cv1, Ch1 and Cd1) using SWT.

Fig. 13.3 Preprocessing of
electromygram signal

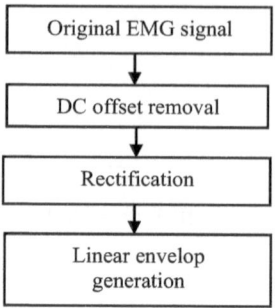

Step 2. Cd1 is further decomposed into four sub bands (Ca2, Cv2, Ch2 and Cd2) using SWT.

Step 3. Binary image is taken and is converted to 1D Vector.

Step 4. Two Pseudo random 2D sequence (PN_Sequence1 and PN_Sequence1 2) are generated by the session based key.

Step 5. Ch1 and Cv1 sub bands are modified followed by the modification of Cd2 accordingly by PN_Sequence1 and 2 relying upon the content of the hidden 1D image vector is to be embedded.

Step 6. Four sub bands of the 2nd level SWT; including modified sub bands are combined using inverse stationary wavelet transform (ISWT).

Step 7. Four sub bands of the 1st level SWT, including resultant 2D signal generated are combined to generate the Watermarked 2D signal using ISWT.

Step 8. Watermarked 2D signal is reshaped into 1D signal.

Step 9. Linear envelope is obtained from the watermarked signal (Fig. 13.4).

Watermark Extraction

Step 1. Session key of the watermark image and watermark image size is sent to the intended receiver through a confidential communication channel.

Step 2. Conversion of the watermarked EMG signal into the largest possible square 2-D signal is followed by decomposition into four sub bands (Ca1, Ch1, Cv1 and Cd1) using SWT.

Step 3. Cd1 is further decomposed into four sub bands (Ca2, Ch2, Cv2 and Cd2) using SWT.

Step 4. Watermark image can be recovered from the Ch2, Cv2 components of the watermarked 2D signal after 2nd level SWT decomposition with the help of correlation function and knowing the modified EMG signal size (Fig. 13.5).

2. Self recovery based watermark embedding and extraction

Watermark Embedding

Step 1. Conversion of rectified EMG signal into the largest possible square 2-D signal is followed by decomposition into four sub bands (Ca1, Ch1, Cv1 and Cd1) using SWT.

Step 2. Ca1 is further decomposed into four sub bands (Ca2, Ch2, Cv2 and Cd2) using SWT.

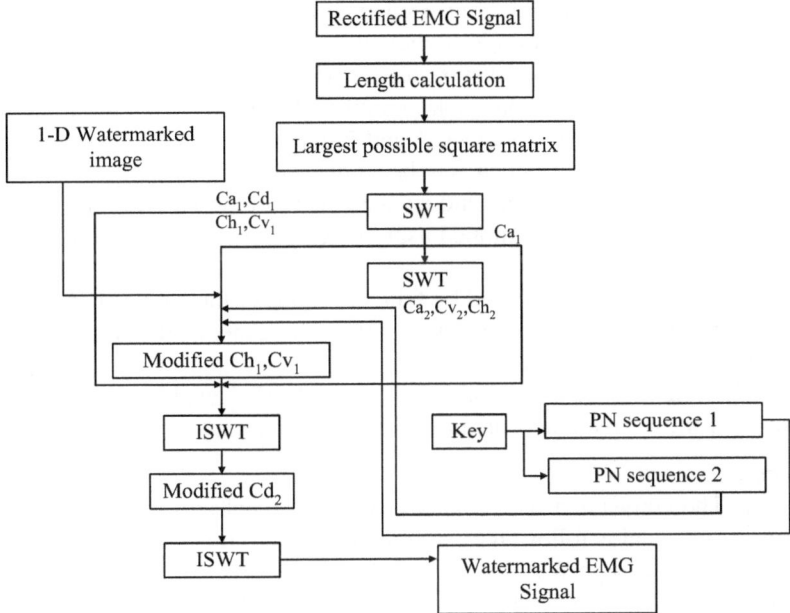

Fig. 13.4 Session key based watermark embedding process

Fig. 13.5 Session key based watermark extraction process

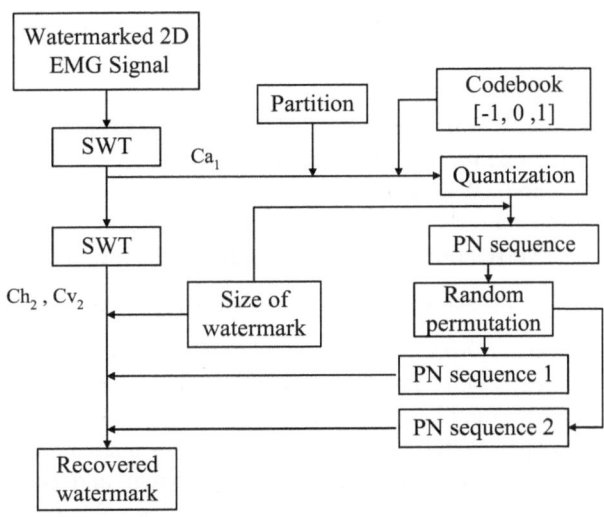

Step 3. A binary watermarked image is converted into 1D Vector.

Step 4. The absolute value of approximation coefficient of the EMG Signal is rounded off.

Step 5. The rounded off values are quantized into steps as specified by partition vector (partitioned into three segments) and encoded based on the codebook vector $[-1, 0, 1]$.

Step 6. Quantized values are converted into 2D matrix.

Step 7. Random permutation is applied twice on the quantized matrix to generate two different pseudo-random sequences (PN_Sequence1, PN_Sequence2).

Step 8. Ch1 and Cv1 sub bands are modified followed by the modification of Cd2 accordingly by PN_Sequence1 and 2 depending upon the content of the hidden 1D image vector which is to be embedded.

Step 9. Four sub bands of the 2nd level SWT decomposed 2D signal including modified sub bands are combined using Inverse Stationary Wavelet Transform (ISWT).

Step 10. 2D signal decomposed by four sub bands of the 1st level SWT including generated resultant 2D signal are combined to generate the Watermarked 2D signal using ISWT.

Step 11. Watermarked 2D signal is reshaped into 1D signal.

Step 12. Linear envelope is obtained from the watermarked signal (Fig. 13.6).

Watermark Extraction

Step 1. The conversion of watermarked EMG signal into the largest possible square 2-D signal is followed by decomposition into four sub bands (Ca1, Ch1, Cv1 and Cd1) using SWT.

Step 2. Cd1 is further decomposed into four sub bands (Ca2, Ch2, Cv2 and Cd2) using SWT.

Step 3. The absolute value of approximation coefficient (Ca1) of the watermarked ECG signal is rounded off.

Step 4. The rounded off values are quantized into steps as specified by partition vector (partitioned into three segments) and encoded based on the codebook vector $[-1, 0, 1]$.

Step 5. Only the watermark image size is sent to the intended receiver through a confidential communication channel.

Step 6. Watermark image can be recovered from the Ch2, Cv2 components of the watermarked 2D signal after 2nd level SWT decomposition with the help of correlation function and knowing the modified ECG signal size (Fig. 13.7).

b. Feature extraction of the original and watermarked EMG Signal

Step 1. Original EMG Signal is reshaped into 1-D signal.

Step 2. Time domain, frequency domain and time-frequency domain features for EMG signal control are obtained.

Step 3. Watermarked EMG Signal is reshaped into 1-D signal.

Step 4. Time domain, Frequency domain and Time-frequency domain features for Watermarked EMG signal control are obtained.

Step 5. A comparative study is done for the features between original and watermarked EMG signal.

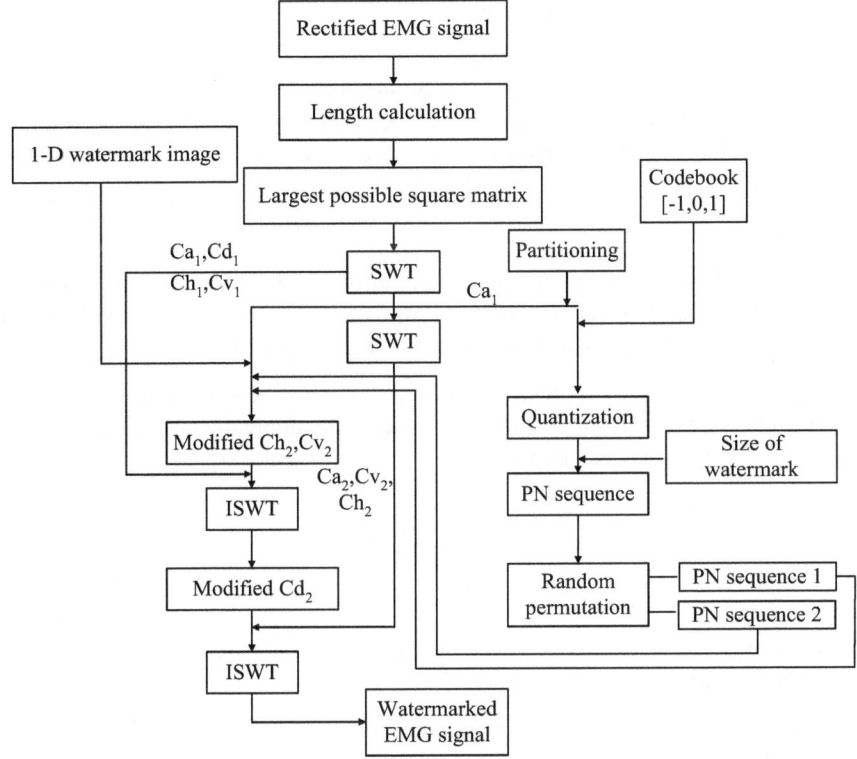

Fig. 13.6 Self recovery based watermark embedding process

Fig. 13.7 Self recovery based watermark extraction process

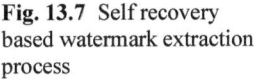

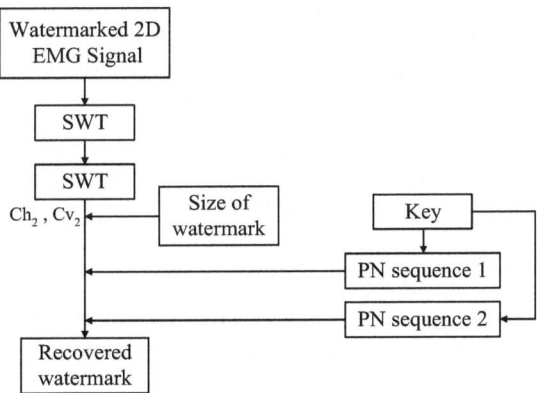

13.4   Results and Discussion

MATLAB 7.0.1 Software is widely used for the study of watermark embedding and extracting in the EMG signal (http://www.enel.ucalgary.ca/People/Ranga/enel563/ SIGNAL_DATA_FILES; Rangayyan 1994, 2002). Related images obtained in the result are shown in Fig. 13.8 through 13.11.

c. Performance Evaluation

This section presents the quantitative evaluation of the proposed methods. The PSNR (Peak Signal-to-Noise Ratio) and correlation is introduced for evaluation of the performance of the presented schemes and signal quality.

Peak Signal to Noise Ratio (PSNR) It is used to determine the quality of the watermarked signal. This performance metric is used to evaluate the perceptual transparency of the watermarked signal with respect to the original signal:

$$PSNR = \frac{MN \max_{x,y} P_{x,y}^2}{\sum_{x,y}(P_{x,y} - \bar{P}_{x,y})^2} \tag{13.3}$$

Where, M and N are number of rows and columns in the input signal, $P_{x,y}$ is the original Signal and $\bar{P}_{x,y}$ is the watermarked Signal.

PSNR between the original and watermarked signal is 20.5038 for watermark embedding and extraction technique using session based key and for self recovery based watermark embedding and extraction technique the value is 16.4344 are shown in Table 13.1. (Amplification value (k)=0.5)

Correlation Coefficient After the process of confidential image embedding, the similarity of original signal x and watermarked signal x' is evaluated by the standard correlation coefficient which is as follows:

$$C = \frac{\sum_m \sum_n (x_{mn} - x')(y_{mn} - y')}{\sqrt{\left(\sum_m \sum_n (x_{mn} - x')^2\right)\left(\sum_m \sum_n (y_{mn} - y')^2\right)}} \tag{13.4}$$

where, y and y' are the discrete wavelet transforms of x and x'.

Correlation (corr2) between the watermark image that is embedded and the recovered watermark image is shown in the Table 13.2 for the amplification value (k)=0.5.

It is observed that the extracted watermark has sound visual quality and this method is best suitable for the copyright protection scheme.

Imperceptibility Test Figure 13.9: (k), (l) show that, the watermark embedding into the original EMG signal using the proposed Self Recovery Based Watermark Embedding and Extraction mechanism does not affect the quality of the signal, which ensures imperceptibility of the embedded watermark.

Fig. 13.8 **a** Original EMG signal, **b** Rectified EMG signal, **c** Linear envelope of the rectified EMG signal

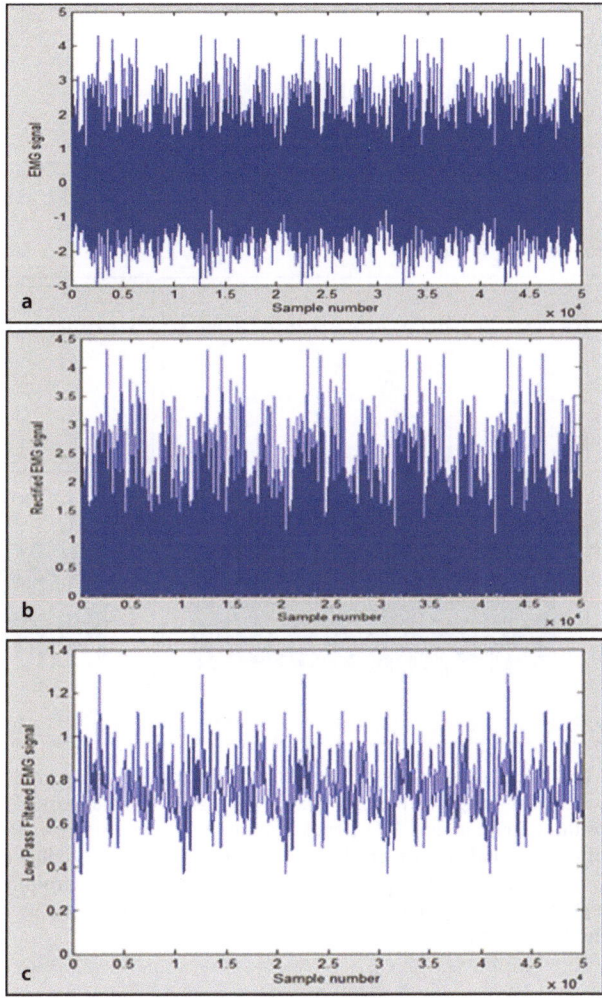

Table 13.1 PSNR value

Original EMG signal vs. watermarked signal	PSNR value for watermark embedding and extraction technique using session based key	PSNR value for self recovery based watermark embedding and extraction technique
	20.5038	16.4344

Table 13.2 Correlation value

Correlation between original watermark image and recovered watermark image	Correlation value for watermark embedding and extraction technique using session based key	Correlation value for self recovery based watermark embedding and extraction technique
	0.8188	0.8858

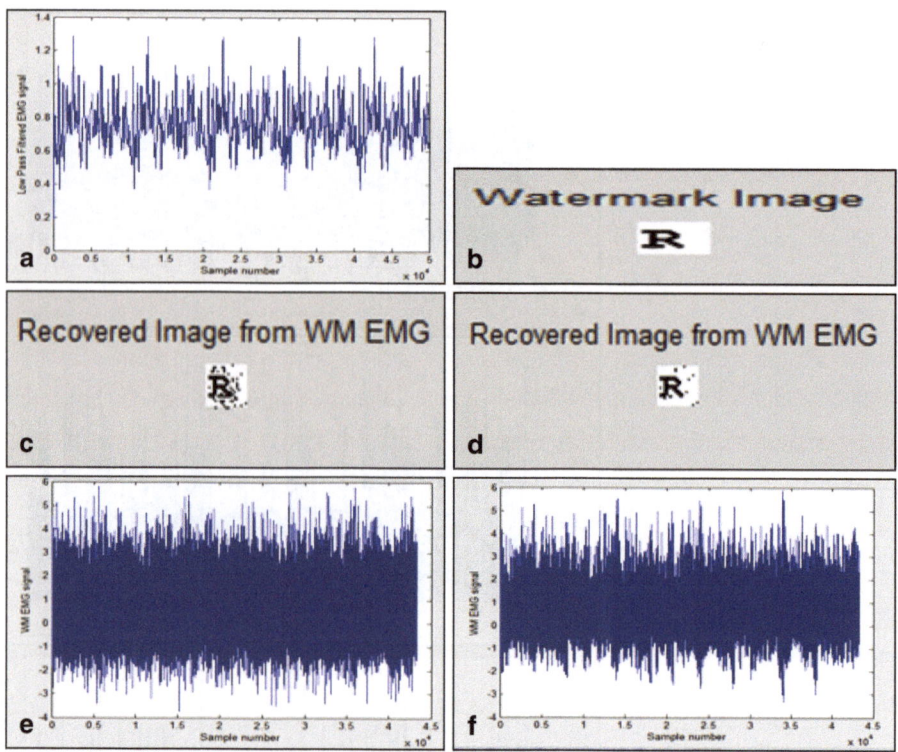

Fig. 13.9 a Original signal, **b** Watermark image, **c** Recovered watermark image, **d** Recovered watermark image, **e** Watermarked EMG signal, **f** Watermarked EMG signal, **g** Linear envelope of the watermarked EMG signal, **h** Linear envelope of the watermarked EMG signal, **i** Overlay of original and watermarked EMG signal, **j** Overlay of original and watermarked EMG signal, **k** Overlay of original and watermarked EMG signal by controlling upper and lower axis limits on a graph, **l** Overlay of original and watermarked EMG signal by controlling upper and lower axis limits on a graph

Robustness Test Different types of digital signal processing attacks can remove or degrade the watermarks. The parameter which measures the immunity of the watermark against such changes by the digital signal processing attacks is called robustness. In this paper the robustness results for three major digital signal processing attacks (Gaussian white noise, DCT based signal compression and Wavelet based signal compression) are presented.

Effect of White Gaussian Noise The following Equation represents a simple model of the EMG signal (Rangayyan 1994),

$$f(t) = s(t) + n(t) \tag{13.5}$$

Where *f(t)* is the vector signal. *s(t)* and *n(t)* denotes EMG signals and White Gaussian Noise $N(0, \sigma^2)$, respectively (Table 13.3).

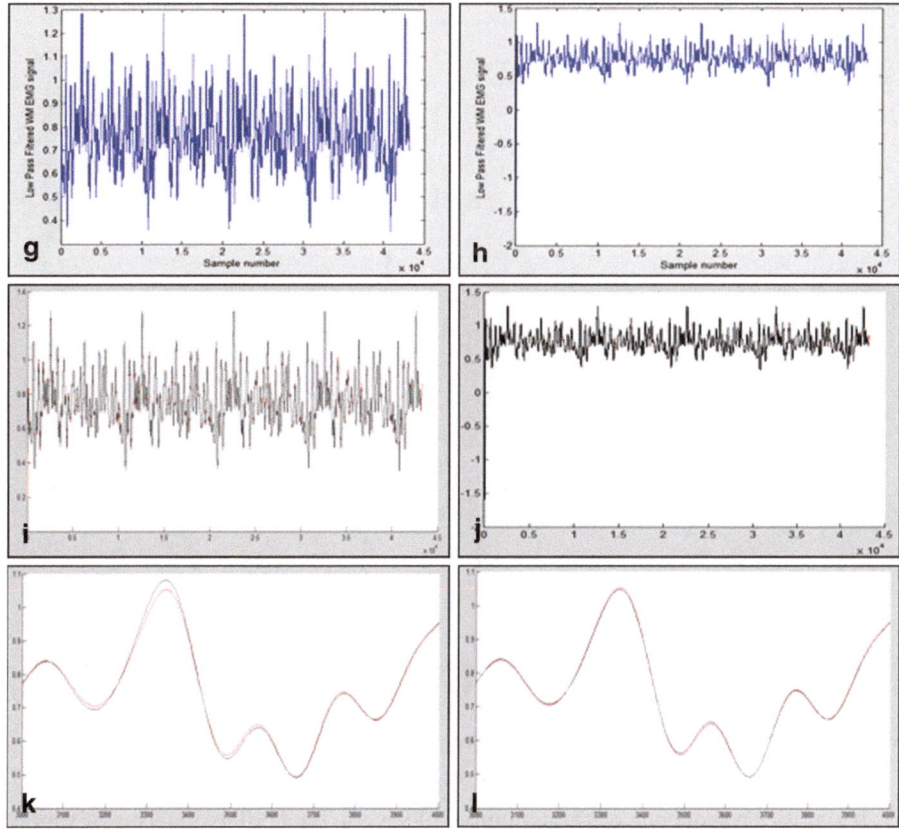

Fig. 13.9 (continued)

Table 13.3 PSNR and correlation as an effect of white Gaussian noise

Signal-to-noise ratio(SNR) per sample (db)	PSNR between noise EMG signal and watermarked EMG signal	Correlation between watermark and extracted watermark
5	11.6828	0.8185
10	11.2564	0.8577
20	11.1129	0.8510
25	11.1242	0.8810

Effect of DCT Based Signal Compression The Discrete Cosine Transform (DCT) converts a signal into elementary frequency components. This is extensively used in signal compression. Test on DCT based compressed EMG signal proves that the proposed Self Recovery Based Watermark Embedding and Extraction Technique gives an effective result which claims the efficacy of the robustness of the technique (Fig. 13.10).

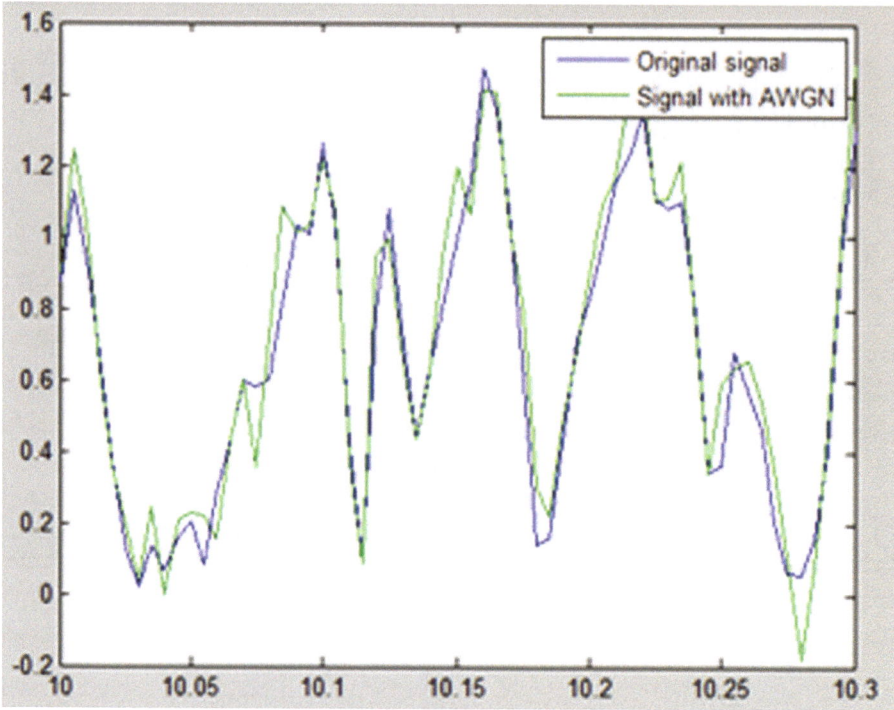

Fig. 13.10 Original EMG signal Vs. EMG signal with Gaussian white noise (SNR=20)

It signifies a sequence of finite number of several data points in terms of sum of the cosine functions which is oscillating at different frequencies. It is broadly used in image compression. The application was launched by Chen and Pratt in 1984.

The discrete cosine transform (DCT) is co-related to the discrete Fourier transform (DFT) with some dissimilarity.

- The DCT is purely real and the DFT is complex (phase and magnitude).
- The DCT has more efficiency in concentrating the energy into the lower order coefficients than DFT.
- The coefficients that are produced by a DCT operation on a block of pixels are similar to the coefficients of the frequency domain produced by a DFT operation. As the N point DCT is correlated to the 2N-point DFT, it consists of the same frequency resolution. The N frequencies of a 2N point DFT corresponds to N points on the upper half of the unit circle in the complex frequency plane.
- The DFT coefficients magnitude is spatially invariant (input phase does not influence) assuming a periodic input, unlike DCT.

For processing 1D (one-dimensional) signal such as waveforms of speech 1D DCT is used. For the analysis of 2D (two dimensional) signals like images, a two dimensional version of the DCT is needed. As the 2-D DCT can be evaluated by applying

Table 13.4 PSNR as an effect of DCT compression

Sl No.	DCT compression by a factor of	PSNR between original rectified EMG signal and compressed signal	PSNR between compressed signal and watermarked signal	Correlation between watermark and extracted watermark
1	2	35.0714	10.9917	0.8768
2	4	26.8446	11.7791	0.8444
3	8	19.9171	9.1539	0.8087

1-Dimensional transforms separately to rows and columns, it can be said that the 2-Dimensional DCT is separable in two dimensions.

For f (x, y), an M × N digital signal its 2D discrete cosine transform and its inverse transformation is evaluated by the following equations (Dey et al. 2012a).

$$C(u,v) = \alpha(u)\alpha(v) \sum_{x=0}^{N-1} \sum_{y=0}^{N-1} f(x,y) \cos\left[\frac{\pi(2x+1)u}{2N}\right] \cos\left[\frac{\pi(2y+1)v}{2N}\right] \quad (13.6)$$

$$f(x,y) = \sum_{x=0}^{N-1} \sum_{y=0}^{N-1} \alpha(u)\alpha(v)c(u,v) \cos\left[\frac{\pi(2x+1)u}{2N}\right] \cos\left[\frac{\pi(2y+1)v}{2N}\right] \quad (13.7)$$

The result of discrete transform is C (u, v), and is also known as DCT coefficient.
Where, u, v = 0, 1, 2,… N − 1, x, y = 0, 1, 2,… N − 1, α (u) is defined as follows:

$$\alpha(u) = \sqrt{\frac{1}{N}} \quad u = 0;$$

$$\alpha(u) = \sqrt{\frac{2}{N}} \quad u = 1, 2 \ldots\ldots N - 1; \quad (13.8)$$

DCT compression is applied on the signal vector of length 43,264. Block size is chosen as (window size) 8192 and the sampling rate is 200. Following table shows the result of PSNR and correlation values changes as an effect of watermarking in the compressed EMG signal (Table 13.4).

Effect of Wavelet Based Compression and De-noising Technique Discrete wavelet transform (DWT) can be used to compress the EMG signal and thresholding method can be used to de-noise it. Wavelets are commonly used for de-noising biomedical signals including the Daubechies (db2, db8, and db6) wavelets and orthogonal Meyer wavelet. This is a well known technique for signal compression process by removing most of the noise (Fig. 13.11).

A. Wavelet Decomposition Based on the chosen wavelet function, the wavelet transformation decomposes EMG signal into multi-resolution components. The resolution of the signal is a measure of the amount of detailed information in the

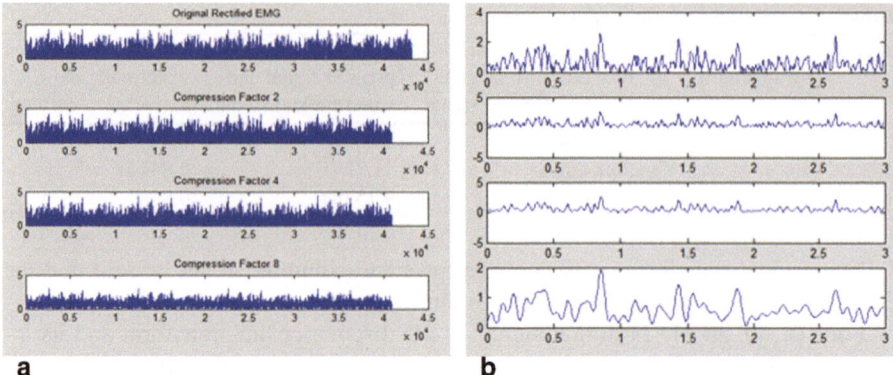

Fig. 13.11 **a** Compressed signal, **b** Controlled graph by upper and lower axis limits of compressed signal

Fig. 13.12 Wavelet tree for db6 of level 4

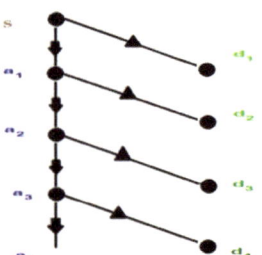

signal. Resolution is determined by the filtering operations. The scale is determined by up sampling and down sampling operations. The DWT is computed by successive low pass and high pass filtering of the discrete time-domain signal.

Wavelet tree is succinct data structure. In wavelet trees strings are stored in compressed space. A wavelet tree for db6 of level 4 is shown in the figure below (Fig. 13.12):

Soft thresholding is applied on compressed EMG signal to remove the artificially added white gaussian noise in the signal (Fig. 13.13).

The following table shows the changes of PSNR and Correlation values for the proposed watermarking method as an effect of Gaussian white noise(SNR = 5) removal using DWT (level 4) and thresholding (Table 13.5).

All the above stated experimental values show the robustness of the proposed watermarking technique.

d. EMG feature analysis

In his thesis Zecca et al. has been said that there are three kinds of features of EMG control systems: Time domain, Frequency domain, Time—frequency domain.

Fig. 13.13 a a4,d4,d3,d2,d1 components of decomposition EMG signal (level 4), **b** Rectified EMG signal, selected co-efficients ($s = a4 + d4 + d3 + d2 + d1$) and rectified de-noised EG signal. **c** Original rectified EMG signal, signal with Gaussian white noise and without Gaussian white noise

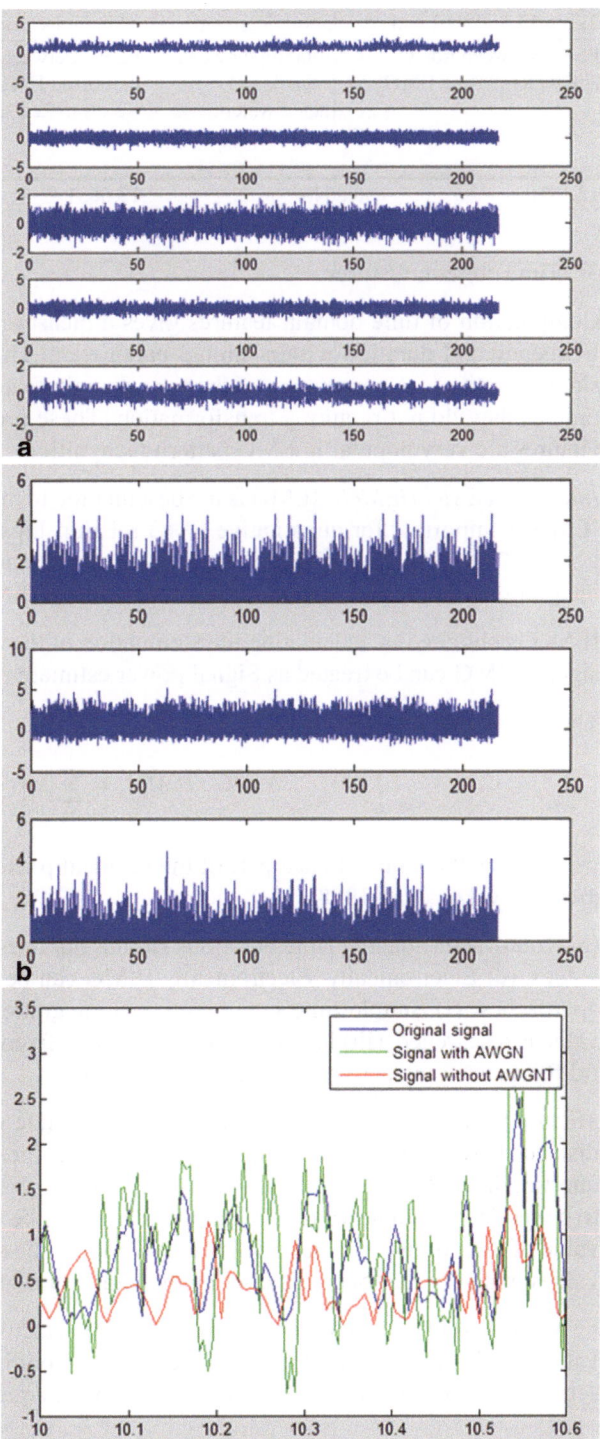

Table 13.5 PSNR and correlation after Gaussian white noise removal using DWT

PSNR between noisy and watermarked EMG	Correlation between watermark and extracted watermark (Noise EMG signal)	PSNR between de-noised EMG and watermarked signal	Correlation between watermark and extracted watermark (De-noised EMG signal)
12.1776	0.8646	13.0631	0.8525

3. Time domain features

Computation of time domain features gives a measure of time domain amplitude, frequency and duration within limited parameters. These are computed based on single amplitude. Computation of the time domain features is easy and takes lesser time as they do not require a transformation. These properties of the time domain features are very popular in EMG pattern recognition.

Integrated EMG (IEMG) IEMG is the best method to measure total muscular effort. IEMG is important for quantitative EMG relationships (EMG vs. Work, EMG vs. Force). There are three different approaches to measure IEMG. (a) Mathematical integration. In this case area under absolute values of EMG time series is calculated.

IEMG is obtained by calculating the summation of the absolute values of the EMG signal. IEMG can be treated as Signal power estimator.

The following equation represents

$$IEMG : IEMG_p = \sum_{i=1}^{N} |x_i| \qquad (13.9)$$

where, X_i is the value of each part of the segment p and N is the length of the segment (Voyatzis et al. 1998).

(b) Root-Mean-Square (Time durations similar but does not require taking absolute values. (c) Electronically. Electronically IEMG can be measured in three different approaches. (i) Simple time integration, (ii) integration & reset after a particular value is researched, (iii) integration & reset after a fixed time interval. IEMG is useful for quantifying activity for ergonomic research.

Mean Absolute Value (MAV) In mathematics absolute value of a number A means distance between the number and 0 on the number line (http://answers.yahoo.com/question/index?qid=20071030083824AABD9K6). As distance can never be negative therefore absolute value of a number can never be negative. Mean absolute value of a set of numbers is calculated by dividing the summation of the absolute values of all the numbers in the set by the total count of the numbers in the set.

Mean absolute value of a signal MAV_p can be calculated by adding the absolute value of all the values of X_i in a segment p and dividing it by the length N of the segment. MAV can b represented by the following equation:

$$MAV_p = \frac{1}{N} \sum_{i=1}^{N} |X_i| \qquad (13.10)$$

Root Mean Square (RMS) To obtain RMS value at first the mean value of the square of all the values of X_i is calculated by dividing the summation of the square of all of the values X_i of a segment by the length N of the segment, and then root of the this mean value is calculated. Root Mean Square can be represented by the following equation (http://rosettacode.org/wiki/Averages/Root_mean_square):

$$RMS_p = \sqrt{\frac{1}{N} \sum_{i=1}^{N} X_i^2}$$ (13.11)

Variance (VAR) Variance is the average of the squared differences from the mean (http://www.mathsisfun.com/data/standard-deviation.html). It can be represented by using the following equation:

$$VAR_p = \frac{1}{N} \sum_{i=1}^{N} (X_i - \bar{X})^2$$ (13.12)

Zero Crossings (ZC) The point where the waveform changes its sign or crosses the zero is known as the zero crossing. For a sine wave or other simple waveform, such situation normally occurs twice during each cycle (http://en.wikipedia.org/wiki/Zero_crossing). To reduce the noise induced the zero crossings a threshold must be included in the zero crossings calculation. If the threshold is Θ, then two consecutive samples X_i and X_{i+1} increases the number of zero crossings if

$$\{X_i > 0 \text{ and } X_{i+1} < 0\} \text{ or } \{X_i < 0 \text{ and } X_{i+1} > 0\} \text{ and } |X_i - X_{i+1}| \geq \Theta \quad (13.13)$$

Weighted Mean Weighted mean differs from arithmetic mean by giving weights to some of the individual values. Weighted mean value does not differ from arithmetic mean value when all the weights are equal (http://ncalculators.com/statistics/weighted-mean-calculator.htm). Data elements with high weights contribute more to the weighted mean than the elements having a low weight. The weights must be positive or zero. But all the weights cannot be zero together. When the values of all the weights are zero then weighted mean will not play an important role in the system of data analysis having its value as zero. Weighted mean can be represented by the following equation:

$$\bar{X} = \frac{w_1 x_1 + w_2 x_2 + ... + w_n x_n}{w_1 + w_2 + ... + w_n}$$ (13.14)

where $w_1, w_2, ..., w_n$ are the weights of the non negative data $x_1, x_2, ..., x_n$ respectively.

4. Frequency domain features:

Frequency domain features are based on estimated power spectrum density of the signal (PSD). Frequency domain features are computed by parametric methods.

Fig. 13.14 Yule AR

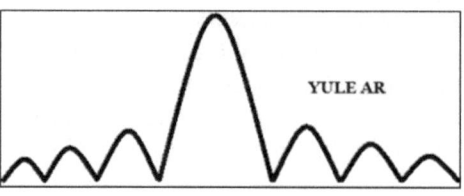

Auto Regressive Coefficients (AR) AR coefficients are used for EMG pattern recognition. Each sample of the EMG signal is described as a linear combination of previous samples plus a whit noise error term by the auto regressive coefficients. AR coefficient is calculated by the following equation:

$$X_k = -\sum_{i=1}^{M} a_i X_{k-i} + e_k \qquad (13.15)$$

Where a_i is AR coefficients, e_k is white noise and M is the order of AR model.

There are various techniques for measuring AR. The main two categories are least squares and Burg method. Least squares method is based upon the Yule-Walker equations.

Yule-Walker Power Spectral Density Estimate The Yule-Walker Method also called the autocorrelation method (http://www.mathworks.in/help/toolbox/dsp/ref/yulewalkermethod.html). This block estimates the power spectral density (PSD) of the input using the Yule-Walker AR method. This method fits an autoregressive (AR) model to the input data. It is done by reducing the forward prediction error in the least squares sense. The diagram below describes Yule AR block (Fig. 13.14).

Power Spectral Density (PSD) Power Spectral Density function shows the strength of the variations as a function of frequency. The unit of PSD is energy per frequency. PSD is computed by the method FFT or computing auto correlation function and then transforming it. PSD is used to identify oscillatory signals and to know its amplitude in the time series data (http://www.cygres.com/OcnPageE/Glosry/Spec.html).

5. Time-Frequency domain features

Englehart has explained in his thesis, that time-frequency representation can localize the energy of the signal both in time and in frequency. Thus a more accurate description of the physical phenomenon can be obtained. But computation of these features is not easy as the feature requires a transformation that is computationally heavy.

Wavelet Transform (WT) Wavelet transform (Selesnick 2007) is a computational tool which is useful for several image and signal processing applications. It is also useful for reducing noise. There are two types of wavelet transforms, one is used in different kinds of image processing application like image compression and cleaning and the other type of wavelet is used in signal analysis. WT is used for the detection of faults in machinery from sensor measurements, for the study of different kinds of biomedical signal like ECG, EMG, EEG, for determining evolution of the

Table 13.6 Time domain features

Self recovery based watermark embedding and extraction (For sample rate 1000 sample distance 0.001)

	Original EMG signal	Watermarked EMG signal
Integrated EMG (IEMG)	32944.3	32960.3
Mean absolute value	0.761471	0.760552
Root mean square (RMS)	0.77597	0.776563
Variance (VAR)	0.0222914	0.02461
Zero crossings (ZC)	0	1
Weighted mean (mean frequency)	2.70966	2.70752

frequency content of the signal over time. Wavelet Transform can be represented by the following equation:

$$W(a,b) = \int x(t) \frac{1}{\sqrt{a}} \varphi * \frac{t-a}{b} dt \qquad (13.16)$$

Where x(t) is the function representing the input signal, $\varphi*$ is the complex conjugate of the wavelet function, $\varphi\left(\dfrac{t-b}{a}\right)$ is the shifted and scaled version of the wavelet at time b and scale a.

Short Time Fourier Transformation (STFT) Applicability of Fourier transform method is extended by Gabor. It is done by dividing the input signal into segments, so that the signal in each window can be assume to be stationary. STFT can be represented by the following equation: For a given signal v(t),

$$STFT_v(t,f) = W * (\gamma - t)v(\gamma)e - ^{if\gamma} d\gamma \qquad (13.17)$$

where W(t) is the window function, * is the complex conjugate, f stands for frequency and γ represents time (Voyatzis et al. 1998).

6. Time domain features (Table 13.6)

7. Frequency domain features

8. Time-Frequency Domain Features (Fig. 13.15 and 13.16)

13.5 Conclusion

Since the application of wavelet transformation in electromyography is relatively a new field of the wavelet technique requires further investigations in order to improve the clinical usefulness of this original signal processing technique. Imperative clinical usefulness is drawn from the innovative application of wavelet transformation in electromyography.

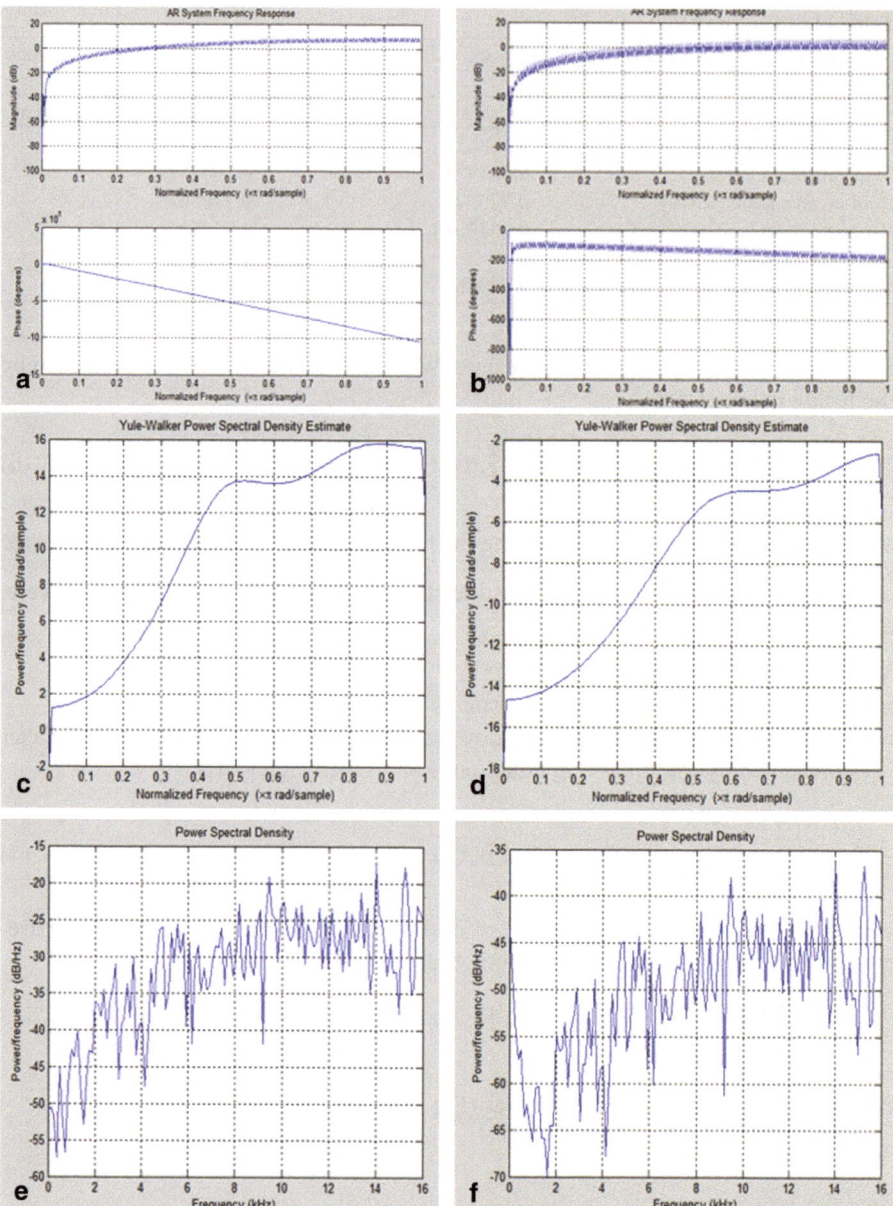

Fig. 13.15 **a** AR system frequency response for original signal, **b** AR system frequency response for watermarked signal, **c** Yule-Walker power spectral density estimate original signal, **d** Yule-Walker power spectral density estimate watermarked signal, **e** Power spectral density original signal, **f** Power spectral density watermarked signal

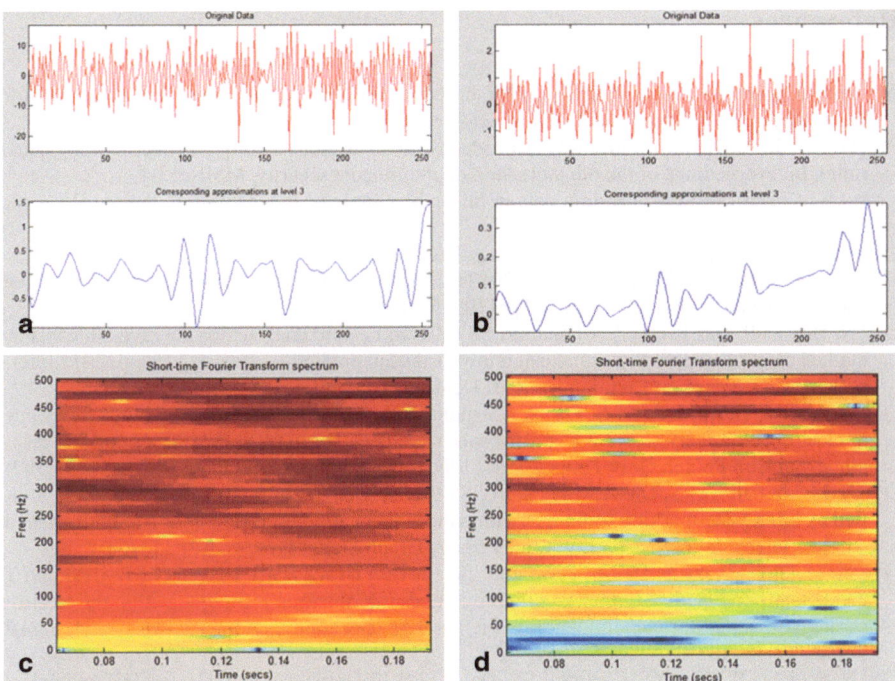

Fig. 13.16 a Wavelet decomposition(Level 3), **b** Wavelet decomposition(Level 3), **c** STFT of the original signal, **d** STFT of the original signal

Proposed techniques of session key based blind watermark embedding and extraction and self-recovery based blind watermark (Dey et al. 2012b, c, e, f) embedding and extraction scheme are appropriate for telemedicine applications. It is used for authentication of the source of the information, verification of the signal integrity, achieving control over the copy process. In this present work, Watermark is embedded in the Cd_2 sub band of the original EMG signal, there is a very minute or negligible difference between the original and the watermarked signal to generate some imperceptibility of EMG data. Due to the strong security aspects of this proposed scheme, this small amount of imperceptibility is acceptable. The correlation and PSNR values are very much promising regarding the credibility and authentic reconstruction of the image. By comparing the correlation value of the two proposed techniques it can be seen that the Self Recovery based blind Watermark embedding and extraction technique is better than the other one. The major advantage of this approach is the self-authentication technique that removes the cumbersome process of adjoining the session key or its transfer from sender to receiver end.

References

Anumol TJ, Karthigaikumar P (2011) DWT based invisible image watermarking algorithm for color images. IJCA Spec Issue Comput Sci—New Dimens Perspect 2(7):73–79

Brachtl M, Uhl A, Dietl W (2004) Key-dependency for a wavelet-based blind watermarking algorithm. In: Proceedings of the 6th workshop on multimedia security, MMSec'04

Chan CK, Cheng LM (2003) Hiding data in image by simple LSB substitution. Pattern Recognit 37:469–474

Chapter-13, Steganography and Watermarking, IV054, ppt

Dey N, Bhattacharya T, Chowdhury SRB (2012a) A session based multiple image hiding technique using DWT and DCT. Int J Comput Appl (0975—8887) 38:18–21

Dey N, Biswas S, Das P, Das A, Chaudhuri SS (2012b) Feature analysis for the reversible watermarked electrooculography signal using low distortion prediction-error expansion. 2012 International Conference on Communications, Devices and Intelligent Systems (CODIS)

Dey N, Maji P, Das P, Biswas S, Das A, Chaudhuri SS (2012c) Embedding of blink frequency in electrooculography signal using difference expansion based reversible watermarking technique. Sci Bull Politeh Univ Timis—Trans Electron Commun 57(71):7–12 (ISSN 1583-3380)

Dey N, Mukhopadhyay S, Das A, Chaudhuri SS (2012d) Analysis of P-QRS-T components modified by blind watermarking technique within the electrocardiogram signal for authentication in wireless telecardiology using DWT. Int J Image Graph Signal Process 4(7):33–46

Dey N, Mukhopadhyay S, Das A, Chaudhuri SS (2012e) Using DWT analysis of P, QRS and T components and cardiac output modified by blind watermarking technique within the electrocardiogram signal for authentication in the wireless telecardiology. Int J Image Graph Signal Process (7)33–46 (ISSN:2074–9074)

Dey N, Samanta S, Yang XS, Chaudhri SS, Das A (2012f) Optimisation of scaling factors in electrocardiogram signal watermarking using cuckoo search. Int J Bio-Inspired Comput 5:315–326

Hernández JR, Amado M, González FP (2000) DCT-domain watermarking techniques for still images: detector performance analysis and a new structure. IEEE Trans Image Process 9:55–68

Hoštálková E, Procházka A (2006) Wavelet signal and image denoising. 14th annual conference technical computing prague

http://answers.yahoo.com/question/index?qid=20071030083824AABD9K6 (Last accessed: 28-05-2014)

http://en.wikipedia.org/wiki/Stationary_wavelet_transform (Last accessed: 28-05-2014)

http://en.wikipedia.org/wiki/Zero_crossing (Last accessed: 28-05-2014)

http://ncalculators.com/statistics/signal-noise-ratio-calculation.htm (Last accessed: 28-05-2014)

http://ncalculators.com/statistics/weighted-mean-calculator.htm (Last accessed: 28-05-2014)

http://rosettacode.org/wiki/Averages/Root_mean_square (Last accessed: 28-05-2014)

http://www.cygres.com/OcnPageE/Glosry/Spec.html (Last accessed: 28-05-2014)

http://www.enel.ucalgary.ca/People/Ranga/enel563/SIGNAL_DATA_FILES (Last accessed: 28-05-2014)

http://www.guluindependenthospital.com/neurophysiology.html (Last accessed: 28-05-2014)

http://www.mathsisfun.com/data/standard-deviation.html (Last accessed: 28-05-2014)

http://www.mathworks.in/help/toolbox/dsp/ref/yulewalkermethod.html (Last accessed: 28-05-2014)

http://www.medicinenet.com/electromyogram/article.htm (Last accessed: 28-05-2014)

http://www.nlm.nih.gov/medlineplus/ency/article/003929.htm (Last accessed: 28-05-2014)

http://www.webmd.com/brain/electromyogram-emg-and-nerve-conduction-studies (Last accessed: 28-05-2014)

Jiansheng M, Sukang L, Xiaomei T (2009) A digital watermarking algorithm based on DCT and DWT. In: Proceedings of the 2009 international symposium on web information systems and applications (WISA'09), pp 104–107

Potdar V, Han S, Chang E (2005) A survey of digital image watermarking techniques. In: Proceeding of 3rd IEEE-international conference on industrial informatics, frontier technologies for the future of industry and business, pp 709–716

Raez MBI, Hussain MS, Mohd-Yasin F (2006) Techniques of EMG signal analysis: detection, processing, classification, applications. Biol Proced Online 8:11–35

Ramirez EJR, Hu H (2011) Stages for developing control systems using EMG and EEG signals: a survey. Technical report: CES-513 in school of computer science and electronic engineering. University of Essex, United Kingdom

Rangayyan RM (1994) Biomedical signal processing, Special issue of the journal Medical and Life Sciences Engineering, Biomedical Engineering Society of India, vol 13

Rangayyan RM (2002) Biomedical signal analysis: a case-study approach. Wiley-IEEE Press, New York, p 516. ISBN 0471208116

Rey C, Dugelay JL (2002) A survey of watermarking algorithms for image authentication. EURASIP J Appl Signal Process 6:613–621

Selesnick IW (2007) Wavelet transforms—a quick study. 27 September 2007

Semmlow JL (2011) Biosignal and Medical Image Processing. CRC Press, pp 1-448

Tao B, Dickinson B (1997) Adaptive watermarking in the DCT domain. ICCASP'97, pp 2985–2988

Voyatzis G, Nikolaidis N, Pitas I (1998) Digital watermarking an overview. Signal processing IX, theories and applications, In: Proceedings of Eusipco-98, Ninth European Signal Processing Conference, pp 9–12

Index